FOUCAULT'S FUTURES

CRITICAL LIFE STUDIES

CRITICAL LIFE STUDIES

Jami Weinstein, Claire Colebrook, and Myra J. Hird, Series Editors

The core concept of critical life studies strikes at the heart of the dilemma that contemporary critical theory has been circling around: namely, the negotiation of the human, its residues, a priori configurations, the persistence of humanism in structures of thought, and the figure of life as a constitutive focus for ethical, political, ontological, and epistemological questions. Despite attempts to move quickly through humanism (and organicism) to more adequate theoretical concepts, such haste has impeded the analysis of how the humanist concept life itself is preconfigured or immanent to the supposedly new conceptual leap. The Critical Life Studies series thus aims to destabilize critical theory's central figure life—no longer should we rely upon it as the horizon of all constitutive meaning, but instead begin with life as the problematic of critical theory and its reconceptualization as the condition of possibility for thought. By reframing the notion of life critically—outside the orbit and primacy of the human and subversive to its organic forms—the series aims to foster a more expansive, less parochial engagement with critical theory.

Luce Irigaray and Michael Marder, *Through Vegetal Being:
Two Philosophical Perspectives* (2016)

Jami Weinstein and Claire Colebrook, editors, *Posthumous Life:
Theorizing Beyond the Posthuman* (2017)

FOUCAULT'S FUTURES

A CRITIQUE OF
REPRODUCTIVE REASON

PENELOPE DEUTSCHER

Columbia University Press
New York

Columbia University Press
Publishers Since 1893
New York   Chichester, West Sussex
cup.columbia.edu
Copyright © 2017 Columbia University Press
All rights reserved

Library of Congress Cataloging-in-Publication Data
Names: Deutscher, Penelope, 1966– author.
Title: Foucault's futures: a critique of reproductive reason / Penelope Deutscher.
Description: New York: Columbia University Press, 2017. | Series: Critical life studies | Includes bibliographical references and index.
Identifiers: LCCN 2016038588 | ISBN 9780231176408 (cloth: alk. paper) | ISBN 9780231176415 (pbk.: alk. paper) | ISBN 9780231544559 (e-book)
Subjects: LCSH: Feminist ethics. | Human reproduction—Philosophy. | Sex—Philosophy. | Foucault, Michel, 1926–1984—Influence.
Classification: LCC BJ1395.D48 2017 | DDC 176/.2—dc23
LC record available at https://lccn.loc.gov/2016038588

Columbia University Press books are printed on permanent and durable acid-free paper.

Printed in the United States of America

Cover design: Lisa Hamm
Cover image: Grete Stern, *Dream No. 30*, c. 1951. Copyright © Estate of Horacio Coppola, Buenos Aires.

CONTENTS

Acknowledgments vii

List of Abbreviations xi

INTRODUCTION
1

1 SUSPENSIONS OF SEX:
FOUCAULT AND DERRIDA
13

2 REPRODUCTIVE FUTURISM, LEE EDELMAN,
AND REPRODUCTIVE RIGHTS
40

3 FOUCAULT'S CHILDREN: REREADING
THE HISTORY OF SEXUALITY, VOLUME 1
64

4 IMMUNITY, BARE LIFE, AND THE THANATOPOLITICS
OF REPRODUCTION: FOUCAULT, ESPOSITO, AGAMBEN
105

5 JUDITH BUTLER, PRECARIOUS LIFE, AND
REPRODUCTION: FROM SOCIAL ONTOLOGY
TO ONTOLOGICAL TACT
144

Notes 191

Index 251

ACKNOWLEDGMENTS

This project began at the Zentrum für Literatur- und Kulturforschung, Berlin, with a research fellowship from the Alexander von Humboldt Foundation and was completed during a senior fellowship awarded by the Internationales Forschungszentrum Kulturwissenschaften in Vienna. I am particularly grateful to Judith Butler, Souleymane Bachir Diagne, Susan James, Elizabeth Wilson, and Ewa Ziarek for their indefatigably cheerful support of the fellowship applications toward this book. These opportunities also opened up through valuable help along the way from Moira Gatens, Elizabeth Grosz, Genevieve Lloyd, Paul Patton, and Quentin Skinner. An important role has been played by the commitment of colleagues in the Department of Philosophy at Northwestern University and in the Dean's Office of the Weinberg College of Arts and Science to a flexible and grant-friendly environment conducive to research.

The book has greatly benefited from colleagues who took time to comment on early versions of manuscript chapters. My warmest appreciation for these stimulating and memorable conversations to Laura Bieger, Astrid Deuber-Mankowksy, Lee Edelman, Estelle Ferrarese, Samir Haddad, Martin Hägglund, Lynne Huffer, Colin Koopman, Christoph Menke, Catherine Mills, Andrew Parker, Francesca Raimondi, Eva von Redecker, Linnell Secomb, Robert Trumbull, and Elizabeth Wilson.

The project has been enriched as well by discussions with graduate students participating in seminars on Foucault, queer temporalities, biopolitics, and necropolitics I have offered at Northwestern; at the Gender, Culture, and Society Doctoral Programme at the University of Helsinki; and at the Department of Gender Studies and the Institut für Medienwissenschaft at Ruhr Universität, Bochum, and particularly the Queer Temporality and Media Aesthetics Workshop convened at the latter. I am grateful to Astrid Deuber-Mankowsky for supporting both a Marie-Jahoda Visiting Chair in International Gender Studies and a Visiting International Professorship at Bochum. This collaboration and the opportunity to work with her innovative graduate students have taught me much about the intersections of gender and sexuality studies and media studies.

A great many colleagues also helped me to acclimatize to new academic environments, generously sharing expertise and friendship during times of transition in Paris, Berlin, and Vienna. My very warm thanks to Laura Bieger, Christine Blättler, Hartmut Böhme, Barbara Cassin, Monique David-Ménard, Estelle Ferrarese, Eva Horn, Rahel Jaeggi, Helmut Lethen, Susanne Lettow, Erik Porath, Christoph Menke, Francesca Raimondi, Juliane Rebentisch, Eva von Redecker, Marlene Rutzendorfer, Miloš Vec, and Ulrike Vedder; to the wonderful staff at the IFK and the ZfL; and to senior and junior fellows at both institutions whose fellowship extended to sharing music, German, and late-night shifts.

A nourishing and distinctive research environment has also been offered by colleagues at Northwestern involved in developing its Critical Theory Cluster. I'm particularly grateful for the trust, wisdom, and practical support of Mark Alznauer, Peter Fenves, Cristina Lafont, Rachel Zuckert, and Sam Weber and for the initiatives, advice, ideas, style, and vigor further contributed by Jorge Coronado, Nick Davis, Ryan Dohoney, Dilip Gaonkar, Bonnie Honig, Anna Parkinson, Alessia Ricciardi, and the cluster's extraordinary graduate students.

I have learned much from the research, tenacity, and independence of spirit of Joanne Faulker, Jack Reynolds, Samir Haddad, Catherine Mills, Wolfhart Totschnig, Eric Jonas, Debbie Goldgaber, Anna Terwiel, and David Johnson, valued colleagues whose futures I look forward to.

On a personal note, Pip's encouragement has been a fundamental force of life. Some of the book was written in the best company in the world—with Alex, Stella, Zach, Tim, and Pip. Michael's solidarity has traversed more than I could have calculated. Dating to Australian days, I am glad to have shared academia and change for almost as long with Alison, Eliz,

Sam, Clare, with Linnell and Diana, with Ross and Lisabeth; and, dating to French days, with Paola, Olivia, and Tricia. And, enfolded in the book's end are some gifts, treasures, and late surprises: Palm Springs; the Eos with my father; Eliz's always best advice; moments of good counsel from my mother; Estelle and Anna's capacity for glamour and a good plan; Apichatpong Weerasethakul in Vienna; and the soufflés, car cakes, and boundless affection of Alessia and Chris. I have been especially fortunate in the combined forces and impact of Monique, Judith, and Astrid. Not least of Monique's many introductions has been to Astrid, only one of whose many introductions has been to *Google Baby*. And no Côte-Rôtie could be adequate to Judith's hospitality—encompassing the ICCTP and Monique's kind of blue—nor to the assistance, over many years, of all three.

Sections of chapter 3 were first published as "Foucault's *History of Sexuality* Volume I: Re-reading Its Reproduction," *Theory, Culture and Society* 29 (2012): 119–37. Early versions of short sections in chapter 4 and 5 appeared in "The Inversion of Exceptionality: Foucault, Agamben and 'Reproductive Rights,'" *South Atlantic Quarterly* 107, no. 1 (2007): 55–70; in "Sacred Fecundity: Agamben, Sexual Difference, and Reproductive Life," *Telos* 161 (Winter 2012): 51–78 (special issue: Politics After Metaphysics); in "Reproductive Politics, Biopolitics and Auto-Immunity: From Foucault to Esposito," *Journal of Bioethical Inquiry* 7, no. 2 (2010): 217–26 (special issue: Continental Approaches to Bioethics); and in "The Precarious, the Immune, and the Thanatopolitical: Butler, Esposito, and Agamben on Reproductive Biooplitics," in *Against Life*, ed. A. Hunt and S. Youngblood (Evanston, IL: Northwestern University Press, 2016), 119–42. A French translation of a section of chapter 5 was published in "Reproduction précaire," *Les Cahiers du genre* 58 (2015): 41–68. A different version of some arguments in chapter 1 can be found in "'This Death Which Is Not One': Reproductive Biopolitics and the Woman as Exception in *The Death Penalty, Volume 1*" in *Foucault/Derrida Fifty Years Later: The Futures of Deconstruction, Genealogy, and Politics*, coedited with Sam Haddad and Olivia Custer (New York: Columbia University Press, 2016).

Tristan Bradshaw's work on the final stages of the book's production was invaluable. At Columbia University Press my very warm thanks to Wendy Lochner, Christine Dunbar, and Susan Pensak.

ABBREVIATIONS

AB   Michel Foucault, *Abnormal: Lectures at the Collège de France 1974–1975*, ed. Valerio Marchetti and Antonella Salomoni. Trans. Graham Burchell. (New York: Picador, 2003).

Bios Roberto Esposito, *Bios: Biopolitics and Philosophy*, trans. Timothy Campbell (Minneapolis: University of Minnesota Press, 2008).

DP   Michel Foucault, *Discipline and Punish: The Birth of the Prison*, trans. Alan Sheridan (New York: Vintage, 1995)

DV   Carol Gilligan, *In a Different Voice: Psychological Theory and Women's Development* (Cambridge: Harvard University Press, 1993).

FW   Judith Butler, *Frames of War: When Is Life Grievable?* (London: Verso, 2009).

HS   Giorgio Agamben, *Homo Sacer: Sovereign Power and Bare Life*, trans. Daniel Heller-Roazen (Stanford: Stanford University Press, 1998).

HS I Michel Foucault, *The History of Sexuality*, vol. 1: *An Introduction*, trans. Robert Hurley (New York: Vintage, 1980).

NF   Lee Edelman, *No Future: Queer Theory and the Death Drive* (Durham: Duke University Press, 2004).

PL   Judith Butler, *Precarious Life: The Powers of Mourning and Violence* (London: Verso, 2006).

PLP   Judith, Butler, *The Psychic Life of Power: Theories in Subjection* (Stanford: Stanford University Press, 1997).
PP   Michel Foucault, *Psychiatric Power: Lectures at the Collège de France, 1973–74*, ed. Jacques Lagrange, trans. Graham Burchell (New York: Palgrave Macmillan, 2006).
SMBD Michel Foucault, *Society Must Be Defended: Lectures at the Collège de France, 1975–76*, ed. Mauro Bertani and Alessandro Fontana, trans. David Macey (London: Picador, 2003).
STP   Michel Foucault, *Security, Territory, Population: Lectures at the Collège de France, 1977–78*, ed. Michel Sennelart, trans. Graham Burchell (London: Picador, 2007).

FOUCAULT'S FUTURES

INTRODUCTION

This is a book about Foucault's children—in a number of senses. It revisits some little-discussed themes in Foucault's work, including the children who are prominent in his Collège de France lecture series *Abnormal* and *Psychiatric Power* and who lurk, also, in his famous books on sex and discipline. These children become the base for a broader reconsideration of Foucault's work on families, procreation, parenting, "optimal" child raising, and the projection of futures as conjoined with specific forms of responsibility—for individual life, societies, and populations.

This is also to reconsider common understandings of the role of procreation in Foucault's best-known work, *The History of Sexuality*, volume 1 (or *La Volonté de Savoir, The Will to Knowledge*). In that work Foucault's repudiation of a repressive hypothesis was also a repudiation of a procreative hypothesis. In other words, he rejected the assumption that nonreproductive forms of sexuality have been discouraged, or socially repressed, to the ends of family-based, heteronormative, procreative forms of sex promoted within, for example, revolutionary France, or Napoleonic France, or Victorian England, or worker-based industrial capitalism. But it would be mistaken to conclude that procreation (unlike the bodies and pleasures with which *La Volonté de savoir* famously concludes) lies entirely outside Foucault's analytic focus or that Foucault denies power's interest in procreation. The right question is: what kind of power?

The mistake occurs because of a phenomenon acknowledged by Foucault: it was easy to be distracted by his revolutionary work on sex. He commented that readers tended to ignore the last chapter of *La Volonté de savoir*.[1] More recent reception of the work has born witness to a dramatic change in this respect. Certainly the first volume of *The History of Sexuality* is now widely recognized—some might say too much so[2]—as concerned with the emergence of biopolitics. This allows more attention to the following point: although not foregrounded in Foucault's overt comments, the significance of children and procreation within the work has been entirely reconfigured by the time one does arrive at the book's concluding pages.

By then, Foucault has accomplished his now celebrated refutation of the hypothesis that power works repressively to prohibit nonnormative sexualities and to promote reproductive union. He has argued that some forms of power are more effective in their capacity to stimulate and produce (for example, forms of desire, interest, identity, knowledge, hermeneutics, identity, administration), rather than discourage and suppress. Wherever this is his point, procreation and children belong differently to Foucault's argument. They surface anew, in his depictions of biopolitical projects to optimize and administer life, in the governmental interest in "birthrate" or "healthy upbringing." In the transition from the repressive hypothesis repudiated by Foucault to his outlining of its alternative, procreation has taken on a new interest, as a problem of trends, patterns, and conduct of and within populations, new concepts of responsibility whose impact includes biomassive futures. Let's, temporarily, deem this phenomenon procreation's "biopolitical hypothesis."[3]

I

This reconfiguration has the potential to challenge an often-noted phenomenon in the many literatures about Foucault's work: a strong separation between the fields engaging his work on sex (for example within sexuality studies and queer theory) and his work on biopolitics (for example, within post-Foucauldian Italian philosophy). This is a surprising prospect because neither of these fields has shown much interest in

"Foucault's children": the role of procreation, birthrate, family spaces, reproductions, and upbringing within, for example, forms of sovereignty, biopower, discipline, governmentality, and security.

Perhaps, one might respond, we should not regret the neglect of these matters in the readings of Foucault dominating biopolitical theory and sexuality studies? There may be children in Foucault's work, but do we lose sight of the specificity of his concerns if we show too much interest in them?

To the contrary. The beginnings of an answering case are outlined from the outset of the next chapter, as follows. According to the multiple approaches to life and death developed throughout Foucault's work, the right question will always be: with *what* life are we dealing, and how do forms of subjectivity emerge in conjunction with the "conduct" of life: for example, formations of moral obligation or freedom or rights or responsibility toward collectivities, futures, or "investment" in futures. Incorporating Judith Butler's interest in related matters of delegitimation and desubjectivation also allows a concentration on subjects variously understood to be responsible *for* life and death and problematized as such. Chapter 5 discusses both the legitimation and delegitimation not just of specific forms of life but also of certain forms of intertwined responsibilization: certain forms of responsibility for life.

How do we come to take for granted the types of problem and the registers (for example, moral, technical, governmental) with which life (what life?) confronts us? What are the corresponding forms of power at work? How can different formations of life be analyzed as the very emergence of those registers that come to seem intuitive: those of epistemology, knowledge, hermeneutics, truth, legality, domination, order, control, duty, police, autonomy, style, aesthetics, political legitimacy, neoliberal investment, ethics, or moral choice?

These are not new questions. But, returning to them, we'll be reminded that the specificity of Foucault's work is not to be found in any one particular status he attributed to sex—or indeed, to children.

Of course, reproduction has been mobilized in promotions of family values, national sentimentalities, idealized or exclusive visions of social futures, normalization, and normative exclusion. Moreover, critique of heteronormative reproductive values has been importantly joined by critique of the homonormative versions—the recentering, and "folding into life," of forms of homosexuality associated with family values.[4]

But to this field of critique we can add the emphasis that reproduction, reproductive agency, and reproductive impact are not always associations with life, nor a route for its agents to be enfolded into life. The question "what kind of life" also leads to reproduction's proximity with figures of death. Associations between reproduction, governmentalities of life, optimal life, and collective futures have (like the association of reproductive life with reproductive futurism) taken shape also as vectors of mortality. The very association of reproduction with life and futurity (for nations, populations, peoples) has amounted to its association with risk, threat, decline, the terminal.

Without minimizing their differences, we can repudiate the oppositional terms (further discussed in chapter 2) in which the interests of queer sex and procreation are sometimes distinguished: antilife versus life. Instead, the discussions of queer politics and the politics of reproduction will take place on a more interesting footing insofar as the latter is more extensively analyzed in the register foregrounded by Lee Edelman: the realm of antilife and the antisocial.

A point to be found in the margins of Edelman's important critique of reproductive futurism is that sometimes women may find themselves ascribed, by virtue of reproductive capacity, with a sovereignlike power over human life. Consider the antiabortion campaigns financed by the Life Always group, who have mounted billboards in a number of American states likening abortion to race genocide. Rerouting the language of reproductive choice, antiabortion extremists have also represented women as making decisions about human life. Uteruses are represented as spaces of potential danger both to individual and population life. To figure maternity, and politicized birth, as principles of life and investments in the future, is to see them as potentially jeopardizing the latter. Reproduction (insofar as it is associated with mismanagement, irresponsibility, failed duty, termination, and a number of threats to life) comes to be seen as potentially impeding futures, the counterside of its promise to ensure them.

Moreover, the attribution of sovereignlike decisions about potential life tends to blur with quite different understandings of interest in life: from concern about population impact to the rerouting of antiabortionism into political pretensions of interest in *women's* lives, their well-being, psychic and physical health.[5] The questions "what life," "what death" help to expand an interrogation of the kinds of problem the formulation of the life decision becomes.

As discussed in chapter 4, forms of responsibility engaged by Foucault—responsibility for life and well-being (of individuals, families, futures, nations, and populations) connect to phenomena embedded in his work but discussed less by him: the attribution to women of the counterpotential for maternal harm, negative impact over life, and negative population or collective impact. Historians such as Gisela Bock, philosophers from Ladelle McWhorter to unlikely candidates such as Roberto Esposito, political theorists and sociologists including Elsa Dorlin and Dorothy Roberts, and scholarship on the complex status of reproduction in the contexts of slavery and its aftermath have addressed the deadly counterpart to the perception of women as life principle.[6] When they are understood to enfold futures, both individual and the future of peoples, and to be the threshold of health, society, defense, or survival (national, ethnic, ethnic-religious, territorial, colonial, or expansionist), the multiplicity of the lives women are considered to enfold may be matched by the multiplicity of the declines and deaths for which they can be deemed responsible. We might call this procreation as the thanatopolitical hypothesis.

What kind of analysis would be adequate to this phenomenon, its bodies, spaces, duties, and temporalities; its making of reproductive futures associated with new hermeneutics, predictive futures, and explanatory pasts; the conjoining of vitalities with mortalities and their "responsibilized" subjects, collectivities, politics, and governmentalities—their biopolitics become thanatopolitics? And, particularly given the multiplication of theoretical options, why turn back to a work as familiar, even exhausted, as *The History of Sexuality*, and to a reconsideration of Foucault's biopolitics, as a means of exploring this phenomenon?

II

So, why Foucault—and how? In fact, this project is also a means of giving closer attention more generally to the way in which absent concepts and problems can be given a shape in potentially transformative ways within philosophical frameworks which have omitted them. This is to elaborate a form of critique which revisits the limits frequently attributed to theorists and philosophers: that interesting gesture of wanting what can't be supplied from a theory understood as having failed to provide it.

More so than is always recognized, that gesture generally involves a two-way direction of traffic and exerted pressure. To identify the limits of theory is, indirectly, also to negotiate with the limits of one's interrogation. In other words, the negative capacities thereby emerging will not be limited to the object of critique, but can be understood as arising from a more productive tension between theorists and critics. Moreover, as I argue about Jacques Derrida's critique of biopolitics in chapter 1, these encounters take place not just between the positions articulated by Foucault and critics such as Derrida but also in the relationship between their omissions, their reserves and suspensions.

I argue that such suspended reserves can be attributed to Derrida's wariness of biopolitics—and also to Foucault's equivalent circumnavigation of sexual difference. Foucault rarely thematized the latter, nor matters of gender. So we might assume the resources of his work would contain few answers to a question that emerges, by contrast, in the course of Derrida's *Death Penalty Seminar*: why was the execution of women a special emblem for nineteenth-century abolitionists such as Victor Hugo of all that was grotesque about a death penalty?

The question is less removed from the present concerns than may first appear. What principle of life was at stake here? It was the potential procreative capacity of woman associated with a principle of life. But this is a formation—women-as-life-principle—by virtue of which, as I further discuss in the subsequent chapters, women have also been associated with the delivery of death. Moreover, it is by virtue of that association that they encounter new kinds of death penalties, some of which have manifested in the politics of abortion. It is as principle of life that some women may be associated with a corresponding capacity to effect harm on embryos, children, and futures which might be formulated in either "pseudosovereign" or biopolitical terms—or both. A number of forms of power and politics will strangely interfold in this regard, multiple languages and projects of biopolitical optimization, the intersection of pseudosovereign life decisions, seemingly sovereign legal measures, and a complex web of bureaucratic distributions of mortality adjacent to legal regimes, the management of forms of "slow death" within populations among women whose relationship to the politics of abortion often manifests as the differential social and political distribution of the perceived worth of different women's lives (according to wealth, age, education, ability, class, immigration status, nationality, mobility, and ethnicity). The various effects can include a concurrent biopoliticization of women, their enfolding into a number of forms of politics, some of which also amount to a depoliticization of women, and underexamined, strange variants on states of exception through which women may be targeted, deconstituted, or abandoned by the law precisely by virtue of seeming to participate in "life decisions."

The resources of Foucault, and of a number of theorists sometimes grouped as post-Foucauldian, can be reconfigured to the ends of such discussions. This contributes to a transformative period for theories of biopolitics, now increasingly reinterpreted as indirect forms of the thanatopolitical. Michel Foucault, Giorgio Agamben, Judith Butler, Lauren Berlant, Roberto Esposito, Achille Mbembe, and Jasbir Puar are among those to have emphasized that projects to govern and optimize life concurrently distribute indirect forms of death, slow death, precariousness, autoimmunity, and the necropolitical. This direction is not a return to a repressive hypothesis, for a number of reasons. Foucault distinctively argued that the formations and distributions of death, which had emerged with biopolitics, tended to emerge to the putative ends of optimizing life. Even when Mbembe rejects the view that modern distributions of death are best understood as typically subordinate to biopolitical ends, still he argues that death, human disposability, disorder, and chaos may be disseminated in some of the contagious, excitable, and proliferating modes Foucault associated with power's capacity to stimulate and not just repress.[7] And even when the category of bare life refers to the capacity to deprive those who might otherwise be rights entitled of that status, this is still a complex understanding of subtraction; as Simona Forti maintains, to dehumanize is to *produce* bare life.[8]

The following question arises: If the government of procreation has never been far from the future-oriented and risk-averse biopolitical aims of managing life and population, and given the trend in post-Foucaudian philosophy to foreground the necro- and thanatopolitical aspects of biopolitics, shouldn't we expect to find some discussion among these theorists of how the biopolitics of reproduction also becomes necropolitical or thanatopolitical?[9] In fact, this thanatopolitical version emerges through the association between reproduction, life principles, the projection of futures, and the conjoined vectors of mortality within them. This suggestion will, in the next chapter, be opened through an indirect route—by first revisiting one of the encounters between Foucault and Derrida concerning their idiosyncratic considerations of capital punishment. Both Foucault and Derrida, albeit via different means, make manifest some of the different types of life constituted before variants of death penalties. Derrida also analyzes the death penalty in terms of a general logic of progress, of "anesthetization," and of claims to a concern for humanity and quality of life whose complex stakes were also registered by Foucault. For Derrida, it also involved problems more specific to his own work: the sovereign decision, the deconstructable instant of a death and of a decision about the moment of another's death, a death penalty's various aspects of spectacle, witnessing, and media technologies. But if Derrida has been brought into the discussion, this is, in part because of an insight he uniquely identifies: that the problem of the death penalty is also a problem of sexual difference.

Derrida did not, however, extend such reflections into the realm of biopolitics. By contrast, the two philosophers most associated with contemporary biopolitical theory, Agamben and Foucault, have been criticized for occluding sexual difference in their considerations, respectively, of bare life and political responsibility for life. The conjunction of these different theoretical foregroundings and occlusions leads to a number of methodological considerations to which I now turn. A potential space will emerge from within such theoretical contexts more adequate to the analysis of thanatopoliticized reproduction, even by virtue of the negative contours of inhospitality to such questions.

III

All the while that biopolitics has increasingly been reconfigured as thanatopolitical and necropolitical, that same development has been accompanied by concern that some of the prominent theorists of the latter have given inadequate consideration to matters of gender, reproduction, politicized maternity, and maternity as depoliticization.[10] The term *bare life* has played a significant role in such discussions. It has been dominant in many post-Foucauldian contexts foregrounding the thanatopolitical. Yet this development has been criticized for failing to differentiate the ways in which subjects might, by virtue of a number of factors, be more or less vulnerable to becoming bare life.

Developed by Agamben, *bare life* is now a ubiquitous philosophical term circulating in the contemporary humanities and social sciences. It refers to the legal and political possibility of depriving human life of its qualified status, in a production of categories of bare life whose extinction or termination may not fully count as loss of life or homicide. One could say it is also the making of forms of death such that these deaths matter less.

Bare life has also become a widely engaged reference point for many contemporary analyses of the ways in which subordination produces, by virtue of sedimented social and historical forces, certain groups of lives deemed to matter less or deemed not worth living. For an account of the circumstances under which some lives are more vulnerable than others to becoming bare life, particularly because of the long-standing hierarchies of race, gender, caste, and colonialist subordination, one might turn, for example, to Judith Butler's *Frames of War*, Achille Mbembe's *Critique de la raison negre*, Veena Das's *Life and Words*, or Alex Weheliye's *Habeas Viscus*. Collectively, such work speaks to the need for genealogies of how colonialism, plantation, slavery, gendered, nationalist, and heterosexual matrices produce the differential vulnerability of certain bodies and subjects.

Butler, Mbembe, Das, and Weheliye all engage critically with Agamben, but they foreground differentials that cannot be expressed by Agamben's more general ontological argument that there is a fundamental and abstract relationship between qualified political life and its possible subtraction. In short, the relationship between deprivation of legal and political status and the historical trajectory of race and gender hierarchies is widely considered—by Agamben's critics among others—to call for different frames of analysis: variously those of genealogy or social ontology, or critical social theory or approaches reoriented toward the ontic, or to the everyday life of violence. Such analyses have been developed through different terminologies, discussed in the following chapters, including precariousness, disposability, and the terrorist assemblage.

Yet it is interesting that some of these terminologies have also been elaborated through a degree of continued conversation with the concept of bare life. And, all the while that a decontextualized version of the latter has moved into wide circulation, Agamben's work has been intermittently characterized by interlocutors in terms of what it does not articulate. That said, if we change the perspective so as to prioritize scholarship on Agamben, the criticism that he fails to attend to the social and historical differentials of race, gender, and genealogy will in turn seem a failure to appreciate his own analytic parameters. This is, in other words, a dialogue habitually organized around the language of failure—on both sides. To interpret primarily in terms of failure is to overlook what is most interesting about this phenomenon: the capacity of the negative contours corresponding to an absent problem to emerge within the work in question.

One might think here of the gesture with which José Muñoz included Theodor Adorno, Ernst Bloch, Giorgio Agamben, and Jean-Luc Nancy among less predictable resources to which he appealed in order to create "new thought images for queer critique, different paths to queerness."[11] If the latter could also be opened through seemingly inhospitable means, distanced from Muñoz's concerns, these might be forms of "failure worth knowing, a potential that faltered."[12] There is more to be said about the very gesture of deeming an intellectual framework a failure with respect to an articulation it ought to be able to provide. These are failures worth knowing, but what *is* failure: particularly where this means assessing a theoretical language or disposition for its potential to accommodate a problem that seems implausible within it?

With respect to the ways in which the term *bare life* has been repeatedly pressed for what it does not deliver, my argument is that the incapacity to articulate gender difference, gender formation, formations of precariousness, and genealogies of vulnerable bodies may—by dint of reiterated attribution—convert to a strong inhabitation by what is missing. For example, an absent conceptual possibility emerges under the pressure of the critical race, gender, postcolonial, and genealogically inflected attention with which Agamben's work has been confronted: a differential and genealogical understanding of bare life jarring with the context in which it emerges. And this is a direction which can always be reversed, as when Ranjana Khanna and Catherine Mills combine feminist critique of Agamben with renewed interest in questions of how legal and political spaces can concurrently protect and expose.[13] This is also to give greater attention to the way in which concepts can emerge through a process of mutual confrontation not just between texts, arguments, theorists, and philosophers but also, and more particularly, through the relationship between their capacities and incapacities.

Accordingly, this exploration involves spending time with some unfamiliar figures and problems: Foucault's remarks on children; some liminal suggestions made about female *sinthom*osexuals in Edelman's *No Future*; some of Agamben's most fleeting remarks about women, reproduction, and sexual violence, and equally brief—and wary—comments about the making of fetal life as precarious in the opening pages of Butler's *Frames of War;* a pregnant woman in a Boston abortion clinic who, in a dissonant passage in Carol Gilligan's *In a Different Voice,* imagines selling her child on "the black market"; Derrida's aversion to biopolitics and his uncharacteristic inattention to both sex and sexual difference when it came to the work of Foucault.

Exploring the quality of futurity with which reproduction emerges within biopolitics—that form of politics assuming responsibility for the management and optimization of life—will take the route of a particular form of dialogue with recent philosophers and theorists who have engaged biopolitical phenomena. This is a turn to what does not lie front and center in these contexts, to what lies held in reserve, even within texts whose resources we may seem to have drained. Critical analysis might use the suspended reserves of the most unpromising theoretical resources to stimulate the emergence of new concepts—from thanatopolitized reproduction to ontological tact to hypergenealogy—whose contours of omission are traced to the ends of a different variant of the productivity of critique.

1

SUSPENSIONS OF SEX

Foucault and Derrida

I am still trying to imagine Foucault's response. I can't quite do it. I would have so much liked for him to take it on himself.
—JACQUES DERRIDA, "TO DO JUSTICE TO FREUD"

It is clear how far one is from an analysis in terms of deconstruction (any confusion between these two methods would be unwise.)
—MICHEL FOUCAULT, "POLEMICS, POLITICS, AND PROBLEMATIZATION"

FOUCAULT'S SURVIVAL

A post-Foucauldian mood characterizes a number of ongoing and galvanizing engagements with Foucault's legacy. In a wide range of disciplines, theorists including Giorgio Agamben, Didier Fassin, and Wendy Brown have continued to respond to elements in Foucault's work awaiting correction[1] or, as Roberto Esposito has formulated this, inevitabilities contained in his work but not articulated by Foucault himself.[2] Fassin responds to the limitations of Foucault's work on life by "enter[ing] it" so as to "get back to where [Foucault] left biopower."[3] Foucault's resources have been profoundly transformed by post-Foucauldian biopolitical theory's interest in inequality,[4] in political legitimacy,[5] in necropolitics,[6] in states of disorder and insecurity, in the extremes of immune paradigms.[7]

These ongoing modes of contesting, correcting, repudiating, or reconfiguring could also be characterized as Foucault's afterlife. Throughout, the very lexicon of challenge (the language, for example, of rectification, of reentering, or of inevitable consequences) has rarely been challenged. Except, a little spitefully, by Derrida. When Agamben finds the direction of his own argument to have been "logically implicit" in Foucault's work, while remaining a Foucauldian "blindspot," Derrida can't help himself: "Poor Foucault! He never had such a cruel admirer."[8] Yet, renewing his own interrogations at ten-year intervals in essays and seminars, Derrida belonged to those who have not wished to take their leave, conclusively, from Foucault's work.

While his well-known criticisms of Foucault's work are extensive, my discussion of their exchange will be oriented by just one element, seemingly brief: the objections Derrida expressed to biopolitics. In fact, this response will allow us to revisit much in Foucault's work: most broadly, his understandings of power, the status of life and death, and the present. The very meaning of Foucault's present has become differently salient with the emergence of theory understood as "post-Foucault." Derrida explored these questions with subtlety: what, for Foucault, would be "post?" In that sense, what, for Foucault, was the present?

This book opens with some of the elements that are most relevant to Derrida's understanding of Foucault's temporality and his survival. The encounter will then lead to a means of thinking about Foucault's reserves, also characterized as his suspended capacities, mobilized in the subsequent chapters.

FOUCAULT'S RESERVES

What if we are sympathetic with the questions directed by Derrida at Foucault's project, yet no less interested in Foucauldian resources for formulating a response? This need not mean claiming that Foucault's texts anticipated Derrida's posthumous questions, nor that they are more deconstructive than it seems. It is a common argument that philosophers deconstructed by Derrida, such as Edmund Husserl or Jean-Jacques Rousseau, had already elaborated the intervention attributed to Derrida. Instead, I propose an alternative means of developing the mutual capacities that emerge in such encounters. Formulated in this way, the encounter between Foucault and Derrida can provide a guiding model for further methodological provocations. For example, how can a productive capacity emerge from the intersection of theorists around the problems they occluded? How might the latter emerge from the analytic pressure each can exert on the other's resources, from the terms of resistance of each to the other, and from the lines of critique stimulated by their more awkward proximities?

As we will see, Derrida interrogated, critically, the status of epoch and threshold in Foucault's work. But I will argue that Foucault offers the resources for calling into question the self-identity of modernity, epoch, mode, tactics, power, apparatus, modernity, present, and gathering principles also queried by Derrida. To ask what, in Foucault's work, is hospitable to such a line of questioning is to go beyond the recognizable limits of Foucault's actual responses to Derrida. It is also to claim that Derrida misses an opportunity to rethink the presence, or principles, of Foucauldian power by means of Foucault's own account of the dehiscence of power's techniques, their perpetual ambiguity and self-differentiation,[9] except insofar as the latter are identified by Derrida's counter-reading. Derrida looks away from interpretative possibilities within Foucault most in affinity with the counter-reading. For example, when Foucault analyzed techniques of power as segmenting and reassembling in multiple temporalities, he offered an alternative to the references to epochs and ages dominating Derrida's response.

This contributes to the complex status of Foucault's "present," whose methodological consequences will prove to be extensive. Working toward this argument, I will first reconstruct four elements presupposed in the more complex versions of Foucault's present. These are, first, Foucault's account of subjects and objects as transactional unities, an account to be conjoined with his accounts of contingent formations of life and death. Second, the dehiscence of the Foucauldian present. This is related to a third: the segmentation, and capacity for decomposition, of Foucauldian techniques of power. The fourth might be characterized as Foucault's suspensions (to use an image from Derrida), his plasticity (to evoke the early development of this term by Catherine Malabou), or (as mobilized in the following chapters) the potential of his work to operate through a transformative proximity.

LIFE AND DEATH—AS TRANSACTIONAL UNITIES

One of Foucault's many rejections of conventional history included a challenge to the status of objects understood as universals: "I start from the theoretical and methodological decision that consists in saying: Let's suppose that universals do not exist. And then I put the question to history and historians: How can you write history if you do not accept a priori the existence of things like the state, society, the sovereign, and subjects?"[10] For example, Foucault repudiated intellectual inquiries for which life or death was "outside discourse" in favor of analyzing the formation of transactional unities in which both subject and object take shape together.

A "critical history,"[11] as Foucault understood the term, would devote itself to the formation of these transactional unities, offering an "analysis of the conditions under which certain relations of subject to object are formed or modified, insofar as those relations constitute a possible knowledge [*savoir*]."[12] In early versions, *The Birth of the Clinic* described the conditions of possibility for the fields of visibility of objects,[13] and *The Order of Things* described the epistemic conditions of a simultaneous emergence of new "knowable objects . . new concepts and new methods."[14] According to Foucault's guiding methodological supposition, as new knowable objects take shape, so do their subjects. "The problem is to determine what the subject must be, to what condition [it] is subject, what status [it] must have, what position [it] must occupy in reality, or in the imaginary, in order to become a legitimate subject of this or that type of knowledge."[15] A corresponding approach to the study of formations of life and death is to be found in much of Foucault's work: in *The Birth of the Clinic*, in *The Order of Things*, and in his work on sex, degeneracy, and biopolitics.[16] He describes the conditions under which life and death differently, and contingently, become possible for correspondingly contingent subjects. In *The Birth of the Clinic* disease and mortality emerge as possible objects of knowledge insofar as their signs and symptoms manifest in organic bodies.[17] *The Order of Things* gives a number of variants in formations of life and death. We find resonances of this analytic disposition at the outset of Butler's *Frames of War*, when she evokes Foucault's archaeological language and its account of the "space" of knowledge, experience, and perception with her reference to the "epistemological" and "interpretive frames" of life.[18] The foundation for her analysis of the making of (differentially) grievable and precarious life is the methodological starting point that "there is no life and no death without a relation to some frame."[19]

The different deaths considered by Foucault (repudiated as universals, described as formations) include death lurking within life, and within the physical bodies of the history of medicine, as a pathological principle whose signs and symptoms make their subjects hermeneutic inquirers.[20] Compare to Foucault's later interest in degeneracy as the preoccupation of those interested in psychiatric medicine, sexuality, early forms of eugenics, and a number of corresponding governmentalities.[21] Again bodies, manifesting such disorders as alcoholism, dissipation, licentiousness and immorality, become symptomatic sites. But the depths in which the knowing subject seeks truth are different. The inquirer preoccupied with degeneration looks into the deep space of a patient's genealogical history for symptoms and their hereditary antecedents understood as explanatory principles. Also the inquirer looks forward, anticipating impact on future generations. The associated conducts are different. The "deep" bodily spaces of *The Birth of the Clinic* are investigated by conducts of the anatomist, the physician, and the clinic. "Degeneracy" integrates with the aim of calculating and managing the threat of a reproduction perceived as destructive for peoples. Compare with *Security, Territory, and Population*'s interest in mortality distributed through populations.[22] The according conducts are not hermeneutic, but those of risk management. Death becomes associated with tolerable thresholds. Its distribution in populations might be understood statistically, as when deaths or diseases are deemed disturbing only above certains rates or levels in the population. Here there is an emergence not only of the corresponding subjects and objects but also of the possibility of administering the "life" of a population, newly understood as an entity with its own patterns, needs, and predictabilities. Here, too, Foucault describes population, understood as a biological collectivity as follows: "a constant interplay between techniques of power and their object gradually carves out in reality, as a field of reality, population and its specific phenomena. A whole series of domains of objects were made visible for possible forms of knowledge on the basis of the constitution of the population as the correlate of techniques of power. In turn, because these forms of knowledge constantly carve out new objects, the population could be formed, continue, and remain as the privileged correlate of modern mechanisms of power" (STP 79 trans. mod.).

FOUCAULT'S PRESENT: THRESHOLDS, DECLINES, AND ADVENTS

Foucault sometimes referred to modes of power as historically consecutive. The anatomo-politics associated with disciplinary techniques are said to have emerged before (and then to have combined with) the biopolitical forms concerned with the management of populations which "formed [s'est formé] somewhat later" (HS I 139). He described the transition from the Roman and medieval variants of legal systems to the modern penal order. In *Security, Territory, Population* he describes having "apparently" given "the bare bones, if you like, of a kind of historical schema" (STP 6). But to confine oneself to such seemingly consecutive narratives would be to overlook much in his work resisting them. Commonly mentioned examples are also available in *Security, Territory, Population*,[23] and in *Society Must Be Defended*,[24] which see Foucault countering just as actively a linear understanding of these modes of power.

He can acknowledge that medieval contexts included elements of disciplinary techniques.[25] But they would not be described as disciplinary societies because these isolated techniques did not belong to a broadly diffused network of interconnecting institutions, forms of knowledge, authority, sciences of efficiency and optimization; psychological individualization, correctability, and normalization; and associated formations of selfhood. There are a number of ways of understanding the point that disciplinary techniques are seen in societies Foucault would not consider disciplinary. For example, the fact that spatial organizations producing a permanent sense of observation and self-judgment manifest in many different contexts, including medieval cloisters, might lead us to ask if these are really the "same" techniques. And, since isolated disciplinary techniques have long and diverse histories, and can manifest without belonging to the capillary forms of power Foucault associates with modernity (the complex interconnection of panopticization, individuation, abnormalization, expert knowledges, institutions, proliferation of interest), this also means, to turn to Thomas Lemke's commentary, that "there is no absolute break between disciplinary and post-disciplinary societies," nor is there a definitive threshold between the disciplinary and the predisciplinary.[26]

Here are some further principles that can be derived from this conclusion. Of any formation or mode of power described by Foucault, one could conclude that its techniques and forms are in the process of transformation. The context of such techniques might be in the process of change, or the techniques themselves might mutate in the sense that they begin to play a role in new types of tactical formations, new modes of power, new types of governmentality, and form new correlations with other techniques.[27]

One can find an extensive metaphorics elaborated by Foucault to describe exactly this possibility. In *Security, Territory, Population* he describes mechanisms of security as having activated (*activé*) and propagated (*fécondé*) techniques of discipline (*STP* 7), in a "reactivation [*réactivation*] and transformation [*transformation*]" of them (*STP* 9). Legal, disciplinary, and security mechanisms, which otherwise might be supposed to replace each other, instead are said to come into new forms of "correlation" (*corrélation*) with each other (*STP* 8). As they do, the techniques in question are described as becoming more complex or as perfecting or as changing (*STP* 8).[28] They might intensify each other, as Foucault suggests is the relationship between modern aims of security which rely on, rather than replace, disciplinary mechanisms. But their coincidence could also be unstable in a number of senses. For example, he also describes the possibility of violent reaction and conflict between the aims of discipline and security (and so an intensification of states of disorder; *STP* 9).

So it is with the relationship between modes of power elaborated in Foucault's work. For the best-known example, consider the relationship between sovereignty and the biopolitical elaborated in *The History of Sexuality* (*HS I*). Generally considered to pertain to a progression of eras, sovereign power is presented by Foucault as the older and now anachronistic formation. In the final chapter of *The History of Sexuality*, we're told that the ancient right to "*take* life or *let* live" (faire *mourir ou de* laisser *vivre*) was replaced by modernity's power "to *foster* life or *disallow* it to the point of death" (faire *vivre ou de* rejeter *dans la mort*; *HSI* 138), or, as Fassin has proposed the translation, a "power to make live and reject into death."[29] Similarly, *Society Must Be Defended* proposes that "the power of sovereignty is increasingly on the retreat and . . . disciplinary or regulatory disciplinary power is on the advance" (*SMBD* 254).[30] Foucault is certainly understood as describing deductive (*HSI* 136) sovereign forms of power as older,[31] and the proliferating, expansive biopolitical modes as more recent—particularly given their emergence in association with new sciences, new technologies, new forms of knowledge (statistics, demography, physiocracy) not available in classical or medieval periods.

Foucault emphasizes that the institutions of the juridical monarchy, its traditions, institutions, forms, and representations are "characteristic but transitory" (*bien particulière et malgré tout transitoire*; *HS I* 89). They emerge with the feudal system that had inherited the Roman legal system and its modes of power, described in terms of deduction (*prélèvement*) centered around appropriation of land, wealth, taxes, liberty, and life. The death penalty expresses this traditional sovereign right over bodies and territories, the right to take, have, annex, deprive. By contrast, as he argues, death penalties are heterogeneous with the emergence of biopower associated with modernity, given that the latter, from the eighteenth century onwards, "took charge [*pris en charge*] of men's existence, men as living bodies" (*HS I* 89) to optimize them.

But despite describing biopower as replacing sovereign modes of power, and the two as having different aims belonging to different ages, he does not deny that many of the legal and political mechanisms of juridical monarchies have also "persisted" (*subsisté; HS I* 89). So, in another formulation, Foucault proposes that such surviving sovereign institutional forms (sovereign state, right, law, logics of appropriation and punishment) have "gradually been *penetrated* [*pénétrée*] by quite new mechanisms of power that are quite probably irreducible to the representation of law."[32] Remarks in this vein have led a number of commentators to emphasize that sovereign power and biopolitics are not simply opposed.[33] The more efficient and productive forms of biopower have not entirely eclipsed modes of sovereign power, just as they don't belong to a clean historical progression.

SEGMENTATIONS, DECOMPOSITIONS

Opening his 1972–73 seminar "The Punitive Society," Foucault argued that strategies and tactics of power could be distinguished, decomposed,[34] segmented[35]— according to their different roles, their tactical functions, and the different economies of power to which they correspond.[36] This is another occasion on which, after a discussion in these terms of a number of forms of punishment, Foucault turns to the example of the death penalty. A death penalty can, but does not necessarily, exclude the condemned from political communities. It can serve to demarcate some as lacking the right to have rights. Or it might involve the expulsion of humans into exposed conditions where the likely resulting deaths will count neither as execution nor as murder. But, in another economy of power, death penalties might be compensatory mechanisms for victims, their families, society, or a governing authority. Alternatively, an execution might be the spectacular declaration of a sovereign's "right to impose justice." Responding to crime, it could be symbolically retributive: understood as "the reply of the sovereign to those who attacked his will, his law, or his person" (*HS I* 137–38). It might serve to demonstrate what a sovereign "pouvait faire du corps d'un homme" (all that he could do with a man's body),[37] as in the grotesquely prolonged execution of Damiens in 1757. By contrast, some modern forms of capital punishment might operate as incarceration's extreme limit, giving the spatial enclosure of the prison the alternative of an ultimate, temporal closure.

Insofar as they belong to different tactics, and to different modes of power, techniques of execution (like techniques of expulsion, fining, surveillance) can be distinguished. These are different techniques of death, as seen in differences in how deaths are effected (as when one compares the elaborate techniques maximally prolonging Damien's expiration with the machinic design with which the guillotine aims at instantaneous and efficient execution). They may be functionally different deaths: operations of retribution or compensation, of desubjectivization or spectacularization. Death penalties are not always primarily punitive. The frenzy of executions during the French Revolution aimed less to punish than to purge the public space of its ever-expanding category of political enemies. Thus it might seem that all executions involve the deaths of individuals.

But not all death penalties individualize. The difference between operations of individualization or deindividualization may characterize a death penalty's specific techniques. An execution might aim to be self-canceling. Its technique might be to retroactively erase its own status as "execution" in its aim to render what is killed, less-than-human life. The difference between these techniques amounts to more than a difference between methods of death or between different aims of imposed death. At stake also is the different deaths of dehumanized individuals, or of political enemies, or of "masses," and only sometimes (through corresponding techniques of individualization) of individuals.[38] It becomes a decisive point for Foucault that the seemingly similar techniques that might otherwise be grouped together as "death penalties" can be tactically differentiated in such ways.

Consider Derrida's comment that "Foucault declares that he could have . . . related the decline of the death penalty to the progress of biopolitics."[39] It is true that Foucault generally describes a decline in the dominance of spectacular, sovereign tactics.[40] But in the passage mentioned by Derrida Foucault offers execution as a further example of how powers of death may be the counterside or underneath (*l'envers*) of biopower (*HS I* 136). Capital punishment can be *consistent* with biopolitical strategies that aim to optimize life. To reinforce that point he turns to a type of justification once provided for the death penalty: "by invoking less the enormity of the crime itself than the monstrosity of the criminal, his incorrigibility, and the safeguard of society. One had the right to kill those who represented a kind of biological danger to others" (*HS I* 138).

So how might the "deaths" ascribed by Foucault to the sovereign power to take life be distinguished from those ascribable to the biopolitical capacity to optimize life? In forms ranging from indirect murder, the rationalization of resources, or collateral damage to massacre, war, and genocide, Foucault argues that biopower has also allowed the formation of strategies of "vital" deaths. Characterizing specifically biopolitical powers of death, Foucault argued they could manifest in forms of war: "no longer waged in the name of a sovereign who must be defended; they are waged on behalf of the existence of everyone" (*HS I* 137). Such "vital" deaths might be surreptitious, meticulously recorded, or meticulously effacing. They might involve complex rationalities, as when some forms of death amount to the prudential disfavoring of certain groups. They might be pursued in the name of security, risk aversion, collective or national interest, or that of rising generations. They may presuppose tacit or overtly declared divisions between more and less valued groups, categories, or forms of life. As Jasbir Puar characterizes the characteristically "vital" aims of biopolitical powers of death: "death is never a primary focus; it is a negative translation of the imperative to live, occurring only through the transit of fostering life. Death becomes a form of collateral damage in the pursuit of life."[41]

This means that the murderousness of biopolitics remains tactically different from the murderousness of sovereign power. But such forms of death can operate together. This is more generally true of Foucault's accounts of the relations between modes of power—they may reinforce each other without becoming entirely indistinct. Foucault characterizes the Nazi state in such terms: as a combination of powers and techniques of discipline, security, sovereignty and biopolitics. The elaborate, mutually denouncing self-scrutiny of neighbors was a disciplinary and panopticized mode reinforcing the Nazi state's sovereign power of death. Its genocides were pursued in a sovereign exercise of powers of death and also in a biopolitical project to optimize Aryan life. Foucault also refers to what he takes to be an extraordinary phenomenon, insofar as sovereign and biopolitical aims were pursued so extremely that they began to merge in their superimposition. As thoroughly biopolitical, the Nazi state was thoroughly murderous (*SMBD* 260). But, even at this point, Foucault is not describing a principle of power that has become self-identical. To the contrary, in a passage elaborated by Esposito (to whom we'll return), what Foucault describes is a "paroxysm" of power in which there are *both* coinciding and conflicted interests, technologies, apparatuses, techniques and modes of power, tactics, aims.

More generally, Foucault argued that the techniques of different modes of power could have multiple valences yet operate in tandem. Life could be optimized in a social body through sovereign aims, anatomo-politics, and biopolitics that are able to articulate with each other. Their modes of power are differentiable technically and tactically, yet come into contact in a number of ways. One reason is that their techniques don't always operate at the same level. From urban planning to the formations of sexuality, as matters of individual conduct and as a regulation of the population, different techniques of different modes of power may simultaneously stimulate bodies, habits, conducts, populations, milieus, trends in different ways, to different ends.

Security, Territory, Population offers a number of examples. Disciplinary mechanisms might also be security mechanisms, factoring in the "likelihood" of recidivism (*STP* 7). Urban planning is a disciplinary mechanism factoring self-realizing standards for bodily conduct, movement, and distribution of bodies (such as one or two individuals per room, one family per house, straight lines of houses forming the thoroughfares of streets, etc.). But it is also a regulatory, optimizing, biopolitical mechanism applied to populations and encouraging overall "patterns" of residential saving patterns, of "levels" of public hygiene, and so on. Sexuality is described by Foucault in disciplinary terms (involving the gridding, disclosure, and normalization of individual sexual behavior) *and* as allowing a governmentality of the life processes of a population (administration in terms of birth, health, death and disease rate, medical and insurance coverage, conducts of sex and reproduction deemed normal and abnormal, prediction and adjustment for their patterns and distributions in populations).[42]

Thus a "same" body (so to speak) is invested, or becomes possible, in a number of different ways at once: as such it is not the same body. Foucault offered a famous definition of the "polyvalence" of discourse: to be understood as "a series of discontinuous segments [*une série de segments discontinus*] whose tactical function is neither uniform nor stable" (*HS I* 100). The formulation can also be used to characterize the plasticity of bodies, conducts, and the tactical segments of modes and techniques of power. This phenomenon is particularly evident, in fact, in a bank of images and lexicon used by Foucault: such as imprinting and availability for penetration, superimposition, polyvalence, coalescing, becoming indistinct, segmentation, decomposition, paradox, transformation, and mutation. This will bring us back Derrida's interrogation of the Foucauldian present. One way to characterize the plasticity of the segments of techniques, apparatuses, and modes of power described by Foucault would be to turn instead to the Derridean term *survivance*: a form of living on that takes place while calling into question what has survived. There is survival without continuity in what survives.[43] In fact, the lexicon employed by Foucault (penetration, superimposition, coalescence, etc.) would lend itself particularly well to such an understanding. This lexicon offers a rich resource for reconsidering one of the problems dominating his ongoing, post-1980s reception: the present, the Foucauldian present, the actuality of Foucault. A good route for this exploration was opened up by the questions Derrida directed at Foucault.

THE FISSURED FOUCAULDIAN PRESENT

Derrida focused on figures that, in Foucault's work, were emblematic of his intermittent tendency to characterize age and epochs in his accounts of epistemic conditions and formations of power. The best-known example concerns Foucault's characterization of Descartes as emblematic of the classical age's confinement of madness.[44] But a number of similar figures emerged in his *History of Madness*. For example, Freud offers an iconic contrasting figure, characterizing a later era's characterization of madness as available to be understood, treated, analyzed, and mastered. Derrida countered that such emblematic figures retained an ambivalent status in Foucault's accounts. In drawing out that ambivalence, Derrida could be said to amplify different capacities of Foucault's work, reworking the status of a Foucauldian present.[45]

For Foucault could describe figures emblematic of an age as *also* foreshadowing later transformations. He makes a number of references to Freud in these different veins. Freud is connected to an earlier lineage of aspirations to moral rehabilitation seen in eighteenth-century treatments of madness developed by Philippe Pinel and Samuel Tuke. Newly deemed an ailment amenable to therapeutic approaches, madness generated an accompanying surplus of enlightened psychiatric authority over it. But Freud also can be connected to entirely different characterizations of human finitude (including what Foucault called man's "empirico-transcendental doublet") associated with later developments in philosophy and the human sciences.[46]

Derrida responds that insofar as Foucauldian figures such as Descartes, Freud, and "psychoanalysis 'itself'" characterize ages,[47] and particularly when such figures or developments are given the status of prefigurations,[48] they challenge Foucault's "present." They destabilize any of the "presents" and epochs Foucault also is prone to characterize. As the imminent advent of other possibilities and ages with different characteristics, they are the anticipatory disturbance of possible transformation (88–90). Thus, in a counter-reading of such figures in Foucault's work, Derrida argues that they challenge the linear sequences and thresholds Foucault also establishes, such as the "partition between a classical and a postclassical age" (77).

> [Foucault] says, in effect, that what is called contemporary had already begun in the classical age and with [Descartes'] Evil Genius, which clearly, to my eyes at least, cannot leave intact the historical categories of reference and the presumed identity of something like the "classical age" (for example).... One may imagine the effects that the category of the "perpetual threat" (Foucault's term) can have on indications of presence, positive markings, the determinations made by means of signs or statements, in short, the whole criteriology and symptomatology that can give assurance to a historical knowledge concerning a figure, an *episteme*, an age, an epoch, a paradigm.
>
> (87)

To return to the example, *The History of Madness* would really have established a psychoanalysis that is "consequently nonglobalizable," "divided and multiple" (114), as are figures such as Diderot, Descartes, and Freud. And once this conclusion is generally broadened to all the figures, knowledges, techniques, and epistemic conditions one might attribute to an "age," one would have to call into question the viability of Foucault's demarcations ("classical," "modern") between them (77). Finally, Derrida claims that this broader expansion could not exempt the "we" who might belong to such ages, nor "time," its "place," its "itself," nor, most generally, Foucault's "present":

> Here is ... according to Foucault, *our* age, *our* contemporareity.... The "we" who is saying "we think in that place" is evidently, tautologically, the "we" out of which the signatory of these lines, the author of *The History of Madness* and *The Order of Things*, speaks, writes, and thinks. But this "we" never stops dividing, and the places of its signature are displaced in being divided up. A certain untimeliness always disturbs the contemporary who reassures him or herself in a "we." This "we," our "we"

is not its own contemporary. The self-identity of its age, or any age, appears as divided, and thus problematic, *problematizable* . . . as the age of madness or an age of psychoanalysis—as well as, in fact, all the historical or archaeological categories that promise us the determinable stability of a configurable whole. . . . The couple Freud/Nietzsche forms and then unforms, this decoupling fissures the identity of the epoch, of the age, of the *episteme* or the paradigm of which one or the other, or both together, might have been the signifiers or representatives. This is even more true when this decoupling comes to fissure the self-identity of some individual, or some presumed individuality, for example, of Freud. What allows one to presume the non-self-difference of Freud, for example? And of psychoanalysis? These decouplings and self-differences no doubt introduce a good deal of disorder into the unity of any configuration, whole, epoch, or historical age.[49]

(109–10)

On Derrida's reading, Foucault would commit to (or declare) the delineation of ages and epochs, while describing phenomena simultaneously undermining such demarcations. In response, Derrida engages in a maximal expansion of the principles attributable to Foucault's account of multiplicity, division, untimeliness, dispersion, extending them back to encompass his work. Thus Foucault would have "ceaselessly" reminded us of powers that were "essentially dispersed" (114; Derrida's point of reference here is the first volume of *The History of Sexuality*). But, Derrida responds, what then allows the coalescence of an apparatus (to use Foucault's term) or allows us to identify the assembling, heterogeneous techniques of a mode of power? Derrida claims that there is a countermovement between its dispersed heterogeneity and a Foucauldian principle of "gathering" (*rassemblement*) (117). Consider Colin Koopman's account of the relations between the elements of an apparatus depicted in Foucault's genealogies. He argues that they allow us "to grasp the coherence of a complex welter of practical material that is contingently interrelated . . . in a way that both encourages respect for the profound stability of this practical material as it functions and also enables acknowledgement of the sheer contingency of this stability."[50]

Accordingly, Derrida directs his attention to a Foucauldian account of power that, finally, must sufficiently amount to a principle of "gathering" for a mode of power or an apparatus to be understood as such. In a Foucauldian apparatus, disparate, heterogeneous elements cohere and interconnect productively. But, as Robert Trumbull interprets Derrida's response: "Once the axiomatic concept of power is put into question, the very project the genealogist undertakes is destabilized. Even if power is irreducibly dispersed, there must be a unity of the concept in order for a genealogy of power relations to get underway in the first place."[51]

This brings me to the fourth guiding theme with which I mobilize aspects of Foucault operative in the following project, the idea of "suspension" suggested by Derrida in his essay on Foucault written after the latter's death, "To Do Justice to Freud." Another term we could propose is Foucault's reserves.

FOUCAULT'S SUSPENDED RESERVES: SEX WITH DERRIDA AND FOUCAULT

Concluding his last published essay on Foucault, "To Do Justice to Freud," Derrida proposed we might return to Foucault's work "by means of a question that it carries within itself, that it keeps in reserve in its unlimited potential," "in suspense, holding its breath."[52] But, in affirming this means of thinking of Foucault's reserves, Derrida holds something back. In rethinking his relation to Foucault, how might he also have interrogated his own reserves? Shouldn't an interrogation of Foucauldian suspensions have provided the context for a corresponding interrogation of the suspensions in Derrida's response? Once amplified and pursued more reciprocally, they contain further possibilities for exploring the suspended dialogue.

When, in "To Do Justice," Derrida imagined the further readings Foucault might have undertaken of the blurred, dual principles of life and death in Freud's *Beyond the Pleasure Principle*, he returned to *History of Madness* and to a number of other texts including Foucault's discussion of Freud and of confessional sex in *The History of Sexuality*.[53] But this was to inhabit a discussion in which Foucault had evoked formations of death in life in a sense not mentioned by Derrida.

One of the most obvious ways in which Foucault described this death in life in *The History of Sexuality* was as a formation of sex. Consider the work's masturbating children, described by Foucault in terms of a late eighteenth- and nineteenth-century preoccupation with death wreaked simultaneously on the child's individual body (vitality sapped in youth and reducing its life by decades) and on the vitality of peoples.[54] Sex in Foucault's work, and its conjoined problems of population, reproduction and transmission deemed individually and collectively deadly, and the biopolitical managements of life and death (in all their extended meaning—futures of bodies, peoples, nations) was not considered by Derrida. Foucault and Derrida dialogued about other questions: about madness, silencing, reason, history, the pretensions of philosophy, their disputed interpretations of Descartes. Lynne Huffer describes Derrida's inattention to the quality, detail, and material character of Foucault's archival work: the latter's minute attention to institutions, architecture, conducts, practices, diagnoses, records, bodies, confinements, timetables, treatments, and cures.[55] Perhaps partly by virtue of this neglect of the details of Foucault's archive, Derrida overlooked the point (recently developed in Huffer's *Mad for Foucault*) that an extensive elaboration of a history of sex was also to be found in *History of Madness*.[56] To recall Foucault's protesting response in 1972 to Derrida's critique of this work: "Derrida thinks that he can capture the meaning of my book [*History of Madness*] or its 'project' from . . . three pages that are given over to the analysis of a text that is recognized by the philosophical tradition. . . . Consequently, there is no point arguing about the 650 pages of a book, no point analyzing the historical material that is brought to bear therein, and no point criticizing the choice of this material, its distribution and its interpretation."[57] Amongst those 650 pages of historical material not considered by Derrida, we'll find (consistent with Huffer's argument) the problematized masturbation, cause of twenty-eight cases of madness,[58] and later deemed one of madness's common causes along with alcohol abuse, communicated viruses, blows, and falls.[59]

It doesn't seem inappropriate to imagine Derrida somewhat averse to engaging the theme that would eventually dominate so many critical engagements with Foucault: the sex. The remark is applicable to Derrida's first critical essay on *History of Madness* in 1963 given the intermittent overlaps between madness and sexual disorder discussed in that work. And in his later responses to Foucault Derrida would prove little more inclined to discuss the sex of *The History of Sexuality*.

For his part, Foucault was not better attuned to Derrida's most specific elaborations. His delayed response to Derrida's critique of *History of Madness* witheringly made Derridean text and textuality seem a preoccupation with language, narrowly defined. *Of Grammatology* had been published five years earlier, in 1967, and contained its now iconic declaration that there was nothing outside of the text (*il n'y a pas de hors-texte*).[60] Foucault seems to have taken this as an indication that there was for Derrida nothing outside "language." At a time when Foucault was diagnosing the conditions of inclusion and circulation of discourse, including the author and commentary functions,[61] Foucault classified Derrida's "text" as commentary—belonging to the phenomenon of commentary on commentary.[62]

The two could find little to say to each other on "text," it was clear. But, by the time of Foucault's sharp remarks in 1972, hadn't Derridean text already become sex in a number of his publications? Think of the early appearance of his readings of Levinasian sexual difference in 1964,[63] and of Rousseau's maternal metonymies and deferred, disseminated desire in *Of Grammatology* in 1967. And what of Rousseau's substitutive "supplements" (masturbation, desire, sex, women, the maternal, nature . . .), which had provided the very context for the Derridean "il n'y a pas de hors-texte"?[64] One could even put the question this way: how did Derrida and Foucault miss the coincidence (and interesting divergences) of their idiosyncratic discussions of masturbation as mortal danger? Everything that was most characteristic about Derridean generalized "text" (allowing him to depart from the limited definition of language with which Foucault had confused his interests) was enveloped in the ambit of Rousseauist masturbation as elaborated in *Of Grammatology's* analysis of the always already substitutive original object of desire. As the deferring and differing "dangerous supplement," Rousseauist masturbation was reinterpreted as deconstructive *différance*.

Foucault would not return to the mortal dimensions of masturbating children until his Collège de France lectures of 1973–74 (*Psychiatric Power*) and then (very extensively) in 1974–75's *Abnormal*. But they had already made their appearance in *History of Madness*. Perhaps everything constituting the philosophical, strategic, and technical gulf between Foucault and Derrida could be located in the different significance of the masturbatory for the methodological intuitions of each.[65] Both extended—to sex, to masturbation—remarkably novel forms of philosophical analysis.[66] Rousseau's masturbation enabled Derrida's first important elaboration of the text of sex and of the sex of text.[67] And the abnormality with which masturbation was associated gave rise to Foucault's discussion of metasomatization and the metabody,[68] the body whose "present" (for example, a child's masturbatory "present") could simultaneously emerge as multiple forms of possible abnormality, connected to a complex, extended hereditary network, and to the collective futures it projected (enfolding potential for transmitting harm to those futures, including a population's impaired vitality or "degeneracy").

So one could conclude there were missed opportunities between the two men and some limitations in their characterizations of distinctive aspects of the other's work. In 1972, neither observed the innovative methodologies available from the other for rethinking sex.[69] Even when Derrida turned to *The History of Sexuality*, in much later writing (in "To Do Justice to Freud" and in his seminar "Beast and Sovereign") he was still problematizing Foucault's epistemes, thresholds, and ages. Interested in the intersections of sex and text, he could have considered Foucault's references to an inscription of sex (*HS I* 69, 95, 96; *SMBD* 251). He might have interrogated *The History of Sexuality*'s account of a replacement of modes of alliance with sexuality and of sovereign forms of power with those of biopower, given Foucault's description of the former as penetrated (*pénétré*) by the latter (*HS I* 89) and of the power to kill as the underside (*l'envers*) of the biopolitical (*HS I* 136).[70] When compared to Derrida's luxuriantly eroticized readings of Genet and Hegel in 1974, or even his exchange with Geoffrey Bennington in *Circonfession*,[71] we could assume there was less pleasure available from the penetrations and undersides of *The History of Sexuality*.

Insofar as each missed the other's sex, it is all too easy to sexualize the image of an avoided encounter between the men. But there is more to be said about their short-circuited potential encounter. The Foucauldian metaphors of penetration characterizing the transformation of modes of power in *The History of Sexuality* could have pulled Derrida's attention to the Foucauldian "techniques" and segmentation providing alternatives to the thresholds, ages, and epistemic ruptures. Derrida missed the complex temporality of the bodies belonging to Foucault's archive. The "metasomatization" of its childrens' masturbatory metabodies alone interrupted the "present" Derrida attributed to Foucault's epochs and figures so as to counter-read. In reverse, the textuality of Derrida's "sex" could have alerted Foucault that Derrida's "il n'y a pas de hors-texte" was not a claim that everything was language. Rather, what we think of as flesh, or matter, or life, or death, or reproduction, or desire, pleasure, bodies, or biography are no less rendered through differing and deferring than the phenomena more readily defined as "language," and "writing."

If we were to explore a possible intersection between Derrida's deconstructive genealogy,[72] and his deconstruction of sex, with Foucault's genealogy of sex, where might this lead us?

SEX AND BIOPOLITICS

Of course, Derrida may have largely avoided Foucauldian sex, but he seems to have been all the more wary of the biopolitics, whose claims are reconsidered at the conclusion to *The Beast and the Sovereign*, volume 1. Distracted by his criticisms of Agamben, Derrida describes Foucault in conjunction with Agamben as succumbing to the "temptation" of "linear history."[73] Repeatedly, Derrida had returned Foucault to a problem of thresholds, now arguing that Foucault's work ought to "forbi[d] our making this history into a properly successive and sequential history of events."[74] But there was more to be said about Foucault as a theorist of biopolitics—its populations and nations, administration of life, birthrates and deathrates, its biologically inflected hierarchies of peoples and state-inflected racisms.

Derrida saw the tendency to suppose a gathering of power as one of the poles of Foucault's oscillations, resisted by the counterforce of the dispersal Foucault also depicted. But, in a sense not factored by Derrida, the biopolitical returned Foucault a number of times to the relation between the alliance model and sexuality in *The History of Sexuality* and more generally to the relation between sovereignty, discipline, and biopower whose elaboration by Foucault would actually interrupt, not reiterate, a linear history.

As it happens, at the time of Derrida's comments about Foucault in his *The Beast and the Sovereign* seminar his archival interests had come into slightly closer proximity with those of Foucault. Derrida had just offered his *Death Penalty* seminar, with its consideration of capital punishment, the latter's phantasmatic sovereign claims, the death penalty's anesthetization, its abolitionism, progress narratives, the ideas and interests of that defense, the concepts of life and death mobilized in the latter. Derrida's several mentions of Foucault in the first volume of his *Death Penalty* seminar took him back to *Discipline and Punish*, but not back to *The History of Sexuality*, nor biopower. Yet we can ask how the biopolitical line drawn by Foucault out of *The History of Sexuality* could bear on the deaths, abolitions, lives, and births of *The Death Penalty*.

With that possibility in mind, let's give Foucault (whom one could imagine hoping to be exempted from the impending discussions of sexual difference) a temporary respite and turn briefly to Derrida's discussions of Victor Hugo in his *Death Penalty*.

DERRIDA AND VICTOR HUGO: THE DEATH OF REPRODUCTIVE LIFE

The abolitionist writings discussed by Derrida include the analogically saturated images from Hugo whose ideals of fraternity Derrida had discussed in his 1988 seminar published as *Politics of Friendship*. There Derrida had presented Hugo's image of a globally expanding fraternity through which Paris would be the embryo of Europe, the world, the future: "It is certain that the French Revolution is a beginning. . . . Take note of this word. *Birth*. It corresponds to the word Deliverance." "O France, adieu! . . . One separates from one's mother, who becomes a goddess . . . and you, France, become the world."[75] Hugo connects this image to that of the temporal and spatial expansions of colonialism: "Under the influence of this motive nation, the incommensurable fallow lands of America, Asia, Africa and Australia will give themselves up to civilizing emigration. . . . The *central nation* whence this movement will radiate over all continents will be to other societies what the model farm is among tenant farms. It will be more than a nation, it will be . . . better than a civilization, it will be a *family*. . . . The capital of this nation will be Paris."[76] As Derrida would observe, reading the related passages together, the same imagery is mobilized in Hugo's strenuous opposition to the death penalty.

This form of opposition reaffirmed distinctions between barbarism and civilization that were just as much to hand when Hugo spoke of France's potential as the embryo for globalist expansion. In this imagery, when the abolitionist movement was associated with the progress of civilization, it was also associated with the progress of life,[77] with organic process, and a seed's development. Derrida points out Hugo's association of this lifelike "progress" with a *"right to life,"*[78] as if progress has its own life, its own life claims on those who would impede it. The deaths effected by capital punishment were considered to impede the "life" of progress as well as those executed. These variants on life were given the metaphors of reproduction, maternity, the *"profound ovary* of a fertilized progress."[79]

Hugo condemned all capital punishment on the grounds of the inviolability of human life. But it happens that he presented the execution of women—wives and mothers, principle of life—as foregrounding the death penalty's egregious character. Why was executing women particularly emblematic of its horror? The putting to death of those associated with the production of life counted as a double infraction of the "right to life," for the death penalty also conflicted with the potential life for which the executed woman would be considered responsible (her real or potential children). A third infraction was also attributed to the execution's forestalling of future collective life with which women as reproductive principle were associated: national, territorial, populationist, colonial, expansionist.

Derrida's elaboration of Hugo's "women and children" is not far from the phenomenon described by Foucault, a body that could be at once considered the embryo of its own life and of the lives to which it could give rise, those of peoples, of populations, and of national futures. To use Foucault's terminology (developed more specifically to discuss the networked multiplicities assumed by the phantasmatic logics of heredity associated with degeneracy), we could see Hugo's objection to harming women and children as an objection to harming the metabody to which they belong, which they enfold, and of which they are the emblem.[80]

THE WOMEN AND THE CHILDREN: DISSEMINATED ANALOGY AND DISPERSED BIOPOLITICS

Could we bring this problem back to Foucault's reserves, to the ends of a productive reading together of Derridean and Foucauldian resources?

Considered by Derrida, these are claims profiting from a concurrent, and very elaborate, literal, pseudoliteral, and analogical status become undecidable. Pursued by Foucault, these are forms of life emerging as relay points of power. In his account of the contingent formations of life, life is never stable or self-present. But, about some of the phenomena he discusses in this context, it could also be argued that there is a blurring between metaphor, figure, symbol, and the literal. To be sure, the instability of these particular distinctions isn't the focus of Foucault's accounts of life. Nonetheless, in Foucault's consideration of the political and biopolitical administration of birthrate to the ends of defending health, peoples, populations, and futures, the reproductive is as much symbolic as it is administered conduct. These registers of maternity (its national meaning and its conduct as national, its meaning as governmentality, its being governed) are saturated with images and figurative significance, its materiality here indistinguishable from metaphor. In other words, the meaning of maternity, children, health, and birthrate intertwines with the way in which these take shape materially: how they are conducted, what forms of birth and upbringing take place, under what (legal, economic, political, policy, insurance, historical, social, technological, epistemological, medical, subjectivizing, dividing, including, discarding, differentiating, securitizing, colonizing ...) conditions.

So when Hugo associates the "true birth" of expansionist-colonialist futurity with women's reproductivity in multiple senses, the literal cancels itself as already figurative, and the analogical cancels itself as not "merely" analogical. Matter, flesh, and figure have already taken shape in a disseminating relation of the "meaning" and "matter" of life.

With some very recent exceptions, Foucault's work is not generally assessed as a contribution to reproductive biopolitics.[81] But there can be no question that, in Foucault's references to the *Polizeiwissenschaft* and biopolitical interest in birthrate, wet nurses, breast-feeding, contraception, and similar "deadly secrets," reproduction takes shape as the concurrent threshold of protection and destruction, as a redoubled and multiple formation of the oscillating techniques of security, life enhancement, and delivery of death. Foucault touches upon exactly these formations, even in his brief mention of these matters in *The History of Sexuality*. He does so by linking the "vital" role of the mother (her good mothering ensuring optimized life in the population) to the negative variant (the problematic, bad, or "hysterical" mother). When he describes the emergence of desirable parental conduct, the duty to maximize health in the family as a threshold of a population's collective health, is juxtaposed with its alternative: the domestic hearth may deliver harm. Thus the new parental obligation is not just that the children be maximally healthy but also that their deaths be averted (*AB* 255; *HS I* 125). I have added a problem not discussed by Foucault. Despite his mention, for example in *Abnormal*, of maternal responsibility, disciplinary (and disciplined) conduct, and elsewhere of the problematization of a maternal conduct understood as vector of risk, he does not describe a thanatopoliticization of women emerging when collective futures are understood to be ensured by optimal reproductivity. But once optimal reproduction ensures the collective future, women also become figures of possible harm to those futures. Once they are the principle of population as national futurity, to execute or kill a woman is to kill those futures. Derrida discusses a number of historical arguments that they should, therefore, be exempt from death penalties. But exactly the same grounds (women-as-life-principle) have also been used to produce women as figures delivering death.[82] And that formation has produced them as figures exposed to the kinds of penalties and new kinds of death penalties and to the modern abortion wars. Women have been attributed a pseudosovereign capacity to harm embryos, children, and futures. They have been targeted not just by biopolitical optimization but also (and with the precariousness of abortion access enmeshed in both) by sovereign legal measures. The latter have survived in strange new forms, new states of exception. It is Derrida, not Foucault, who astutely recognized that the death penalty is a scene of sexual difference. But it is Foucault, not Derrida, who developed the corresponding biopolitical meanings of optimized and administered life. Foucault returned a number of times to the phenomenon of biopolitical projects to take care of life that incorporated a conjoined taking of life.[83] Certainly, we would turn to Derrida for his engagement with the special significance taken on by women in relation to death penalties. But, as I will argue, we can then turn to Foucault's work to find further resources for analyzing the conjoining of a biopoliticized and thanatopoliticized reproduction.

THE RESERVES OF PROXIMITY: FOUCAULT AND DERRIDA

For his part, Derrida had identified the importance of "the woman, the mother, sexual difference," and their role in the "true" birth of the nation, in their emblematic and exceptional status when confronted with the death penalty. Foucault analyzed the emergence of reproduction, birth, breast-feeding, child raising as biopolitical principles of life, such that we can better understand what principle women have become when they stand before a death penalty in the sense evoked by Victor Hugo in Derrida's *Death Penalty*. Of the two, it is Derrida who made it a regular practice to consider the analytic necessities of factoring sexual difference. In chapter 3 I will draw attention to a number of moments when Foucault, averting sexual difference, habitually converts the life duties of the "mother" to those of the nondifferentiated "parent." Uncharacteristically, given how attentive he was to the repeated occlusions of sexual difference in a great number of philosophers, Derrida missed the opportunity to consider this issue in Foucault's work. At the conclusion of "To Do Justice," he tried to imagine Foucault's response to questions directed at him posthumously. Again sexual difference is far from this scene. But it's appropriate that a missed meeting not be the encounter one might have anticipated.

An unexpected question, explored by neither in relation to the other, would be how sexual difference intertwines with the biopolitical. It can be dislodged by working with the suspended reserves of both Foucault and Derrida. This is not an intersection of the arguments each directed at the other. Rather it is an intersection in abeyance: of themes respectively explored by each (for Derrida, the regular occlusion of sexual difference, for Foucault, the biopolitical), but not explored by each in the other. Derrida averted an attention to Foucault's interest in biopolitics;

Foucault paid no attention to Derrida's general interest in sexual difference, although that resource might have alerted Foucault that his own references to undifferentiated "parents" and "couples" were in error. In the working space opened up where Foucault and Derrida's reserves held a suspended capacity to engage each other, a sovereign ability to deliver life and death was linked to a woman rendered principle of life. She had become the emblem of what was abhorrent in the death penalty, of the forces impeding progress. She, and the "the children," had come to enfold the promise of, and the threat to, an expansionist (bio)political, territorial, national, and metasomatic future.

My suggestion is not that the deconstructibility of analogy would be particularly galvanizing for Foucault.[84] Nor should we minimize the tension between the ways in which Foucault and Derrida referred to the biopolitical. Yet, at the point of contact between Derrida's capacity to think the simultaneously literal and analogical and Foucault's capacity to think together multiple corporeal spaces and times which enfold each other, a form of materiality can be articulated as a productive mutation engaging the capacities of each. Foucauldian reserves, and those of Derrida, allow us to consider (just where Derrida's intriguing use of the term *suspension* stops short) something new emerging from the confrontation between their suspended reserves, reconceived as transformative capacities.

BEYOND FOUCAULT'S SUSPENSIONS

Foucault has been supplanted, discarded, rebutted, buffeted, repudiated, completed, or modified, living on in fields including contemporary Italian philosophy, thanato- and necropolitics, affect theory and race studies, queer and feminist theory, new queer Deleuzeanism, and some of the "beyonds" of *Beyond Biopolitics*.[85] As a guiding methodological principle for the following chapters, the terminology of suspended reserves will be close to hand in a discussion of some of the more transfiguring engagements with Foucault's work: Derrida's *survivance*,[86] Giorgio Agamben's bare life, Roberto Esposito's immune paradigm, Lauren Berlant's slow death, Achille Mbembe's necropolitics, Jasbir Puar's terrorist assemblages, Wendy Brown's waning sovereignties, Judith Butler's precarious life, and Lee Edelman's reproductive futurism.

The pursuit of Foucault's children will take us to Foucault's discussions of family spaces and child-raising manuals, elements which might have been given a place in *La Croisade des Enfants* (one of the never-realized volumes of *The History of Sexuality* as he first conceived it), the making of children as bodily spaces which were at risk but also posed risks, published as brief comments on the dangers delivered by masturbation, wet nursing, insufficient surveillance, irresponsible strangers and family members, the need for marsupial mothers, optimal child-rearing understood as defensive, neo-Malthusian responsibilization, reproduction made a matter of biopolitical optimization and security, the harm to a future seeming to threaten children (but which they were also understood as effecting), and the corresponding responsibilization of maternities and governmentalities. We'll also consider less literal references to the making of children as futures: the phenomena described by Edelman as reproductive futurism, reproblematized by Puar as a biopolitical formation that comes to enfold a nationalism which is both hetero- and homonormative.

Problems not quite belonging to the theorists considered in the book will be reconfigured as transformative capacities. The proximities of Foucauldian and post-Foucauldian theorists will emerge, sometimes insofar as they miss each other on points which can be better articulated together and through the miss. In the following pages Foucault's suspensions become productive insofar as they are considered alongside a repeating phenomenon: the liminal making of women's (biopoliticized) reproductive life as principle of harm, death, or precariousness in the work of a number of post-Foucauldian theorists.

2

REPRODUCTIVE FUTURISM, LEE EDELMAN, AND REPRODUCTIVE RIGHTS

A queer theorist, driving down a highway, finds himself addressed by the abortion wars: "Not long ago, on a much traveled corner in Cambridge, Massachussetts, opponents of the legal right to abortion plastered an image of a full-term fetus, larger in size than a full-grown man, on a rented billboard that bore the phrase: 'It's not a choice, it's a child.'"[1] This is one of the encounters framing Lee Edelman's critique of reproductive futurism. So Edelman begins to attune us to the imaginary figure of the Child, a heteronormative fixation, a conservatism (and conservationism) of the ego, a Ponzi scheme promoted at the expense of those who do not seem to serve its interests. Edelman queried the terms with which (for example) Republican senator Rick Santorum's case against gay marriage was refuted by gay activist Dan Savage's family values: "we're moms and dads, too."[2] Edelman promoted the alternative possibility of occupying the space of queer negativity—and the very extensive debate to which the work gave rise has concentrated on this proposal.

No Future opened with reflections on the political profit accrued when Bill Clinton campaigned for the "children." By its third page, these reflections on public and political profiting from the (imaginary) Child were formulated as a challenge not only to the reproductive futurism of gay rights activism, and also of reproductive rights politics. Was Edelman broaching a timely coalition between the contemporary reflections of queer and abortion politics?[3]

True, he defended a queer politics capable of the declaration "*we* are the advocates of abortion" (*NF* 31). Arguing for an understanding of negativity as an ineluctable part of psychic and social life, he proposes a reclaiming of negativity by those to whom its antisociality is, in any case, attributed. Yet, temporarily, the framing, trenchant question, who would come out "*against* futurity and so against *life*?" (*NF* 16), was conjoined with another, "who *would*, after all, come out *for* abortion or stand *against* reproduction?"[4] A proposal was extended also to abortion rights activists: to rethink the strategy that, "while promoting the freedom of women to control their own bodies through reproductive choice, recurrently frame[s] their political struggle, mirroring their anti-abortion foes, as" (Edelman cited Donna Shalala) a "'fight for our children—for our daughters and our sons,' and thus as a fight for our future"? (*NF* 3).

There is, he argued, a "common stake in the militant right's opposition to abortion and to the practice of queer sexualities" (*NF* 15). In the name of the imaginary Child, both queer politics and feminists have been depicted as threatening the interests of reproductive futurism. Both have been denied rights on this pretext. But there was another affinity. Both gay rights activists and abortion rights activists have sometimes promoted rights by means of espousing a reproductive futurism shared with their opponents. Gay, feminist, liberal, or conservative, all parties would accept, overtly or tacitly, the "meaning of politics [as] . . . a fantasy frame intended to secure the survival of the social in the Imaginary form of the Child" (*NF* 14).

No Future is not widely considered to be engaging feminism. Certainly not positively,[5] and it is hardly the book's main concern. But its provocations extend in multiple directions. Among these, one can amplify the proposal to direct attention to the costs (I will discuss this term later) of the tacit or overt reproductive futurism of reproductive politics and the telos of reproductive rights. This would prompt closer scrutiny of the abjected figures produced by their projected futures and the Ponzi schemes taking place at someone's expense.

FARING EVEN BETTER

No Future responds to the representation of gay men and abortion rights activists as "embrac[ing] a culture of death" (*NF* 40).[6] But contemporary gay politics have also included rights claims to raise children under legally and socially equal conditions, including the right to adopt; the right to recognition of the joint parental status of same-sex couples; the right to health care benefits for one's partner and children; the right to equal access to assisted reproduction technologies; equal taxation, financial, and inheritance rights; the right to equal legal recognition of parental unions. There has also been a rhetorical and legal blurring of these aims with those of gay marriage rights. Public and political discussion of gay marriage in 2013 in France and America saw considerable citation by public commentators and politicians of the views of putative experts and studies assessing the "psychological impact" on children raised by gay couples.[7]

So Justice Antonin Scalia could include among his arguments against the federal recognition of state legalized gay marriage: "there's considerable disagreement among—among sociologists as to what the consequences of raising a child in a—in a single-sex family, whether that is harmful to the child." The *Washington Post*'s Ezra Klein could answer: "We should be begging gay couples to adopt children."[8] These, too, are instances of how idealized forms of parenting attach to Edelman's imaginary Child. Just as the emblem for striking down DOMA was the gay couples who had been together for twenty years,[9] the accompanying discussions of gay parenting were not disinclined to promise two loving parents, sharing child-raising work equally,[10] willing to parent the otherwise unadopted, producing particularly happy and successful children. This was to hold the bar of marriage and reproduction well above the average to low standards long set by heterosexuality: both rejection and legitimization of claims to gay and reproductive rights ramp up unreal fantasies of perfect, idealized parenting, relationship stability, children who might fare "even better."[11]

Like the planned parenthoods of abortion rights, the imaginary Child of gay parenting is the thoroughly chosen and willed Child—sometimes the result of elaborate planning and negotiations with surrogates, technologies, and greater legal and bureaucratic restrictions, including access to adoption, assisted reproduction, and the latter's transnational markets. So we are brought to another of the overlaps between the reproductive futurisms attributed by Edelman and the imaginaries of abortion rights and gay rights: the delivery of hyperwilled, optimally raised children by maximally attuned parents.

However, perhaps the central question arising from *No Future*'s case for negativity still lingers: what, in fact, is so wrong with reproductive futurism?

THE FIGURAL BURDEN OF QUEERNESS

When some are represented, as in homophobic contexts, as the "gravediggers of society" (*NF* 74), they are considered an obstacle not just to society and to its reproductive interests, but also, Edelman argues, to the interests of an imaginary ego. Because a vilified other (the gay man, the woman who will not reproduce) appears to threaten continuity into the future, one could imagine such continuity to be possible—absent the forces impeding it. A psychoanalytic account of this threatened phantasmatic continuity leads Edelman to remind that neither inert fixity, self-presence, nor perpetuation of that self-presence into the future is available to any of us.

This leaves open the question whether Edelman could affirm an unpredictable, unanticipatable future (a future that by definition could not be "our future").[12] Edelman identifies in the conservative hope for persistence the defensive ramparts of the ego, attached to an always already lost, illusory image of stasis and unity in which we misrecognize ourselves and that we retain as an ideal. It is projected forward as the survival of a fictional self-presence.[13] To those accused of endangering the welfare of imaginary Children attributed with the characteristics of "Tiny Tim," we must respond, he argues, by insisting that "Tiny Tim is always already dead" (*NF* 48–49). But Audre Lorde's words, "we were never meant to survive,"[14] can also be engaged by Edelman's seemingly echoing "we're destined all to vanish" (*NF* 33). His declaration puts into question not just the cost of forward projection but also the presupposition of the "we" in question. We could imagine him answering: yet "we" have already not survived. We have never been "us." This gives a first answer to "what is so wrong with the future": one variation of the futurism repudiated by Edelman is a future whose imaginary is the persistence of the same.

Second, this imaginary continuity of impossible self-presence is peopled by card carriers for its preservation (hence the ideal of protecting the imaginary Child's "Future"). More important, it is peopled by card carriers for its obstruction (thus the "Child" must be defended against those representing the death of its interests). Here Edelman identifies the interconnection between the fantasy of a continuous future as conservation of a continuous "us" which cannot survive (for we have never been fixed and so *have* never survived) and the vilification of others considered obstacles to the future, to survival, and thus to the social. This vilification is premised on the supposition that the future and the social could be accomplished absent those obstacles.

In short, Edelman is opposed not to "children" but to the use of sentimentalized representations of the imaginary Child justifying the abjection of those who seem not to favor its interests, particularly where a) that abjection serves to reinforce the phantasmatic, countering possibility of conservative continuity and persistence, and b) manifests, according to the concluding lines of *No Future*, in brutal outbreaks of violence. This is one of the simplest answers Edelman offers to the question what could be wrong with the future? It leads him to another redefinition of queer: to be queered is to have the death drive projected onto you (*NF* 30), sometimes with murderous consequences.

WHY NOT US?

According to Edelman's argument, those long vilified as impeding social futures might prefer to embrace that association, if the alternative is an alignment with the interests of social futures that redistribute burdens of queerness onto others. Why shouldn't the fantasy beneficiary of one's politics be "us" rather than the (imaginary) Child? But this is not in question: let's take a moment to think about what that formulation would mean. Edelman is challenging a conservatism he associates with ego attachment to a fixity that appears to have been lost in the past, never was present, and becomes a projection of an impossible preservation and endurance.

Thus this is not a matter of "us" versus "them" or of "present" versus "future" any more than it is a matter of "queer politics" versus the interests of "children." This clarifies a version of the argument touching on abortion politics. In the latter context, the interests and rights of the woman and the imaginary fetus or "potential Child" are sometimes considered to be competing. Again, one would oppose the very opposition. When imaginary Children become idealized figures of continuation, in a vilification of those who seem to thwart such ends, idealized "Mothers" are similarly stimulated. The latter are associated with societal aims of preservation, continuity, futurity, growth, flourishing. The question would be: how do these aims, and their imaginary Mothers, similarly "shif[t] the figural burden of queerness to someone else?" (*NF* 27). This is to extend the argument further than does *No Future*. But it does bring us to another liminal problem in its pages: the female "*sintho*mosexual."

*SINTHO*MOSEXUALS AND FEMALE *SINTHO*MOSEXUALS

Edelman defines the *sintho*mosexual as the queer figure of antisociality and "anti-meaning," those on whom the death drive is projected. They are figures of impediment to, or annihilation of, the socially legible pursuits of others (*NF* 113). They may refuse attachment or their attachments may be strangely incomprehensible. Thus *No Future* considers a number of media, literary, and film representations of the childless and child-hating, cruel, or impervious "machine-like men." They are indifferent to the "natural" order of human reproduction (*NF* 165*n*10). Randomly callous, they thwart the aims of the future, the hero, the heterosexual union, the happy ending, the teleological narrative, the hope of children. These are the figures either coldly or cruelly or willfully opposing the winsomeness of Tiny Tim or the emerging aims of *North by Northwest*'s Roger to unite with Eve Kendall or *Bladerunner*'s Deckard to unite with Rachel. Thus among Edelman's examples of the *sintho*mosexual are *Bladerunner*'s Roy,

A Christmas Tale's Scrooge, and *North by Northwest*'s henchman Leonard. Their sometimes intense alternative attachments— whether to profit, subterfuge, employers, or the available time—comprise an inscrutability and absence of sense in their drive to impede, harm, or terminate.

As a figure of "resistance to the viability of the social" (*NF* 3),[15] exemplars of this *sinthom*osexual are also to be found in Hitchcock's *Birds*, whose malevolent entities attack children without cause and obstruct the trajectory of Melanie and Mitch. And, in a note, Edelman includes the possible contours of the female *sinthom*osexual as well (*NF* 165n10). Who, then, are the childless, callous, or sexually ambiguous women, unmotivated, or motivated by incomprehensible attachments, blocking the aims of protagonists and their heterosexual unions with their own aims to spoil, impede, and harm? Briefly, he proposes the housekeeper Mrs. Danvers from Du Maurier's,[16] and Hitchcock's, versions of Rebecca and *Leave Her to Heaven*'s strangely jealous and murderous Ellen Berent, who causes two deaths and her own miscarriage before taking the step of killing herself so she can machinate the prosecution of a hated rival for her death. Perhaps, he speculates, we could add the initial, "untamed" Katherine in *The Taming of the Shrew*, striking her sister and her suitor, breaking the lute she might otherwise learn, seemingly obstructing the marital and familial ends of all. As queer figures of femininity, they are antimaternal while lacking a coherent expression of alternative aims. Ellen has murdered her husband's adolescent brother, but indirectly, in a vague and passive reverie, without formulating the intent. These women will neither reproduce nor marry; nor do they espouse a legible alternative. Compare to the feminist who has also, historically, been accused of antisociality, yet lays claim to greater intelligibility in the form of organized political claims or claims to realize personal aims: they embody legibly alternative routes (albeit those of social resistance or transformation) into public or political life.[17]

Thus it comes as no surprise that when Edelman turns to a discussion of Antigone as a possible candidate for female *sinthom*osexuality, he does not decipher in her, as many have, a motivated and intelligible challenge to authority.

REREADING ANTIGONE

For Judith Butler, by contrast, Antigone is almost if "not quite a queer heroine."[18] Insofar as Antigone defends the claims of kinship against the state, she is an emblem of kinship trouble and a possible, but unpredictable, transformation of kinship relationships. She defends their claims, but she has departed from the norms of kinship. She is described as "manly," she is sister to her father and pursues the suicidal ends of burying her brother in lieu of marriage, children, and, finally, life.[19] In response, Edelman suggests that Butler nonetheless returns Antigone to a counterteleology, to the *promise* of the future. She represents to Butler, positively, the possibility of transgression rather than its incalculability. According to Edelman's repudiation: "Butler's reading . . . buries in [Antigone] the *sinthom*osexual who refuses intelligibility's mandate" (*NF* 105). So where she is, for Butler, "almost queer," for Edelman, she is almost the *sinthom*osexual. She is neither machinic nor automatic nor birdlike;[20] she is not vengeful, but she does obstruct the interests of reproduction and of the social order. Her actions can appear to be giving pointless trouble to all.

Also (to build on Edelman's argument), consider the memorable speech in which Antigone explains the rationale for her devotion to accomplishing the funeral rites in defiance of the laws of the city. It is an intriguing passage if we are asked to look for the *sinthom*osexual. Less interestingly, she names her childlessness a tragic fate.[21] More strangely, she offers some calculations. She has flaunted the rules of the city, and Creon's edict, in burying her brother, though she would not have done so for a child of her own. If she lost a child she could always have another. A husband would also be replaceable. But her parents are dead, and so it is her brother who cannot be replaced:

> For never, had children of whom I was the mother or had my husband perished and been mouldering there would I have taken on myself this task, in defiance of the citizens. In virtue of what law do I say this? If my husband had died, I could have another, and a child by another man, if I had lost the first, but with my mother and father in Hades below, I could never have another brother. Such was the law for whose sake I did

you special honor, but to Creon I seemed to do wrong and to show shocking recklessness, O my brother. And now he leads me thus by the hands, without marriage, without bridal, having no share in wedlock or in the rearing of children.[22]

That is her algorithm as she compares attachments and kinship relations: "never, had children of whom I was the mother . . . perished . . . would I have taken on myself this task." To die for a child would be a poor economy for, according to this ranking of the significance of her family members, it could always be replaced.

Antigone adds to Edelman's emphasis on the unintelligibility of the *sintho*mosexual by reminding us of the strangeness of their calculations. Investing in their personal and national futures, the reproductive futurists are the great calculators. But the *sintho*mosexuals also—in their own way—may commit to calculation. Preoccupied with their mysterious attachments (Ellen to her dead father, Mrs. Danvers to the "first Mrs de Winter"), *sintho*mosexuals function according to their own incomprehensible algorithms—obstruction, profit, replaceability or irreplaceability, revenge, self-interest, refusal, resistance, or a revenge to be delivered by arranging their own death. Scrooge calculates on the rewards of financial profit. Mrs. Danvers's principle is that "Rebecca" cannot be replaced and that those who try should die. Roy is calculating the time remaining.[23] Some of these figures go to their death. Some find themselves converted to the meaning of Christmas or to spousal obedience. But, converted or not, and with different outcomes, they calculate ("I could have another") while also bearing witness to the opaqueness of their own efforts.

THE COST

So the figure of the *sintho*mosexual also serves as a reminder of how often even a figure standing for unintelligibility or negativity will return, or be returned, to logics of calculation. This is not an indication that such calculations are possible, but rather that they are a compelling draw. The *sintho*mosexual reminds us to look again at the recurrence of their algorithms, in all their incalculable madnesses, no less than the equally mad investments by the reproductive futurists in calculability. In a small way *No Future* bears witness to this also.

This brings us back to implications of Edelman's suggestion: "make no mistake, then: Tiny Tim survives at our expense" (*NF* 48). Edelman's challenge is communicated with the metaphorics of cost and benefit. Economic metaphors are present in his assessments of the negatives of reproductive futurism: it is too expensive.[24] Also, it "shifts a burden" as a bad form of finance: "the figural Child alone embodies the citizen as an ideal, entitled to claim full rights to its future share in the nation's good, though always at the cost of limiting the rights "real" citizens are allowed" (*NF* 11). Reproductive futurism is, above all, the Ponzi scheme. But even the costs of a Ponzi scheme can resist calculation. Eventually it self-destructs, but, for as long as incoming investors sustain the seeming profits, it is uncertain exactly which of them will finally prove to have been robbed.

The two elements I have so far characterized as liminal in *No Future* have been, first, the female *sinthom*osexual and second, an intermittent language of cost and expense. A third concerns the relationship between the pregnant woman and the fetishized child, given *No Future*'s discussion of P. D. James's novel *The Children of Men*. It opens the door to an exploration of the relationship between the reproductive futurism of interest to Edelman (the negativity that ends up attached to "nonproductive," illegible sexual agents) and reproductive futurism as it attaches to the politics of reproduction.

REREADING P. D. JAMES

In James's novel the human race, having become nonfecund, is threatened with imminent extinction. There is neither human biological posterity nor more generally human teleology. Without reproduction, sex has become meaningless gymnastics. Global salvation could be offered only by procreation.[25] A caustic feminist and queer reaction to *Children of Men*'s pronatalism was only to be expected.

While they blur, let's consider the pregnancy and the pregnant woman separable, though connected, fetishes. Both fetishes—the miraculous Child and Julian, the last Pregnant Woman—are present in the novel, but the latter is amplified in the movie adaptation. Here the pregnant woman is the refugee Kee, a figure of wonder whom a number of protagonists covet or struggle to protect. Edelman does not direct our attention to the difference between these fetishes, nor consider fetishizations of the pregnant woman. In his response to the reproductive futurism of *Children of Men*, he slips between this figure and that of the fetishized imaginary Child as if they need no distinguishing.

Similarly, he notes that the "parent" is very often depicted as an intrinsic social and political good. He expostulates, in response to one rallying cry for a "parent's bill of rights," "what 'greater electoral clout' could fathers and mothers *have*?"(*NF* 111). But some degree of differentiation could make sense here also. There have been different trajectories in the politics of "mother's" and "father's" rights. In historical context, these have also been taken to conflict with each other.[26] Also, the overvaluation of the "parent," and of "parent's rights," is not the same project, nor the same kind of reproductive futurism, as the overvaluation of the pregnant woman. And the overvaluation of the pregnant woman is itself a principle of division: some pregnant women are overvalued, while others (figures of surplus pregnancy, of welfare benefit abuse or other kinds of irresponsibility) may be under- or devalued, and some pregnancies (such as the pregnancy of the illegal immigrant) are entirely debased. The pregnant woman may be a figure of superabundance or of abuse of the "system" or a figure of undisciplined reproductive excess. Despised or sentimentalized, she bifurcates easily between her status as guaranteeing or threatening the future, as does the potential child she bears.[27] In short, the making and disparagement of the queer negativity that interconnects with fetishes of the anticipated Child also interconnects with that of the Pregnant Woman in expressions of national, familial, and individualized reproductive futurism.[28] And that last also interconnects with the making and disparagement of some pregnant women against others. This point does not conflict with Edelman's analysis, but, in *No Future*, it is not factored by him.

To focus on this phenomenon might bring us back to his discussion of the giant image of a fetus on a billboard. As he says, the billboard extends an invitation to consider this an image of a "future Child." Here too, we might add to the discussion a long trajectory of feminist arguments that criticize the visual elimination of the woman carrying this fetus, so that it can appear an autonomous entity making its own rights claims.[29]

To fetishize the figure of the imaginary Child can also be to indirectly produce, presuppose, *and* render invisible the role of the woman as subordinated to the ends of reproduction and collective futures.[30] For, embedded in the billboard image of a fetus's miraculous, apparent autonomy is the concurrent invitation to challenge reproductive rights attributed to the pregnant woman carrying the future Child. Considered a possible threat to the claims of the imaginary Child, the pregnant woman can certainly be added to the account of those held hostage (no less may she hold herself hostage) to reproductive futurism.

Reproductive futurism involves a) a phantasmatic "we" (to which one may respond, "we" have never been "us"; b) the casting of an imaginary Child extending the continuity of that we; c) the casting of "antisocial" figures deemed to obstruct the interests of the imaginary Child and "our" future; as well as d) a division between the imaginary forms of reproduction, also understood to serve or obstruct that future; and e) an infusing of the woman's phantasmatic pregnant body in terms of the reproductive futurism she either is taken to serve or, alternatively, obstruct.

If one extended this reflection, one could explore the contours of the imaginary Mother who is complement to the imaginary Child. This imaginary Mother is an unselfish, responsibilized moral agent, conduit of individual and social hopes. Primarily facilitating the latter, her independent demands and needs are not excessive. She is a social factor maximizing health and well-being (of children and communities—thus she is also a biopolitical figure, both individualized and understood as a factor in the health and future of populations). She is not selfish, indifferent, cruel, or incomprehensibly harmful. The Child of the Future is associated with this concurrent imaginary pregnant mother, whether her role is highly visible, fetishized, or invisible in the teleology of the Child's value. What Edelman sees, in considering *Children of Men's* pregnant mother, is a representation of the redemptive Child. This is to look through the associated making of women's imaginary pregnancies to the ends of the former. Yet his own point is that reproductive futurism also manifests in reproductive politics. This is not to reduce his analysis of the former to an interest in the latter. But, when these overlap, imaginary Mothers of all kinds (idealized and obstructive) may intertwine with the imaginary Child of reproductive futurism.

This raises the question of how reproductive futurism conjoins with the politics of reproduction. This is not to confuse the latter with the former. It is to ask how we can repudiate the former while *also* paying attention to its making (and bifurcating) of a phantasmatic Mother as well as a phantasmatic Child. Can we add to the point that "we" have never existed, and that "Tiny Tim" has never existed, the further point that the "Mother" (as morally or practically oriented material conduit to the future; hyperresponsible unselfish carrier; life-, family-, and nation-optimizing child raiser, devoid of the death drive) has never existed? Are variants of *sintho*mosexuals generated by the politics of reproductive futurism and even by feminism's rights claims more generally? Does the latter's elaboration of reproductive rights generate disturbing figures of political and futural impediment, antisociality, and an absence of meaning and purpose?

ILLEGIBILITY AND REPRODUCTIVE RIGHTS

In an argument not unsupportive of reproductive rights, the philosopher Ronald Dworkin has described decisions about abortion as a "a dramatic and intensely lit example of choices people must make throughout their lives, all of which express convictions about the value of life and the meaning of death." He ups the ante: abortion involves a "terrible conflict," this decision can be for any woman an "awful" one. He discusses the subjects confronting abortion in Carol Gilligan's *In a Different Voice*. Each woman had to weigh up (as Dworkin saw it), the value of her own life and "a new life," and, as he claims "each was trying, above all, to take the measure of her responsibility for the intrinsic value of her *own* life . . . to see the decisions about whether to cut off a new life as part of a larger challenge to show respect for all life by living well and responsibly herself."[31]

Let's stipulate that these are some of the imaginary women peopling the reproductive futurism of reproductive choice. Their choices are oriented toward their own future and the future of those for whom they do, or might, care. If so, perhaps, we'd say of this context that its own *sinthom*osexual is sitting in a number of medical offices, waiting rooms, and other spaces, offering a conundrum to counselors, friends, ethicists, and moral philosophers. She is the woman who seems to be having too many abortions, who seems to choose irresponsibly or to be indifferent to the consequential narratives expected of her reproductive decisions. Perhaps she seems feckless, has an insufficient or inappropriate account of her reproductive life (or, more generally, her life decisions). Perhaps she does not seem to care sufficiently how and why she got pregnant or under what circumstances she might again. Perhaps she presents a certain recalcitrance or illegibility in this regard. Or she may be unconcerned about her own decisions, or incoherently reckless, or accused of abusing the health system or of refusing reproductive responsibility. Perhaps, when it comes to her pregnancy, or her abortion, she is not a good storyteller.[32] The reproductive futurism of much reproductive rights discourse can be seen in an uneasy response to those on whose behalf rights are claimed, if the latter's aims seem to be antiaims: indifferent, destructive, disorganized, or perversely obstructive. Such figures do not accord with the imaginary contours of the responsible decision makers associated with the hopes of reproductive choice.

Extending this line of inquiry out still further, one could diagnose a related form of reproductive futurism in some prominent historical feminist claims.

CALCULATING WITH FEMINISM

The complex rhetorical history of women's rights claims includes, as Joan Scott has argued, the tensions between asserting sameness and difference.[33] Both variants have attached rights claims to forms of reproductive futurism. The most obvious versions can be identified in historical feminisms that affirmed women's maternal role as vital to social and political futures.[34] Sometimes such claims have been attached to those of an imaginary Child.

To be sure, many prominent feminist thinkers rejected the view of women as primarily maternal. But, to pinpoint the reproductive futurism in question, take one of the nineteenth-century feminists best known for her outright rejection of maternity: Claire Démar. Author of the aptly named *Ma loi d'avenir*, Démar's vehement declaration is "No more motherhood, no more law of blood. I say: no more motherhood."[35] But this does not amount to the declaration "The future stops here!" To the contrary, her reclamations concerned how social life could be reoriented toward an ideal future offering new roles for sexual difference.

Démar's is not the only declaration of women's rights whose politics included the question of how children might best be brought up. A number of historical feminists have offered images of young children dangerously exposed to harm or death and linked those images specifically to the vindication of women's rights. In *Ma loi d'avenir* Démar identified this threat as coming from two quarters—first, from selfish fathers regretting the pregnancies resulting from their sexual activity. Such fathers, she argued, warm only temporarily to their children. Once their interest tired, they gave regular beatings and lessons in injustice, with the child emerging as "un monstre hideux."[36] Here were the evils of a long-standing patriarchal power associated with bloodright, dating back at least to the Roman law which recognized paternal authority over the life of offspring.[37] Because women are themselves prone to egoism and not necessarily good mothers,[38] Démar calls for children to be raised by professional nurses. Thus her claim "no more motherhood," is not a feminist antifuturism.[39] Women's rights will be in everybody's collective interest, including those of their children. For women to undertake paid work according to their abilities, and be liberated from exploitation and "le loi du sang,"[40] was also to ensure that the children were best raised by those most competent to do so. The future thereby ushered in would be one of "concorde et harmonie."[41]

Or consider how Mary Wollstonecraft's claims to women's rights in 1792 also concerned their impact on children and the future. An improvement in education for women would enable them to better raise children, endowed with the qualities and capacities best ensuring responsible social life. Women's rights were presented as serving women's interests, to be sure, but they were also affirmed as serving children's interests, national interest, and, above all, futural interest. Wollstonecraft proposed an algorithm for the claims of women: "Would men but generously snap our chains, and be content with rational fellowship, instead of slavish obedience, they would find us more observant daughters, more affectionate sisters, more faithful wives, more reasonable mothers—in a word, better citizens."[42] This might have been the strategic calculation of the feminist reproductive futurist, but how reliable was that outcome?

This brings us back to the question: what could be wrong with the future? In this case, reproductive futurisms produces a conditional feminism pegged to promises—for example, for better-raised children and societies, whose interests would not be obstructed by bad mothers and antisocial women. Perhaps an alternative feminism defended in terms of unpredictable ends and uncertain futures seems a bridge too far, yet consider the extent to which Wollstonecraft's feminism is peopled by the imaginary, rights-endowed Woman with very specific characteristics: she will be observant, affectionate, faithful, reasonable, better. Condorcet might have identified these claims as too circumscribed. Claims to education, voting, and workers rights tended not to be conditional in this sense.[43] Those understood to have the right to enjoy them certainly included the negligent, the distracted, the unfeeling, the faithless, and the foolish.

THE *SINTHOM*OSEXUAL OF FEMINISM?

Feminism has sometimes manifested this tendency to overpromise, given that many will exercise reproductive rights, just as many exercise voting rights, vaguely and incomprehensibly. Some of the canonical texts of the history of feminism have a frequently noted tendency to depreciate many of the women on behalf of whom they speak, particularly those considered to undermine social aims.[44] A vindication of women's rights might promise, for example, the emergence of improved human character. The texts of Wollstonecraft, Anna Wheeler, John Stuart Mill, or Simone de Beauvoir defended universal rights and principles of justice and recognition. But they also described contemporary women as trivial, superficial, stupid, vain, pretentious, and mannered, preoccupied with seduction, unproductive, pleasing, careless, unjust, immoral, selfish, competitive, jealous, negligent, narcissistic, cruel, or vicious. Condorcet found it not untrue that women lacked the sentiment of justice. Wollstonecraft saw the undereducated, bougeois women of her day as vain, superficial, and dangerously lacking in principles.[45] Beauvoir describes the irrational jealousies and obstructive hostility of many disappointed, thwarted middle-aged women and mothers. Such arguments are not incoherent: they make the case that women's rights (education, work, independent income, meaningful occupations, franchise, equal status, reciprocal recognition) would improve women's qualities, among the positive transformations. Eighteenth-century arguments for women's education had promised that women would be more socially useful, wise, judicious, improved, principled. Even allowing for the emphasis on the distorting role of environment described by writers from Wollstonecraft through Condorcet, Taylor, Mill, and Beauvoir, some of these texts give a striking characterization of women's destructive capacities, ranging from manipulativeness to trivial interests occupying extremes of libido, even to the detriment of their children. A memorable image from Mary Wollstonecraft is the lady who takes her dogs "to bed, and nurses them with a parade of sensibility, when sick," taking her lapdog "to her bosom instead of her child."[46] She argues that an appropriately structured education is necessary to the development in women of regulated sentiments less driven by antisocial neglectfulness. One could say that their queer (in Edelman's sense) and even their antiteleological animal devotions are emblematic of their irresponsible, ill-distributed interests. Conjoined with arguments that women's inequality is harmful to children, such negative representations have played a role in the history of women's rights vindications.[47] These are also calculating arguments; attached to the promise of alternative outcomes (if they would "but generously snap our chains . . . "). Their vindications would deliver better outcomes for nations and peoples ("they would find us . . . more reasonable mothers—in a word, better citizens").[48] In short, a rich dialogue is available by considering feminism's archive from the perspective of the recent critiques of reproductive futurism.

The vindications of *No Future* are not antichild, but anti-Child. Edelman opposes the sentimentalized images of future generations as continuing the hopes of the present and the vilification of those cast as impediments to the former. But its liminal elements also brought queer and abortion debates into proximity. In chapter 4 I further explore the problematic figures generated by the reproductive futurism of reproductive rights, arguing for a detachment of the latter from the former.

Perhaps such analyses could lead to more differentiating typologies of reproductive futurism. How can a politics of reproductive choice be dissociated from overpromising the advent of *responsible* individuals, *better* parents, producing the *wanted* children? Martha Shane and Lana Wilson's documentary *After Tiller* (2013) depicts the desperation of those—many very poor—who have needed third-term abortions. It also includes, and has been surrounded by, debate emphasizing the extensive moral reflection brought to such decisions. Given the extreme difficulty of access to abortion services for many in the United States, the bureaucratic obstructionism and absence of clinics which in some cases has made late-term abortions necessary, and the accompanying blame, hardship, and expense, does it alleviate or add to those burdens to emphasize the extent to which many of these women morally reflect? The legitimacy of abortion services should not be subordinated to the thickness of the moral life of those who turn to them,[49] not least because this can only stimulate contrasting images of antisocial feminine irresponsibility.

STRANGE COALITIONS: QUEER NEGATIVITY AND REPRODUCTIVE POLITICS. AND WHAT IS SO WRONG?

In reiterating the question "what is so wrong with reproductive futurism?" I have explored a number of answers. Edelman is widely considered an advocate of a pure political negativity,[50] but, as he clarifies in his dialogue with Halberstam, it is very different from the targeted antiestablishment "No Future" of, say, a punk sensibility. Edelman explores a queer negativity without meaning, aim, and targeted good: "dare we trace . . . the untraversable path that leads to no good and has no other end than an end to the good as such?"[51] This is not a matter of smashing specific idols or figures of authority—certainly, not in the name of alternative idols, political positions, or competing principles.[52]

However, a number of different renditions have been given of this case for antisociality, and I turn now to mention one version suggested by Jack Halberstam, another from Heather Love, and a third from Tim Dean.

Recognizing the argument that the "queer subject stands between heterosexual optimism and its realization,"[53] Halberstam takes this to be the argument that the queer subject "has been bound epistemologically to negativity, to nonsense, to nonproduction, and to unintelligibility, and instead of fighting this characterization . . . [Edelman] proposes that we embrace the negativity *that we anyway structurally represent*."[54] Heather Love, by contrast, has proposed a different inflection, one I emphasized earlier: "Edelman argues that rather than trying to deny [queer] associations with the antisocial (or the death drive), queers should take up the 'figural burden of queerness'[55]—the burden of representing the dissolution of the social—*and not shuffle it off to someone else.*"[56] And as a means of clarifying this interpretation, compare both these versions (from Halberstam and Love) to the characterization by Tim Dean. In the face of: "the viciously homophobic representation of homosexuality as sterile, unproductive, antifamily, and death-driven, Edelman insists that 'we should listen to, and even perhaps be instructed by, the readings of queer sexualities produced by the forces of reaction' (16). If there is a germ of truth in homophobic stereotypes of queerness as destructive, then we might heroically identify with those negative stereotypes in order to short-circuit the social in its present form."[57]

While Edelman would specifically repudiate a *heroic* identification with negative stereotypes, it is easy to see how Dean could arrive at that wording. Doesn't this seem just one further increment to the view mentioned by Love—that embracing queer negativity avoids *shuffling the burden of queerness off onto someone else?* If converted either to heroism or to ethics, the project would be prone to generate new, contrasting figures, the unheroic who deflect a burden. Carrying a load of queer negativity in a stance of heroism isn't Edelman's style: too principled, too teleological for one thing. Notwithstanding one reference in *No Future* to an alternative route for queer ethical value,[58] Edelman does not speak to a queer ethics so much as the sheer appeal of siding with the birds.

What if these variants on *No Future's* antisocial thesis also offered a number of means to reconsider queer's twin: abortion? According to the first version: the queer subject has been bound to negativity, to nonproduction, to unintelligibility, to the grave: instead of fighting this characterization, the subject of abortion might embrace of the negativity she "*anyway represents.*" There is good reason to resist the attachment of reproductive rights to productivity and intelligibility, and an abortion politics could endorse the absence of the moral field, and the role of the intermittently incoherent, unresolved, irresponsible, selfish, terminal, "instead of fighting this characterization." On this variant the stress would fall on the latter: *anyway,* reproductive rights are going to take place around this specter.

According to variation two, upping the ante of accountability and moral subjectivity produces an unreal fantasy about reproductive choice, whose claims are thereby subordinated to an excessive onus on an appropriately narrativized phantasmatic reponsibility, delegitimating subjects who do not conform to its contours. Here the point would be that in reproductive rights contexts, also, reproductive futurism *shuffles the burden to someone else.*

Reproductive futurism *makes and renders* its figures of impediment, the antisocial others lurking in the frames of heteronormativity and in the canon of feminism's history. But a methodological orientation alert to this making of figures of expense—abject and illegible figures—must also forgo the assumption we can calculate that one subject's pursuit of the normal of reproductive futurism is directly connected to another subject's consequent role as the impediment to reproductive futurism. We can identify the relation between the normal of reproductive futurism and the production of its antisocial other while also exercising caution about that calculation: "make no mistake, Tiny Tim survives at our expense."

Edelman notes that the putative agents of death sometimes undertake what he sees as a reactive, answering project, proclaiming themselves the agents of life. Doing so contributes, indirectly, to the scapegoating of abject and attacked representatives of the obstruction of social interest. But we can recognize this expense, without assuming it can be computed exactly. We can look for the production of abject, unintelligable, and queer figures, while also allowing that we cannot always calculate exactly where their cost falls.

CALCULATING, STILL DRIVING: MORE BILLBOARDS

In fact, an important resistance to calculability is also shared by queer politics and the politics of abortion. Think of Wendy Brown, reflecting on the complexities she encountered in her engagements with reproductive rights: "in the clamour for the right to abortion . . . we were missing out on the extent to which reproductive freedom takes different forms for different populations. The constraints on reproductive freedom are different for different classes, castes, races, geographical locations and sexualities."[59] We could add, in different ways, to Edelman's confrontation with that giant roadside invitation to consider a fetus as not a "choice" but a "child." We could turn to another series of billboards he might also have encountered in a number of American cities. Here a reproductive futurism addressed African American women in particular with the charge that the implications of their abortions were negative for racial equality.

In November 2011, as the Republican primary debates continued, all leading Republican candidates were aggressively antichoice. The American organization Planned Parenthood was targeted by several candidates, including Herman Cain, who agreed with claims that abortion disproportionally impacted the future of African Americans and could be likened to genocide.[60] In the same year billboards were to be seen in Atlanta, Oakland, and New York City declaring "The Most Dangerous Place for Black People Is the Womb."[61] The campaign attributed to women a procreative responsibility not just toward their potential offspring but to population and racial futures they could preserve or betray.[62]

Brown included reproductive rights in her well-known essay on paradoxical rights, an essay which reminds that the rights achieved by some may be accomplished at the expense of others. They may submerge differences or they may conceal, or generate, power differentials between those who can and can't enjoy them.[63] The paradoxes she highlights are also an important reminder to hesitate before simple calculations of impact. It is not just that the reproductive rights of women of color have also been held hostage to a race-conscious reproductive futurism. For some, reproductive rights claims have included the right not to undergo forced, coerced, or unduly encouraged sterilization, and the calculations of pro- and antiabortion politics ("at whose expense?") have been complicated by inequalities of race, poverty, and class. Moreover, reproductive rights offer a good example of forms of agency, freedom, and responsibility considered to be threatened by, but only arising in the wake of, the biopolitical interest in reproduction they often resist. Chapter 4 will consider several accounts of the intersections of reproductive futurism with visions of national and population futures in relation to which women's bodies may be figured as thresholds of risk and defense, erosions and growth.

This brings me to an intuition very briefly shared, albeit differently, by Heather Love, Jack Halberstam, and by Jasbir Puar[64]—that *No Future* might also be brought into proximity, indirectly, with a theorist rigorously absent from its pages: Michel Foucault.[65] Arguably, Foucault was interested in the conditions and costs of reproductive futurism, from its responsibilizations to its tolerable thresholds. He resisted identifying a direct relationship between profits and expenses (such as a profit for family values or expense incurred by delegitimized abnormals). But there is another reason, also—not an obvious one—for a turn to Foucault amidst this discussion.

If there is one major theorist to whom one might best turn for an account of the circumstances in which queer politics and the formation of reproductive rights could strangely connect, it was Foucault. This intersection was one of the most curious and opaque aspects of a work with an ambiguous status in the emergence of queer theory: Foucault's *The History of Sexuality*, volume 1. The work proposed an intersection with which many readers never quite made their peace: between, on the one hand, the formation of sexualities, abnormalities, perversions, confessions, models of psychic depth and sexual truth and, on the other hand, the broader formation of the biopolitical—its preoccupation with matters such as hygiene, the relation of birthrate to death rate, harmful and healthy pregnancies, child raising, urban planning, alimentary trends, the interests of populations. This intersection is the navel of *The History of Sexuality*, volume 1.

Edelman has claimed that reproductive futurism is also a kind of disciplinary Panoptimism.[66] With an important exception, the concerns of biopower have not, for the most part, been brought into dialogue with Edelman's work. But there is a possible biopolitical aspect to *No Future*, despite the absence of the corresponding language and problematics in his work. Opening this chapter, I speculated about a possible model allowing the tension to better abide,[67] between (for example) *No Future*'s psychoanalytic orientation, and its possible dialogue with other explorations of reproductive futurism: those of reproductive politics, even reproductive rights, feminism, and biopolitics. How could these push well at each other as a more transformative provocation?

Situating Edelman on a biopolitical terrain leads Puar to argue that he means to oppose but ends up presupposing a reduction of sexuality to a "thin biopolitical frame of reproduction."[68] The argument, I think, is that futurity for Edelman ends up being reproductive in a narrow sense: as if the futurists put the interests of *children* first, giving preference to reproduction and normative kinship. Attributing to Edelman a preoccupation with the costs of privileging the literal children (and so, in that sense, with a reproductive biopolitics), Puar suggests that Edelman misses the mark. On her reading: "he ironically recenters the very child-privileging, future-oriented politics he seeks to refuse."[69] If Puar's reading, in turn, misses a mark, this is only because one can imagine the arguments of Puar and Edelman, on their marks, containing far more interesting suspended reserves for the other. Given the psychoanalytic inflections of Edelman's argument, the point cannot be the child but the structure: conservationism, projection of the death drive. His argument targets whatever stands in for the Child and the associated (redistributive) projection of its "obstruction." Is *No Future* really at odds with what Puar presents as an alternative view? "The biopolitics of regenerative capacity already demarcate[s] racialized and sexualized statistical population aggregates as those in decay, destined for no future, based not upon whether they can or cannot reproduce children but on what capacities they can and cannot regenerate and what kinds of assemblages they compel, repel, spur, deflate."[70]

Both Puar and Edelman invite us to consider the highly flexible possibilities for all that can stand in for the Child. Those possibilities can certainly be seen in governmental and often nationalist calculations relating to populations, their futures and logics of conservation, their flourishing and tacit and overt "expenditure." Puar and Edelman might agree on the remark that "the child is just one such figure in a spectrum of statistical chances that suggest health, vitality, capacity, fertility, 'market virility', and so on."[71] Because Edelman's argument was not pursued in a biopolitical register, we might seem to have traveled far from his concerns and the phenomena to which he directs an acute eye. But, from the outset of *No Future,* the specter of the child-refusing *sintho*mosexual, associated with the negation of life, is said to represent a negative impact on "community" and "nation."[72] As he notes, reproductive futurism (and we are going to add—not to confuse them but to consider their points of contiguity—biopolitics) names agents of death and pursues, indirectly or directly, strategies of death.

In the next chapter I take up the possibility that reproductive futurism includes the aims and by-products of the biopolitical. In arguing that Foucault's work encompasses some biopolitical variants of reproductive futurism, I will expand some largely unexplored figures in Foucault's work: the child (and concurrently the nation) at risk of harm or death from poor parenting practice, the Malthusian couple, contraception, masturbation, marsupial mothers shadowing their children to avert risk. This will bring us to the biopolitical "children" who emerge as the threshold figures of national and population flourishing.

3

FOUCAULT'S CHILDREN

Rereading *The History of Sexuality*, Volume 1

Four figures emerged [se dessinent] from this preoccupation with sex, which mounted throughout the nineteenth century—four privileged objects of knowledge, which were also targets and anchorage points for the ventures of knowledge [les entreprises du savoir]: the hysterical woman, the masturbating child, the Malthusian couple, and the perverse adult. Each of them corresponded to one of these strategies which, each in its own way, passed through [a traversé] and made use of the sex of women, children, and men.

—MICHEL FOUCAULT, THE HISTORY OF SEXUALITY, VOLUME 1

Perhaps we will never have done exploring all the analytic potential compressed in that familiar, tiny, and exploratory volume, *The History of Sexuality*, volume 1? Here is a strangely unfamiliar point that ought not be novel, nor controversial: the administration of reproduction (in particular of "birthrate," but also maternities and parenting) was included by Foucault under the modern biopolitical concerns discussed in *HS I* and elsewhere.[1] Moreover, this provokes a question: does this inclusion mean that something is missing from Foucault's account?

For, as we have seen, Foucault also argued that powers of death accompany the biopolitical as its counterpart or underside: the byproduct of its pursuits of life. So shouldn't Foucault's elaboration of this complex relationship between biopolitical powers of life and death have included some kind of discussion of the reproductive variants of the latter? We could ask the question this way: if reproduction becomes (as Foucault indicates) biopolitical, then (given his own understanding of the latter) does this mean, as some have suggested, that reproduction also becomes *thanato-* or *necro*political?[2] And in what way? Certainly, one could turn to a number of theorists for accounts of reproduction rendered economically or politically significant to nationalism, race hierarchy, colonialism, slavery, and genocide.[3] As such it has been the grounds (and means) for exposure to forms of control, various legal regimes and force, incitement to harm, states of chaos, anxiety, and death.

I will focus on the point that it also produces female subjects understood as having the capacity to propagate death (to futures, races, peoples, and nations) through reproductive transmission, a possibility presupposing the legibility of procreation both as conduct and also as the conduct of a conduct Foucault called governmentality. We can see the articulation of this possibility as one of the suspended capacities of Foucault's work. This chapter discusses a number of preconditions for setting it in play, concluding with an eightfold definition of thanatopolitics, the eighth prong of which is the thanatopolitical constitution of figures of impediment to putative biopolitical and futural interest.

In the previous chapter we saw a conjunction identified (albeit fleetingly) by Edelman: the perverse male and the aborting woman as figures of impediment associated with the refusal of "life" (*NF* 31).[4] In this chapter we'll see related figures (those considered to be sexually perverse, and those considered to impede reproduction through the use of "deadly secrets"), aligned in the nineteenth- and twentieth-century concerns about population degeneracy discussed by Foucault. If we depart now from Edelman's discussion and return to the first volume of *The History of Sexuality*, we can locate its conjunction of bodies individualized by power relations stimulating interest in, and extorting truth from, the forms of sexuality deemed perverse, but also from "the child's body, à propos of women's sex, in connection with practices restricting births and so on" (*HS I* 97). Foucault makes special mention of the masturbating child, the hysterical woman, associated personages such as "the nervous woman, the frigid wife, the indifferent mother—or the mother beset by murderous obsessions" (*HS I* 110, translation modified)—and the dissipated men or socially conscientious Malthusian couples who impede or control reproduction. Foucault presents these as "strategic ensembles [*ensembles*] forming specific *dispositifs* of knowledge and power centering on sex" (*HS I* 103, trans. mod.). But insofar as they become hermeneutic figures of intense scrutiny, his account depicts these as unities centering (also) on heightened possibilities of death. The masturbating child jeopardizes its own childhood and adult vitality as well as that of the nation. The psychically and physiologically disordered women associated with hysteria are nervous, neurotic, or harmful child rearers.[5] Birth control practices are said to have a pathogenic value "for the individual and for the species" (*HS I* 105), as in the widespread view, vividly depicted in Zola's *Fécondité*, of interrupted coition as destroying human vitality, just as do women's interruptions of their pregnancies.[6] Edelman describes one type of "crusade for the children," and Foucault described another,[7] in which concern for a child's individual well-being becomes coextensive with concern for their collective health and that of population.

The perverse male, masturbating child, and hysterical women discussed by Foucault are, as he famously argues, not best understood as the objects of repression. Instead, they are intensifying figures of interest, interpretation, identity, identification, self-identification, and problematization.[8] For the human sciences of the late nineteenth and early twentieth century, they could also be the manifestation of degenerate "types." Signs of degeneracy might be seen in perverse pleasures or sexual dissipation or fecundity control. Such signs come to be linked with the associated logics of truth, secrecy, identification, and disclosure. With its proliferating figures of impediment to the "healthy futures" of individuals and peoples, this typology serves as a reminder of the contingency of its forms of life, death, and responsibility.

BODIES AND POPULATIONS

To return to the surprises *HS I* continues to hold: at one point in *Terrorist Assemblages* Jasbir Puar hinges together an initially implausible characterization of intersectionality with the following characterization of Foucault's account of sexuality: "Foucault's own provocations include the claim that sexuality is *an intersection*, rather than an interpellative identity, of the body and the population. . . . Unlike intersectional theorizing which foregrounds the separate analytics of identity that perform the holistic subject's inseparableness, the entities that intersect are the body (not the subject, let us remember) and population."[9] Of course, it's counterintuitive to claim, as Puar does, that "intersectional models cannot account for the simultaneous or multifarious presences of both or many."[10] The founding impulse of intersectionality has been to do exactly that, particularly by means of seeing race and sex as always inflecting each other.[11] While Puar recognizes this, her argument is that the study of intersectional identities is prone, nonetheless, to betray that founding impulse: "taking imbricated identities apart one by one to see how they influence each other."[12]

In *HS I* Foucault describes the formation of a sexuality that becomes associated with soul, back history, case, explanatory principles, identity claims, depth models of the self and of desire. However much he denaturalizes these by describing their conditions of formation, perhaps such an analysis breaks insufficiently with their parameters, Puar speculates.[13] She agrees with the Foucauldian point that the complex and unstable forces at work in such formations are not to be understood as "power" working on "identities," for the latter emerge only through the former. But, just as (she might argue) an intersectionality theorist who refutes the separability of imbricated identities may betray this impulse by separating them *so as* to show their imbrication, the Foucauldian who does not mean to see "sexualities" as worked on by "power" may, nonetheless, do so, "presum[ing] the automatic primacy and singularity of the disciplinary subject and its identitarian interpellation."[14]

Working in the wake of Foucault, one would not assume the interests, concerns, or organizing principles of "homosexuality," the "child at risk," or the "bad mother," nor take them to preexist the forms of power seeming to target them. Instead, the aim would be to ask how identities generate, unstably, in the intersections of bodies and populations.

Now consider a proposal from Rey Chow, for whom this Foucauldian thinking of body-population intersections gives a further result: "seen in the light of biopower, sexuality is no longer clearly distinguishable from the entire problematic of the reproduction of human life that is, in modern times, always racially and ethnically inflected."[15] A complex intervention into a body of literatures is being effected here. First, Chow follows Ann Stoler's watershed intervention into the occluded role of colonialism, colonial sexuality, race, and ethnicity in *HS I*.[16] Second, she joins a number of theorists in noting an odd phenomenon that has arisen in the wake of its publication: a bifurcation of the secondary literature concerned with the status of sex in the work and the secondary literature engaging its biopolitics.

Asking if these concerns really disconnect so easily, Chow returns us to Foucault's claim that the formations of race and ethnicity as internal forces against which a society "must be defended" amplify the murderous aspect of biopolitical formations (*SMBD* 256). In consequence, a genealogy of biopolitics, and of the control and "entry of ['biopoliticized'] life into history,"[17] is, at the same time, a genealogy of the ascendancy of whiteness.[18] This should not be neglected by sexuality studies, for Foucault's "analyses of the various institutional practices devised in European society since the Enlightenment for handling human sexuality lead him finally to the conclusion that such practices are part of a biopolitics: a systematic management of biological life and its reproduction."[19] A reading disconnecting the "sex" from the "biopolitics" would, in neglecting their intersection, occlude what Chow and some others have claimed is the *reproduction* of race and race hierarchy forming at that intersection, in the aspirations of colonialism, nationalism, security, "peoples." Also, Foucault's genealogy suggests that many of the classifications of sexuality in nineteenth-century sexology emerged in tandem with the preoccupation with race-hierarchical theories of degeneracy and its transmission (by sexual disease, reproductive transmission, contact, or social influence). Stoler has argued that these similarly overlap with a period in colonialism in which sex and reproduction become thresholds of individual, population, and racial harm.[20] It does seem, then, that the aspects of *HS I* speaking to this connection will be lost by secondary literatures separating the account of "sex" from the account of "biopolitics."

In response, Puar certainly agrees that this separation is curious and infelicitous. Yet she has had misgivings about Chow's means of considering the racism of biopolitical formations described by Foucault. Of course the integration of a Foucauldian analysis of the making of sex with that of race hierarchy is welcome. But the interest in this overlap can also bring the focus back to preoccupations *HS I* specifically deflected: as if the aims of heterosexual reproduction are dominant and organizing.[21] One could see *HS I* as demonstrably *about* the vicissitudes of reproductive heterosexuality, albeit showing that its ends are not produced as one might expect (not primarily through repression of abnormality or of "nonproductive" sexuality, nor through reduction of discourse about or interest in abnormality, nor through normalization, not primarily through the promotion of economically useful and predictable reproduction). Yet even this reading would similarly fail the specifics of Foucault's analysis if it presupposed that the interests of a productive and reproductive heterosexuality were the organizing principle of the contingent formations he describes (*HS I* 38, 45, 103).

Moreover, Puar's question is this—why do the analyses of biopoliticized race, colonialism, and Empire, insofar as they undertake to highlight the concurrent importance of biopoliticized reproduction, then seem to occlude the intersection of perverse sexualities with race and racism? The problematic bifurcation of literatures cuts both ways. If much sexuality studies literature has neglected the biopolitics and the genealogy of racism offered by *HS I* and the associated Collège de France lectures, some of the literatures amplifying the genealogy of racism in Foucault's work have seemed prone to neglect the perverse sexualities.[22]

This response to Foucault embedded in *Terrorist Assemblages* adds to his genealogy of the intersection between race division and biopolitical governmentalities an analysis of the association of stigmatized race identities and perversions. Puar shows that the latter are racialized and the former sexualized *and* that this very intersection has become a mode of population management, a technique of security, and of proliferating control. Population logics, biopoliticization, sexualization, *and* racialization are shown to be interlocking modes of circulating politicized affect and governmentality. For example, she analyzes the fearmongering circulation of images of Muslims as imminent terrorists whose foreignness is associated with their supposed repudiation of homosexuality and who may incur a retaliating aggression whose race vilification comes to merge with homophobically inflected attack in which they are savagely associated with the perverse sexuality they are supposed to find intolerable. Thus race-based attack merges with homophobic forms of sexualization.

Despite the differences between their Deleuzean and psychoanalytically inflected analyses, Puar and Edelman share the concern that the claims to family values by gay politics can occur at the expense of sexualities not encompassed within such claims: those associated with "antilife" and unintelligibility.[23] As Puar puts this, a newly sanctioned homosexuality is "folded into life" (associated with the values of life) through "market virility . . . and 'regenerative reproductivity.'" But, focusing more than *No Future* on the interlocking of race, sex, reproduction, and biopolitics, Puar notes the generation of figures of less tolerant nations, religions, and foreigners now reconfigured as challenging this new variant on American (and European) claims to a (sexual) exceptionalism. The attribution might amount to its own form of death mongering—as when the ascribed intolerance of other nations, religions, or peoples is used to justify differential immigration policies, occupation, or war. So when (some) gay and queer subjects are positively associated with the values of "life," Puar argues for a closer and more critical attention: in fact, "how queerness folds into racialization is a crucial factor." Offering a critique of homonationalism allows her to show how sexual and queer politics can integrate with "patriotism, war, torture, security, death, terror, terrorism, detention and deportation."[24]

Countering the division of literatures, Puar offers a distinctive working together of the aspirations of sex, race, biopolitics, *and* reproduction. Yet there is one respect in which she limits her attention to the role of reproduction in this cluster. She discusses its association with inclusive claims to be enfolded in life, rather than the conducts of reproduction understood as forms of death and death mongering. Yet the routes through which procreation can also be understood in the latter terms are consistent with her analyses.[25]

To return to the theme of suspension: when Puar offers a critique of Foucault, she also favors the least identitarian (to use Puar's term) Foucault. But we can favor a different reading of *HS I* by foregrounding its most flexible, segmented, and disassembled dimensions. We've seen the possible view that a Foucault returned to reproductive sexuality will be less favorable for a queer reading. But I will argue that another variant of analysis of Foucault on reproduction is available.[26]

WHAT CAN REPRODUCTION BE?

According to a Foucauldian analysis of sexuality, its "terminal forms" (*HS I* 92) must not be presupposed in genealogical analysis. That approach can similarly be extended to his references to "life," "birthrate," "reproduction," "birth," "family." How should we approach some of the most liminal figures from the work: "phthisic child," "erotomanic aunt," "neurasthenic mother" (*HS I* 125)? According to a possible rereading of *HS I,* the making of perverse sexualities *is* also a making of hysterical, absent, or failed, irresponsible, harmful, or deadly mothers. The material, if not its dominant rhetoric, directs us to the contingency of procreation. It can be individualized or massified. It can be a passivity or an agency, belonging to nature or humans. It can be prepolitical, extrapolitical, or thoroughly political. It can be nature, fate, or personal project, conduct, moral choice, or technology. It can be the figure of security or jeopardy—the maintenance of family bloodlines or the defense of a society or the flourishing of a nation—or the figure of their various declines. It may be ateleological or any number of teleologies, convergent and divergent.

How to pursue the analysis so that a discussion of *HS I* in terms of its procreation does not reduce to what we think we know about procreation's agencies, aims, and interests? How, in this context, to generate an appropriately segmented, decomposed, and dehiscent "reproduction?" How to undertake the analysis of a figure such as "mother," so as to resist the "knowing, naming and thus stabilizing of identity across space and time" for which both Foucault and Puar invite alternatives? The project serves as a reminder that the resources of Foucault's analyses and *their* (self-) identity are also not definitively resolved.

I argued in chapter 1 that Foucauldian segmentation resists the periodization attributed to him, offering reserves of resistance to aspects of Derrida's critique. The following section will propose some similar implications of this segmentation for the seeming self-identity of "race," "sex," "mothers," procreation, and "reproduction" and for alternatives to what Derrida refers to as the principle of gathering.[27]

THE PARALLEL LIVES OF *THE HISTORY OF SEXUALITY*'S VOLUME 1

To continue an exploration of untried readings of *HS I*, although Foucault's *dispositifs* read most effectively when their elements are understood as interconnecting, in this chapter I argue for a provisional disentangling of the terms: sexuality, life, reproduction, and population, for a specific, and temporary, reason. This allows a closer focus on procreation as a hinge between Foucault's account of sexuality and his account of biopolitics operating in a society which "must be defended."

So why do we hear so rarely of the procreation of *HS I*? The work had a number of parallel lives. Looking back twenty years, and considering the figurings of Foucault from Agamben (1998), Rose (2006), Esposito (2008), Bernasconi (2010), Jones (2010), and Weheliye (2014), on the one hand, and Halperin (1995), Eribon (2004), Sedgwick (1990), and Halley (2006),[28] on the other, it might indeed seem as if there had been (at least) two quite different *HS I*s, depending on whether the work has been read though the prism of sex or life. Sex is presented as the means of "access" in a number of ways, but one might focus in particular on the stimulated interest in confession and the will to talk about interior desires. Confessional sexual subjects fascinated by the presence of the possibly abnormal deep seat of a sexual self, talk, and want to talk, as Foucault noted, to all and sundry. Discursive explosion and expert knowledges intersect with the data of statistics and demographics—all critical to the possibility of biopolitical governmentality.

Given the very widespread concerns of biopolitics, it might appear unclear why Foucault would attribute any special significance to sex in thinking about the relation between (disciplined) bodies and (biopoliticized) population (addiction, for example, will also link individualized confessional selves with the concerns of managing population). Here is Foucault, presenting sex as the hinge or link between these. It is given a special status insofar as it is particularly involved in the scrutinizing, gridding, differentiating, normative, and individuating work of the disciplines, but is also the concern of the biopolitical management of populations:[29]

> Why did sexuality become a field of vital strategic importance in the nineteenth century? ... On the one hand, sexuality, being an eminently

corporeal mode of behavior, is a matter for individualizing disciplinary controls that take the form of permanent surveillance (and the famous controls that were, from the late eighteenth to the twentieth century, placed *(exercés)* both at home and at school on children who masturbated represent precisely this aspect of the disciplinary control of sexuality). But because it also has procreative effects, sexuality is also inscribed, takes effect, in broad biological processes that concern not the bodies of individuals but the element, the multiple unity of the population.... It is, I think, the privileged position it occupies between organism and population, between the body and general phenomena, that explains the extreme emphasis placed upon sexuality in the nineteenth century.

(*SMBD* 251–52)

This passage from *Society Must Be Defended* specifies (perhaps more clearly than *HS I*) that this is "*because it also has procreative effects (effets procréateurs)*" (*SMBD* 251, my emphasis).[30] My intention is not to misleadingly suggest that Foucault gives a greater focus to procreation than is the case, but I do want to draw attention to the reasons that *this* (procreative) variant of sex is said to link the biopower of (disciplined) "bodies" and of (biopoliticized) "populations." In the secondary literature (both the reception of Foucault in biopolitical literature and in sexuality studies), this is one of the least emphasized aspects of Foucault's discussion, although an attention to this question has emerged.[31] We tend to accept the account of sex as critical to biopolitical management, because of its role in normative individuation in the libidinized practices of disclosure and confession, examination, and self-presentation. Thus it is said to be the key hinge between the bodily life of the disciplines and the government of the biological life of "populations." Indeed, the same incited interest in identity will stimulate one-to-one scrutiny and "gridding" of parallel *types* of identities (for example: the "delinquent," "the addict," the "anorexic," the "fundamentalist," the "terrorist") about which population, administration, and expert and scientific inquiry may also come to be most interested (as distributions within populations).[32] Many types of hermeneutically inflected identities (including some not considered by Foucault: those identified with ADD or anorexia) emerge in accordance with what he describes as a sexual identity model (psychic depths or secrets, disclosure, discovery, gridding, norms, classifications, the "case" of which one comes to understand oneself as an instance). The models Foucault particularly associates with sex (the charge of interest with which confessing and interrogated bodies with hidden depths are stroked into individuality) become paradigmatic for other forms of close examination and interior truth (*HS I* 44–45).

Thus, when we ask what is this "life" (of the "body" and of the "species") to which sex (on Foucault's account) supposedly gives access (*HS I* 146), we will find we are dealing with multiple forms and makings of life. Sex has a great number of lives from a biopolitical perspective. It is just one subdomain of biopolitics (it becomes governmental, as does health, aging, etc.). It is also depicted in *HS I*, but less so in the prevailing biopolitical literature, as the *critical* means of power's access to life. And it stimulates the *kind* of interest, and the contours and mode of examined, individualized corporeal information, and disclosure models, the corresponding "*perpetual spirals of power and pleasure*" (*HS I* 45) proliferating in the relevant expert knowledges, human sciences, and governmentalities.

But we saw in the passage quoted earlier another point to which Foucault refers: the "sex" managed biopolitically is also procreative: it is concerned with birthrate, with population futures, with the way in which reproductive "health" impacts the population. This domain also bears its corresponding hermeneutic dimension; Foucault describes the hidden secrets and disclosures associated with heredity.

While queer theory will readily recognize sex as interconnecting with the biopolitical vicissitudes of life and death, it has shown less interest in some of the biopolitical preoccupations mentioned by *HS I* that seemingly have less to do with sex (biopolitical interest in alimentation, healthy circulation in urban environments, for example). With respect to the question "what is this life" of the "body" and of the "species" supposedly accessed by biopolitics, we'll find different answers to the question if we turn to the Italian philosophers Roberto Esposito and Giorgio Agamben (both considered in the next chapter), or to Didier Fassin,[33] to those who (for example) return Foucault's interest in life to his dialogue with Georges Canguilhem[34] or to the epistemes described in the *The Order of Things*.[35] Life can be a reference to biological process, to species, to formations of life as contingent, as open to chance and error, or as having epistemic conditions. It can be a reference to the possible objects of governmentality, taking shape in tandem with the latter. Minimally, reproductive biopolitics belong to the prisms of life through which one can read *HS I*, operating at the nexus between the biopolitical administering of life and the biopolitical intensification of sex. So let's now reconsider procreation's transition in *HS I* from the conservative teleology supposed by the repudiated repressive hypothesis to a significant biopolitical preoccupation.

HS I AND THE PROCREATIVE HYPOTHESIS

Foucault's engagement with the status of procreation is present from the first pages of *HS I*.[36] In rejecting the repressive hypothesis so stimulating to confessional sexual selfhood, he rejects the view that the perversions were subdued as illicit or illegal to the ends of a Victorian and capitalist-friendly sexuality oriented to the reproduction of the family unit. According to the view of repression he repudiates, excessive and unproductive desires, pleasures, and symptoms—those of homosexuality, masturbation, hysteria—are rendered problematic not just because they offend declared norms for sex but also because they compete with the requirements of a nonsquanderous reproductive sexuality. He depicts the received narrative of a repression of sexuality in relation to which the perversions would have to be pursued covertly: "sexuality was carefully confined; it moved into the home [*emménage*]. The conjugal family took custody of it [*la confisque*] and absorbed it into the serious function of reproduction.... The legitimate and procreative couple laid down the law. ... A single locus of sexuality was acknowledged [*reconnue*] in social space as well as at the heart of every household ... a utilitarian and fertile one: the parent's bedroom" (*HS I* 3). So procreation's stakes are first at work in *HS I* in the guise of this *replaced or rejected* repressive hypothesis. Revisiting our suppositions about the latter, he was also revisiting suppositions about a *reproductive* hypothesis, asking: "was this transformation of sex into discourse [*mise en discours du sexe*] not governed by the endeavor [*ordonnée à la tâche*] to expel from reality the forms of sexuality that were not subordinated [*soumises à*] to the strict economy of reproduction: to say no to infertile [*infécondes*] activity, to banish casual pleasures [*les plaisirs d'à côté*], to reduce or exclude practices whose object was not procreation?" (*HS I* 36 translation modified). He answers:

even if the apparent aim is to deter nonprocreative, sexual activity,[37] *even if* "all this garrulous [*bavarde*] attention which has us in a stew over sexuality [*dont nous faisons tapage autour de la sexualité*] is . . . organized by [*ordonnée à*] one basic concern: to ensure population, to reproduce labor capacity . . . to constitute a sexuality that is economically useful and politically conservative" (*HS I* 36–37 translation modified), "reduction has not been the means employed for trying to achieve it." Here, the "it" refers to the (putative) economically useful reproduction.

The implantation (in Foucault's sense) of pleasures figured in the nineteenth century as abnormal and perverse—from masturbation to homosexuality—could, in fact, be depicted as an excellent "means" to generate the most calculable, normative, statistically comprehensible, fully administered, gridded, procreative heterosexuality at the level of population. But that is not quite the point, not least because Foucault resisted reducing an apparatus to a uniform aim. What then, is the role of newly biopolitical formations of procreation in his account of the formation of perverse sexualities?

THE PROCREATIVE HINGE

When Foucault considers the formation of sexuality as interconnecting with regimes of truth, expert knowledge, and biopolitical administration, notice how one can substitute the terms *procreation* or *procreative sex,* for the word *sex* (as I have done in the following passage):

> At the heart of this economic and political problem of population was [procreative] sex: it was necessary to analyze the birthrate, the age of marriage, the legitimate and illegitimate births, the precocity and frequency of sexual relations, the ways of making them fertile or sterile, the effects of unmarried life or of the prohibitions, the impact of contraceptive practices—of those notorious "deadly secrets" which demographers on the eve of the Revolution knew were already familiar to the inhabitants of the countryside.
>
> Of course, it had long been asserted that a country had to be populated [*peuplé*] if it hoped to be rich and powerful; but this was the first time that a society had affirmed, in a constant way, that its future and its fortune were

tied not only to the number and the uprightness [*virtu*] of its citizens, to their marriage rules and family organization, but to the manner in which each individual made use of [their] sex [*chacun fait usage de son sexe*].

(*HS I* 25–26)

Now consider the following citation as encapsulating the more specific hinge that takes place in *The History of Sexuality* and in the last lecture of *Society Must Be Defended*, between Foucault's concept of those mechanisms of power addressing themselves to life and those mechanisms of power addressing themselves to sex or sexuality. Small as it is, this intersection is the reproductive "hinge" in the work, a hinge that is identified by Foucault, but not greatly emphasized as such: "We . . . are in a society of 'sex' [*du sexe*], or rather a society 'with a sexuality' [*à sexualité*]: the mechanisms of power are addressed to the body, to life, to what causes it to proliferate, to what reinforces the species, its stamina [*sa vigueur*], its ability to dominate, or its capacity for being used. Through the themes of health, progeny, race, the future of the species, the vitality of the social body, power spoke *of* sexuality and *to* sexuality; the latter was not a mark or a symbol, it was an object and a target" (*HS I* 147).

Clearly, most of Foucault's references to sex are not procreative. But for Foucault it is (procreativity oriented) sex and (biopolitically oriented) reproduction in populations that hinge together, as when he describes the formation by which: "sex was not something one simply judged; it was a thing one administered. It was in the nature of a public potential [*il relève de la puissance publique*]; it called for management procedures" (*HS I* 24). Introducing *this* administration of sex, Foucault mentions its becoming a "police" matter (the reference is to discourses of management—as in the eighteenth-century meanings of *Polizeiwissenschaft*). He cites Johann von Justi's 1757 text on the importance of having knowledge about the assets of those who belong to the Republic, to "make them serve the public welfare." The example Foucault gives of the regulation of sex is that of birthrate in the population and healthy or optimal reproduction.[38] If, in this one sense, the sex formations discussed by Foucault are somewhat more procreative than it may appear—so, too, with his biopolitics. My point is that *when* biopolitics intersects with sex in Foucault's own references in *HS I* (in association with what he describes as the management of "life") both are procreative.[39]

In other words, at several points in *HS I* Foucault brings together two problematics that do not necessarily fit together. One can, for example, describe the process by which from the eighteenth century onward births are increasingly counted and recorded in the registers of churches, parishes, in medical and local government contexts in relation to the rates of death and marriage.[40] The other problematic relates to the conceptualization of "population" and the broader beginnings of demographics. Although Foucault discusses in *HS I* the nexus of the policing of sexual (reproductive) habit and the conceptual formation of an interest in population, it helps to separate these concerns (rather than assuming their coincidence) just long enough to pay closer attention to the conditions under which they come to overlap. But in his work he presents their overlap in such a way as to occlude a question that is germane for his own purposes: how does reproduction come to present as a mode of responsibility toward "population" or its future? How does it become a problem of both bodily conduct and of governmentality (including the administrative conduct of conduct?) What kind of responsibility is this, and how can we best highlight its contingency? Who comes to be understood as bearing it? Under what conditions?

WHAT CAN POPULATION BE?

That an account must be given of how population comes to include the *conduct* of procreative sex is apparent from his variously faceted discussions of the former in a range of projects from *Security, Territory, Population*, back through *The Order of Things*. There, referring to the formation of the concept of population and its movements, Foucault first discusses a 1740 text by Nicolas Dutot, and the belief that "population tends to move in the contrary direction to money . . . the poorer countries thus have a tendency to become depopulated." A number of subsequent accounts referenced in the work describe how population levels might be impacted by stimulation of coinage,[41] by the level of wages (188, and see 259), by availability of food and natural resources (256), movements in levels of industrial profit (258–59), or the relationship between the value of the commodity and the value of labor (260).

More in line with these comments, in *HS I* Foucault mentions Claude-Jacques Herbert's 1753 *Essai sur la police générale*: "men multiply like the yields from the ground and in proportion to the advantages and resources they find in their labors."[42] Foucault continues with an account of how an interest in managing population can include patterns of sexual behavior, marriage, births in and out of wedlock, and the use of mechanisms to interrupt pregnancy (*HS I* 25–26). But in other work we are offered interestingly different accounts of what may be understood to determine levels of population: sex only appears to be the most obvious agent.

The Order of Things is a resource in this respect, with its account of Smith's law of population according to which better wages are conceptualized as the population stimulus; "the demand for men, like that for any other commodity, necessarily regulates the production of men."[43] The tacit idea might still be that increased or decreased wages stimulate or deter rates of marriage or procreation yet the determining factor is not necessarily depicted as *sexual*, and so may not be considered a matter of the "conduct of sex," nor of the governmental conduct of that conduct. This is just to make the obvious point that a management of population is not necessary a management of either sex or sexual "agency." A governmental conduct of conduct aiming to impact population levels might, for example, aim to act on wage increases (for example, by modifying taxation conditions). And the relevant governmentality might target the overall patterns of abstract masses rather than the behavior of individuals. As Foucault elaborates most extensively in *Security, Territory, Population*, concepts of population will reconceive of peoples in terms of multiplicities whose trends may be collectively affected by action on their "milieu" (*STP* 21)

Lars Behrisch has discussed eighteenth-century calculations of how the availability of sufficient looms could stimulate population levels in Lippe.[44] Thomas Robert Malthus does consider, despite his attention to the "geometric" impact of sex as on population, other factors with "arithmetic" impact: war, emigration, wages, and food availability. *Security* discusses a great number of eighteenth-century accounts of how population varies (and may, or may not, be directly or indirectly manageable) according to the variables of climate, commerce, and currency flows, the use of wet-nursing, the availability of subsistence, the demand for exports, and the availability of work (*STP* 70–72). Thus Foucault's remark, "At the heart of this economic and political problem of population was sex" (25), can be reconsidered. The contingency of this formation is highlighted by alternative approaches to population levels, many of them discussed by Foucault himself. What, then, is significant about sex?

POPULATION, PROCREATIVE AGENCY, AND WOMEN

As described in *HS I*, one eventually sees an individualized "responsibilization" (*HS I* 105) with respect to procreation: a responsibility associated with sexual, or reproductive, conduct as moral or civic duty toward populations. That biopolitical responsibility comes to include maternal duty. He will eventually refer to the twentieth-century responsibilization of the "Malthusian" couple,[45] and we could compare that phenomenon to a variant manifesting a century earlier in Malthus's *Essay on the Principle of Population* (1798): the formation of a relevant concept of moral duty.[46] This contrast helpfully highlights the contingency of associations between moral duty and reproduction and their agents, telos, substance, and practice. Malthus explores a concept of reproduction as morally reprehensible toward one's own offspring if the agents lack the means of supporting them. He also conceives individual reproductive duty in terms of one's reproductive impact on the abstract collective entity: "population," reconfigured as the matter of moral teleology.

But who is the agent? Where this is a moral duty concerning the conduct of procreative sex, we can ask: does this moral duty *have* a sex? Is this moral duty sexed? Yes, and very specifically. Malthus recommends a mindfulness concerning population impact such that individuals should delay marriages. He imagines the premarriage years to be passed in celibacy. Here those who would bear this responsibility for delayed marriage unions are male: "It is clearly the duty of each individual not to marry till he has a prospect of supporting his children; but it is at the same time to be wished that he should retain undiminished his desire of marriage, in order that he may exert himself to realize this prospect, and be stimulated to make provision for the support of greater numbers."[47]

This individual duty is born by a potential reproductive agent toward immediate offspring and concurrently toward a collective future (general happiness) negatively impacted by "geometrically" expanding population.[48] Here we will see vivid illustrations of the absence of an equivalent concept of reproductive agency attributable to women. Malthus does at one point acknowledge that reproduction is dependent on something specific to women: their childbearing "power." But when he does so, he is not discussing a female reproductive agency but a natural law: "The fecundity of the human species is, in some respects, a distinct consideration from the passion between the sexes, as it evidently depends more upon the power of women in bearing children, than upon the strength or weakness of this passion. It is, however, a law exactly similar in its great features to all the other laws of nature. It is strong and general . . . it is an object of the Creator, that the earth should be replenished . . . and it appears to me clear, that this could not be effected without a tendency in population to increase faster than food."[49] It is tempting to interpret this as an occlusion of the mother as a maternal agent. But Malthus is associating the ethics of reproduction with an agency to instigate marriage whose social and legal possibility did not belong equally to women. Malthus's suppositions invite us to consider the conditions under which contemporary versions of women's reproductive agency eventually take shape.

If women will come to be considered as agents exercising reproductive choice, they also come to be reproductive thresholds of the health of nations, populations, peoples, and futures in a number of ways associated with norms for responsible conduct.[50] But the plausibility of that association ought not be taken for granted. It has a number of conditions, and these include a different configuration of procreation's association with maternal agency, conduct, telos, outcomes, and associated obligations. These might include the survival, health, or growth of offspring and the nation; the competitiveness of the latter, its colonial expansion; a continuing or thriving family unit; the transmission of the bloodline, the family name, property, genealogy, as well as reproduction of the labor force; maternal, religious, or social duty. Eventually it can be associated with such matters as individual flourishing, domestic or personal happiness, personal freedom, reproductive autonomy, individual rights.

HS I can therefore be read in terms of its "nonstaging" of a question that can, nonetheless, be thought with its capacities: How can we understand the genealogical conditions for the problematization of the procreative conduct of women? The preliminary questions include, first, an analysis of the conditions under which procreation can be understood as "moral conduct" at all.[51] Also, it includes an analysis of the conditions under which women, more specifically (rather than men) emerge as plausible agents in relation to that conduct.

THE PROBLEMATIZED MOTHER

What are the suspended resources of Foucault's work in this regard? Under the rubric of the "socialization of procreative conduct [*conduits*]," Foucault describes incitements and restrictions, beginning in the eighteenth century, "brought to bear on the fertility of couples; a political socialization achieved through the 'responsibilization' of couples with regard to the social body as a whole" (*HS I* 104–5). It is here that he averts a discussion of the sexual differentiation of this reproductive responsibilization. Not differentiating this "couple," he is not prompted to include a fuller discussion of the respective (and different) roles and responsibilizations of the "man" and "woman" in the nineteenth and twentieth centuries.[52] For (and unlike the forms of responsibility imagined by Malthus) forms of neo-Malthusianism would address women with new understandings of reproductive choice. (Indeed, this responsibility would be enthusiastically embraced by a number of turn-of-the-century feminist movements.)[53]

It might seem that Foucault considers specific forms of responsibility attributed to women in his discussions of families, although he does not do so in his discussion of population impact and management. Katherine Logan belongs to a group of researchers to have recently revisited Foucault's work on families and to have argued that "when Foucault refers more generally to 'the family', we ought to take this as lacking its necessary specificity in terms of the way in which the members of the family are individuated."[54] Other commentators, including Foucault's contemporaries, had considered the roles more specifically assumed by women. In the first major Foucauldian study in this area, *The Policing of Families*, Jacques Donzelot described the emergent forms of parental responsibility newly informed by expert knowledges giving mothers the authority of the expert's opinion. Women have been the latter's auxiliaries within the family space,[55] despite also being (socially and legally) subordinated to their husbands and (differently so) to medical and lay figures of expertise.

But Foucault reroutes the specificity of the woman's or mother's role to that of a fairly consistent reference to "parents," as seen in his discussion in *Abnormal* of family spaces mediated by expert concern about the effects of masturbation for which the parents are held responsible (*AB* 244). He describes the consequent injunctions on parents, the techniques for linking "the parent's body to the child's body [insofar as] . . . the child must be prevented from arriving at the state of pleasure," the "instruction for the direct, immediate, and constant application of the parents' bodies to the bodies of their children" (*AB* 247). This systematic favoring of the "parent" is seen in his discussions of eighteenth-century child-rearing tracts. He included a recommendation from P-M. Rozier's early nineteenth-century *Des habitudes secrètes* that a mother should closely shadow her child. By almost encompassing it, through a marsupial-like corporeal proximity, she can deter its masturbation.[56] But Foucault follows Rozier's commentary on how responsibility falls on "parents":

> Children's bodies will have to be watched over by the parents' bodies in a sort of physical clinch. There is extreme closeness, contact, almost mixing; the urgent folding of the parents' bodies over their children's bodies. . . . This is what Rozier says about the example I have just given: "The mother of such a patient is, so to speak, like the wrapping or the shadow of her daughter" . . . The parent's body envelopes the child's."
>
> (*AB* 248)

Similarly, Foucault speaks to the "urgen[t] [enjoining] of "parents . . . to reduce the large polymorphous and dangerous space of the household," the overlaps of the doctor-patient relationship and the relationship between parents and children (*AB* 250), the antimasturbation campaigns which took place in the broader context of invitations at the end of the eighteenth century to parents to prevent children from dying, watch over them and train them, to take responsibility "for the child's body and life" (*AB* 255).

We see the degree to which Foucault is averting a differentiation—which in this case would be available and meaningful—between the ways in which mother and father become responsibilized within family clusters. In none of these discussions (including Foucault's references to an emergent, widespread concern about the importance of women breastfeeding their own children as a matter of the latter's health and survival)[57] is there a discussion of the different roles of fathers and mothers as "parents,"[58] whereas, revisiting the many eighteenth- and nineteenth-century texts discussed by Foucault, one will find this difference.[59]

On the other hand, turning back to Logan's critical response to the lack of sexual individuation in Foucault's discussion of families,[60] she continues: "within the family, the mother can be described as a central figure and maternal power as a central mechanism in the deployment of sexuality.[61] While the mother is necessarily linked to the father within the sovereign realm of the family, the mother ought to be regarded as having been quite distinctly individuated with respect to familial participation in the deployment of sexuality." Thus, Logan also touches on the contexts when Foucault most demarcates the significance of sexual difference. For, as is rarely observed, the family formation is, in Foucault's work, *also* depicted as the locus of sovereign spousal formations whose function, as Foucault describes these, is primarily to individuate husbands and fathers. In *Psychiatric Power* he describes the family, in the period immediately following the institution of the French civil code, as an "alveolus of sovereignty" (*PP* 83). It is based in relations of domination between men and women, and over children: "What do we see in the family if not a function of maximum individualization on the side of the person who exercises power, that is to say, on the father's side?.... The father, as bearer of the name, and insofar as he exercises power in his name, is the most intense pole of individualization, much more intense than the wife or children. So, in the family you have individualization at the top, which recalls and is of the very same type as the power of sovereignty, the complete opposite of disciplinary power" (*PP* 80, and see 115).

I had asked what a Foucauldian approach could offer, more specifically, to this question, particularly when thinking in terms of his suspended reserves. A first step directs attention to locations where Foucault either does—or could—distinguish the sexual difference of the parents. A second step considers the registers of power described here. We have, first, the sovereign mode. But we also have disciplinary modes. The husband and father is individualized by the former. The mother (in addition to the children) is individuated by the latter. The regimes of parenting informed by the "expert" knowledges described by Foucault also distinguish good and bad mothers, let's say: those said to raise their children responsibly or irresponsibly. In this sense, the mother is individuated, and becomes a vector of the disciplines, in tandem with the child.[62]

As we follow Logan's gambit and reinstate (where plausible) the sexual difference sometimes lost in Foucault's own references to the roles of parents and couples, a complex account emerges of coinciding, inconsistent techniques of power. The family is depicted by Foucault as a space of historical, social, or legal subordination of mother to father, a phenomenon whose history is that of sovereign authority, and this he deems persistent. The family space is also one in which "parental" authority is described as becoming subordinate to expert authority. In fact, in *Psychiatric Power* that expert authority is also described as a kind of sovereign authority or as partaking in some of its aspirations and resonance, also. Thus the "parent" in the family is both the expert's auxiliary, subordinate to the latter, but *also* newly authorized by expert knowledge. The resulting techniques and stimulations of disciplinary power are not to be understood in sovereign terms. This gives redoubled (but also conflicting) techniques and apparatuses of paternal authority over children and the overall project of a conduct of conduct: of parenting, by parenting. And other commentators (among them Donzelot)—albeit not Foucault—have added that this new subordination of parents to the expert, complex as it already is, *also* could give the mother a new authority as medical ally within the family space.[63] Yet that does not mitigate women's concurrent subordination in other ways, patriarchal, legal, traditional, as wife and mother. In short, the techniques associated with the relevant, coinciding apparatuses of power in which women are intertwined are multiple and not necessarily consistent. It's common to think of Foucault as describing the coincidence of elements working strangely well in conjunction.[64] But Foucault also describes spaces of coinciding modes and techniques that don't necessarily work in this way: they may also be disjunctive and contradictory. All such elements, and not only the most consistent, are at work in this enmeshing of the apparatuses of discipline, biopower, pastoral interest, and various forms of sovereign power, for example.

Consider another of Foucault's discussions of family spaces, this time his collaborative work with Arlette Farge, published as *Le désordre des familles* (1982).[65] Here the intersection of a number of forms of sovereignty with family constellations is described. In the century leading up to the French revolution, the authority of French monarchs vested in their local auxiliaries might intervene into "disordered" family spaces, both wealthy and poor. Charged with an interest in maintaining domestic order, they could confine, through *lettres de cachet*, those accused of dissipation, licentiousness, alcoholism, brutality, vagrancy. Thus this was also a type of sovereign authority secured, as Deleuze has emphasized, as much from below as from above.[66]

Sexual difference is distinguished in these discussions. Discussing specific archival cases, Farge and Foucault emphasize that women no less than men could and did successfully appeal for the confinement of their violent or dissipated spouses and children. The family is a space in which women may suffer (as amply illustrated in *Le désordre des familles*'s archival material) the violence of spouses, and it is also separately described by Foucault as the space of subordination of the wife to the husband, but we'll *also* find an account of the woman's multiple and complex roles in the relays of sovereign power, in their ability to confine husbands and children by means of the administrative auxiliaries of monarchic authority.

But there is an eventual "withdrawal of sovereign interest" from the (sometimes) minor discords of family order, for this was a relatively inefficient, individualized form of management. The result for women is a reconfiguration of male authority within the private, domestic sphere: "reproduction will henceforth be managed by the masculine domain." According to Foucault and Farge's commentary in *Le désordre des familles*: "Families are no longer a royal matter, and gradually a domestic space emerged in which the man laid down the law. Suddenly detached from the fabric of public events, the woman was obliged by the life of the couple to quit the scene. In this sense there is no longer a reciprocal relationship between the state and the woman. Their spheres disconnect, fairly definitively, with men now serving as their point of connection. Women are relegated to the confined space of private life. The Civil Code will complete this shift."[67]

We are brought to the conclusion that Foucault most distinguished the sexes when discussing sovereign authority in the family, complex as these analyses are.[68] This is not to say that the family is only (in Foucault's work) or even best thought in these terms (and Foucault's work includes a number of different discussions of families and of different types of families).[69] But Foucault disaggregated father and mother most, to whatever extent that techniques within families and relations between the sexes were understood in terms of sovereign power. Otherwise (and sometimes in conjunction—both variants are present in *Psychiatric Power* and in *Abnormal*) we are more likely to see a reference to the (sexually indistinguished) "parents" of the disciplines, and of normalization, who monitor, defend, spatially separate, stimulate. Similarly, "parents" and "couples" tend not to be distinguished where Foucault refers to biopolitical aims such as the conservation and maximization of life, the defense against degeneracy or reducing the overall child mortality rate, the new importance of medical authority, itself integrated with the state and practices of good government.

So women in the family are (legally, traditionally) under the sovereign authority of their husbands, who become the point of connection between women (in the private sphere) and the state. And women (and also men) in these contexts are *also* differently individuated by way of the disciplines, with the result being that they are nexus points and relays of multiple modes of power. But they *also* take on a new significance in the biopolitical interests of child raising and of healthy reproduction: "The family will change from being a model to being an instrument; it will become a privileged instrument for the government of the population rather than a chimerical model for good government. . . . From the middle of the eighteenth century, the family really does appear in this instrumental relation to the population, in the campaigns on mortality, campaigns concerning marriage, vaccinations, and inoculations, and so on" (STP 105).

In other words, once we begin to differentiate the sexes in Foucault's various accounts of family spaces, we can pay attention to a different phenomenon, relevant for our purposes. First, it is not only that Foucault has more to say about families (and sexual difference) than is sometimes perceived. More importantly, insofar as Foucault's accounts of the family can therefore be understood as contexts in which he is outlining the coincidences of multiple, differently, and concurrently functioning techniques and modes of power (sovereignty, discipline, biopower, biopolitics, security, and governmentality, and later neoliberalism), we again see him troubling the more linear models with which he is sometimes associated.

In the introduction we considered a number of commentators interested in the different ways in which biopolitics and governmentality seem to "replace," but may also "rearticulate" sovereign power. Discussions of the coincidences of sovereign, disciplinary, and biopolitical modes often default to his brief mention of the Nazi regime in the last lecture of *Society Must Be Defended* (259). His account of "penetration" (of sovereign by biopower and the contrary) and of the coincidence of modes (most typically of discipline, sovereign, and the biopolitical) has not, by contrast, been extensively explored by means of revisiting Foucault's discussion of family spaces.[70] Yet they offer an excellent elaboration of the nonlinearity of modes of power, and of the correspondingly segmented and divergent techniques in family, reproductive and child-rearing contexts. They foreground the point that these are complementary (in the fortuitous interconnections of apparatuses) but *also* divergent.

"Penetration" and similar metaphors used by Foucault to discuss the relationship between sovereign power and biopolitics have allowed much debate among scholars interpreting the status of sovereignty in Foucault's work. It is sometimes proposed that new modes replace and absorb older modes or the reverse (that sovereignty is penetrated by biopower—or vice versa)—as also seen in the language of "rearticulation" of one mode by another. But, I am suggesting, this replacement can amount to a simultaneously complementary *and* conflicting survival of the replaced mode, a "survival" containing dehiscence as well as absorption. This is the line of interpretation I propose as the best means of understanding the status of women and of the family in these discussions.

Consider, in particular, the eight or so pages on "alliance" (the "system of marriage, of fixation and development of kinship ties, of transmission of names and possessions," HS I 106) in *The History of Sexuality*, volume 1.[71] It is particularly in Foucault's discussion of a transition from alliance models that terms proliferate reiterating the image of power's rearticulation, if not "penetration" of,[72] or in, new formations. The discussion of reproductive aims and unions indicates concurrent connection and disconnection of the sovereign mode of power corresponding to marital alliance and the biopower corresponding to sexuality. He stresses there is no simple replacement of the one by the other; rather he identifies the "interchange" (*l'échangeur*; *HS I* 108) between them, their "interpenetration" or "coupling" (*épinglage*; *HS I* 108, 113), that the one is "propping up" (*soutenir*; *HS I* 113) superimposes (*superpose*; 106) on or "covers up" (*recouvrir*) the other, while not rendering useless or obliterating (*il ne l'a pas effacé ni rendu inutile*) what it covers up (107). Rather they operate in conjunction or in relation to each other (*par rapport à*; 108); the one gains "support" from (*en prenant appui sur*; 108) the other. It is not exact to say that alliance is supplanted (*s'est substitué à*) by sexuality, even if one day it will be replaced (*remplacé*) by it (107). Foucault's point is that the family form of alliance (a space of sovereign modes, of prohibition, of the law) is *also* the site where sexuality (and its techniques of incitement and interest) is the most active (109):

> The family cell, in the form in which it came to be valued in the course of the eighteenth century, made it possible for the main elements of the deployment [*dispositif*] of sexuality (the feminine body, infantile precocity, the regulation of births . . . the specification of the perverted) to develop along its two primary dimensions: the husband-wife axis and the parents-children axis. The family, in its contemporary form, must not be understood as a social, economic, and political structure of alliance that excludes or at least restrains sexuality, that diminishes it as much as possible, preserving only its useful functions. On the contrary, its role is to anchor [*ancrer*] sexuality and provide it with a permanent support [*le support permanent*]. It ensures the production of a sexuality that is not homogeneous [*homogène*] with the privileges of alliance, while making it possible for the systems of alliance to be traversed [*traversés*] by a new tactic of power.
>
> (*HS I* 108, trans. mod.)

While interpretation of *HS I* has generally concentrated on the point that sexuality was *not* being repressed in the family, and on Foucault's innovative concept of productive power, Foucault's text erupts with multiple images providing alternatives to the consecutive replacement of modes of power: here sovereign v. biopower, alliance versus sexuality. Foucault promotes a relinquishing of repressive understandings of forms of power better understood as productive, to be sure. But he also invites attention to the *exchange* and persistent *coincidence* between *disparate, incongruous, concurrent, modes* of power and their segmented techniques.[73] Just one of the many conclusions to be drawn from Foucault's explosion of images (I have suggested these be grouped as the images of "penetration") would be a very obvious point: we can't stabilize the mother as one thing or as belonging to one mode (one role, one technique, one vector): her role is a remnant of a sovereign mode, she is both object and subject of pastoral and panopticized modes of examination, of scrutiny and self-scrutiny for conduct, of normative individuation, of "birthrate" and responsibility for birthrate. She belongs to a milieu on which governmentality might hope to act. She belongs to the techniques of security that aim at the regulation of the uncertain, or at disturbing trends in reproduction, and she belongs to the conduct of family investment and self-investment. She is the coincidence of multiple modes. She is, among other things, a multiplicity of techniques, operations, individualizations, statistics, trends, risk factors, forms of human capital.

Rereading *The History of Sexuality* from this perspective, we find it presents a family space to be understood in just such terms:[74]

> It's often said that modern society has attempted to reduce sexuality to the couple—the heterosexual and, insofar as possible, legitimate couple. There are equal grounds for saying it has, if not created [*inventé*], at least carefully arranged [*soigneusement aménagé*] and made to proliferate, groups with multiple elements and a circulating sexuality: a distribution of points of power, hierarchized or brought into apposition [*affrontés*]; "pursued pleasures [*des plaisirs poursuivis*]" that is, both sought after [*désirés*] and hunted down [*pourchassés*]; fragmented [*parcellaires*] sexualities that are tolerated or encouraged; proximities that serve as surveillance mechanisms and that function as mechanisms of intensification; contacts that operate as inductors. This is the way things worked out in the case of the family, or rather, the household, with parents, children, and in some instances, servants. Was the nineteenth-century family really a monogamic and conjugal cell? Perhaps to a certain extent. But it was also a network of pleasures and powers [*plaisirs-pouvoirs*] linked together [*articulés*] at multiple points and according to transformable relationships. The separation of grown-ups and families, the polarity established between the parents' bedroom and that of the children,[75] . . . the relative segregation of boys and girls,

the strict instructions as to the care of nursing infants (maternal breast-feeding, hygiene), the attention aroused [*éveillée*] concerning infantile sexuality, the supposed dangers of masturbation, the importance attached to puberty, the methods of surveillance suggested to parents, the exhortations, secrets, and fears, the presence—both valued and feared—of servants; all this made the family, even when brought down to its smallest dimensions, a complicated network, saturated with multiple, fragmentary, and mobile sexualities. . . . Educational or psychiatric institutions, with their large populations, their hierarchies, their spatial arrangements, their surveillance systems, constituted, alongside the family, another way of distributing powers and pleasures, but they too delineated [*dessinent*] areas of extreme sexual saturation, with privileged spaces or rituals such as the classroom, the dormitory, the visit, and the consultation. The forms of a nonconjugal, nonmonogamous sexuality were drawn there and established.

(*HS I* 45–46, trans. mod.)

Clearly, the significant claim here is that apparently repressive mechanisms of supervision and control (parental, expert, and institutional) in fact constitute a proliferating distribution of nonmonogamous sexualities. But Foucault's notoriously counterintuitive account of power has been so transformative that we can overlook other points made in such familiar passages. What if we return to the misleadingly simple use of the term *aussi* to discuss the multiple techniques and modes of power for which the elements of the family are vectors? "Was the nineteenth century family really a monogamic and conjugal cell?" (*HS I* 46). Perhaps, we are told, and Foucault considers what it was *also*. What are the consequences for the woman in this family? As part of a conjugal cell, her role as wife and mother is (on Foucault's account) one of subordination to a husband individuated as such and understood in terms of sovereign conjugal authority. Concurrently interconnected with networks of expert advice and surveillance systems, she is also addressed by norms for parenting: newly negative views about the involvement of household servants in childcare, the biopolitically inflected injunctions to women to breast-feed, rather than using wet nurses. As "parent," the mother could share with her husband what Foucault describes as a sovereign authority over the child, but she is described as sharing the child's subordination to the father's sovereign authority. The intense interest in the child's health and sexuality is also disjunctive with this subordination: for the child is not just "subordinate" insofar as it becomes a point of inscrutability, depth, secrecy, hermeneutics, and fascination. The same point is widely made of the mother's negative images: such as the "hysteric." The woman bears an individualized responsibility for the "child's body and life," but is also critical in the instrumental relation the family will play as vector in the government of "population.[76] We can recognize in Foucault's "also" the different techniques in play, corresponding to the coincidence of sovereign, disciplinary, governmental, biopolitical, and security apparatuses. This "also" is the work not just of conversion, not just of addition, nor transformation, survival, nor even plasticity, but in all of these, their concurrent divergence.

Similarly, consider Foucault's argument that the disciplines are not modeled on the tradition of family discipline, and, to reverse the point, "family" discipline is not to be confused with Foucauldian discipline. This point rightly takes the focus. But there can be an *incongruent* coincidence of these modes. As we have seen, the former is that of the sovereign cell-like unit organized in terms of a sovereign father's authority to discipline its child. Foucauldian disciplines are capillary-like multiplicities (laterally connecting techniques within families with those of institutions ranging from schools to prisons and with associated expert knowledges) differentiating behavior in relation to gradations of abnormality and stimulating individuation. Yet the "same" family *and some of the same techniques* (segmented, and correspondingly belonging to different, mutually repelling but also complementary apparatuses) may be loci of both kinds of discipline. In fact, Foucault argues that one factor enabling the disciplinary work of normalization is the availability of sufficiently adapted bodies. Some role is *also* played in this respect by conventional family disciplines, even while the family is also a vector of "Foucauldian" disciplines. The latter's individuation in relation to norms will stimulate categories of extreme recalcitrance or disobedience: the undisciplined, the delinquent, the nonresponsive, the poor learners, the nonadaptive. The warning issued within the family is that the child's abnormality destines it for the prison, but the family can also be considered the space to which those who cannot be disciplined may be returned.[77] The family space is multispatial. It is both hierarchical and horizontal, both cell-like and enveloping of populations, a vector of the interconnected, linked, multiple bodies of the disciplines, a necessary "prior" to the disciplines, and seemingly also a surplus to the disciplines. Thus we would attribute to Foucault's family "a complicated network, saturated with multiple, fragmentary, and mobile sexualities" and of conflicting modes and techniques of power.

With respect to debates in Foucauldian commentary about the relationship between sovereignty, biopower, and their mutual penetrations, this brings us back to the powers of death elaborated by Foucault in relation to both. Let's return to Foucault's point from *HS I*, mentioned earlier (and also developed in *STP*), that the family *also* becomes an instrument in the management of "populations." It *also* becomes a vector in techniques of security. This means that the child's life is both principle of life, a body at individual risk, *and* a likely mortality *rate* (sometimes a body at risk *and* a potentially dangerous transmission factor). It is both a governmental problem to which an administrator should attend and also a problem of government at the level of family. This may be seen in the view that family practice or child mortality rates are amenable either to administration or to modification through stimuli by governmental conduct, for example by changing their conditions and milieus.[78]

This offers a new inflection to the dehiscent complexities to be registered at the level of the family space and to the senses in which the family becomes a milieu for the child's life or death. As a milieu, the family is a zone of risk. As the space of the child's desirable survival, it also becomes the context for calculating its likelihood of death. A practice such as breast-feeding might be a normalizing, expert-inflected "discipline" (targeting individual maternal conduct) and the topic of a biopolitical aim to modify overall rates of breast-feeding. Thus it emerges as the context for different types of management of (individualized, collective, and multitemporal) health, vitality, and mortality. In 1778 Jean-Baptiste Moheau, proposed by Foucault as "no doubt the first great theorist of what we would call biopolitics, biopower" (*STP* 22),[79] joined other early demographers in accumulating data about birthrate and death rate from parishes, establishing disturbing trends in infant death, at a time when this could be attributed to factors ranging from smallpox to inoculation practices to the impact of unhealthy climates or to the perceived trend toward the use of wet nurses or more generally deficient mothering.[80]

> Population ... is dependent on a series of variables. [It] varies with the climate ... the material surroundings ... the intensity of commerce and activity in the circulation of wealth ... the laws to which it is subjected, like tax or marriage laws ... with people's customs, like the way in which daughters are given a dowry for example, or the way in which the right of primogeniture is ensured, with birthright, and also with the way in which children are raised, and whether or not they are entrusted to wetnurses ... with the moral and religious values associated with different kinds of conduct ... with the condition of means of subsistence.
>
> (STP 70–71)

Like the formations of "sexuality," those of "maternity" and "children" also assemble *and* disassemble at the interfaces and overlaps of concurrently sovereign, disciplinary, biopolitical, governmental, pastoral, security, and neoliberal modes and their aims, techniques, conducts, and forces. Practically disseminating and stimulating biopolitical preoccupations, a maternal body is simultaneously subordinate to the husband; scrutinizing *with* the husband, jointly subordinate to the expert's authority, and authoritative as the latter's auxiliary in the home, the vector of overlapping normalizations (both of children *and* of maternal conduct) linking the disciplinary, individuating and differentiating work of normalization with governmental interest in population trends and risk factors—all the while that maternal conduct could also come to play a role in some neoliberal understandings of self-investment in family capital, choice, or self-making. These conduct and their effects may be contradictory. There may be an expectation of deliverance, by parents or public authorities, of care, safety, order, liberty, and autonomy. Children or mothers might be positioned as deliverers of the future, as rights claimants, as entities "at risk," or as harmful—to individuals or collectivities. Moving forward, I focus on the latter possibility: the concurrent making of childhood and maternity as thresholds of harm, death, insecurity, threat, and exposure in divergent and concurrent multiplicities: linking child, parent, authority, law and state in sovereign, security, disciplinary and biopolitical forms of power, and in correlates of defense and exposure.

FROM THE BIOPOLITICAL TO THE THANATOPOLITICAL

While incorporating references to an optimal management of death, Foucauldian biopolitics are most commonly associated with his interest in power as a capacity to foster life (*HS I* 138).[81] Biopower was galvanizing in the context of Foucault's work insofar as it allowed him to attend to what had been less commonly attributed to power: its capacity to enhance and maximize, to make and produce rather than limit, repress, marginalize, constrain, and subordinate. An emphasis on its concurrently deadly, subtractive, or negligent components may initially have appeared to be a mistaken focus on the repressive function from which he was importantly differentiating biopower.[82]

As we've seen, what makes such dimensions part—arguably an indissociable part—of any biopolitics is, as Foucault argues, the new logics provided to what might otherwise appear to be its repressive, subordinating, depriving, or deadly components. The biopolitical power of death is distinctively characterized by its putative justification in terms of overall health and well-being, good management of the population, its overall needs and its "collective" and futural interest. Its mode, similarly, is proliferating rather than repressive.

The stimulations of the biopolitical also include its making of figures of death. The thanatopolitical understanding of Foucauldian biopolitics (its making of death) is not always evident, but it is rarely far from the scene. It is seen in his reference to sexual, reproductive, parental, and maternal agents of biopolitical harm. If we turn back again to Donzelot's *The Policing of Families* we will similarly find repeated elaborations of children variously deemed at risk. On the one hand, we have Donzelot's definition of the so-called *Polizeiwissenschaft*, in other words: "The proliferation of political technologies that invested the body, health, modes of subsistence and lodging—the entire space of existence in European countries from the eighteenth century onward. All the techniques that found their unifying pole in what, at the outset, was called *policing*: not understood in the limiting, repressive sense we give the term today, but according to a much broader meaning that encompassed all the methods for developing the quality of the population and the strength of the nation."[83]

Here we have the well-known analyses of techniques of power as productive in the aim of an optimal administration of life. Yet it is not difficult to relocate the powers of death in the aims described by Donzelot to enhance the quality of the population and the nation's strength. Those aims optimize presupposed differentials of worth in the distribution of resources. For example, Donzelot presents calculations made by philanthropic movements in late eighteenth-century France concerning the groups they might most productively assist: children rather than the aged. Women in preference to men, since this concurrently preserved their children also. Poor mothers were to be preferred—but only those mothers who agreed to breast-feed their own children and not to abandon them to wet nurses (whose use was associated with higher mortality rates).[84] In this context, saving the children really does amount to denying resources to the aged while also differentiating the lesser value of recalcitrant mothers.[85] Thus biopolitical calculations can (and, some would argue, always) carry their thanatopolitical component. Perhaps they always stimulate their figures of death, complements of the figures of life: the children whose masturbation was sapping their future strength *and* that of any lives to which they might give rise: "The child ... was in danger of compromising not so much his physical strength as his intellectual capacity, his moral fiber [*devoir*], and the obligation to preserve a healthy line of descent for his family and his social class" (*HS I* 121). The negligent mothers who sent their children out to wet nurses delivered similarly redoubled negative effects for the individual and the collective, the short and the long term. In its figures of harm, a biopolitical governmentality includes this proliferation of thanatopolitical imaginaries and identities.

To differentiate the role of mother and father in relation to this proliferation is to be confronted with the redoubled role of mother. At the level of individual bodies, conduct, discipline, individualization, there was the problem of "the individual diseases that the sexual debauchee brings down upon himself" (*SMBD* 252). Foucault will include women among this group of debauchees and will emphasize that the dissipation and death incurred is individual, yet also considered to collectively weaken the nation. But they are being transmitted through the generations as well: here women have the extra role as principle of their (reproductive) transmission: "debauched, perverted sexuality has effects at the level of the population, as anyone who has been sexually debauched is assumed to have a heredity. Their descendents also will be affected for generations. . . . This is the theory of degeneracy: given that sexuality is the source of individual diseases and that it is the nucleus of degeneracy" (*SMBD* 252). Similarly, we have the child who, in masturbating too much, "will be a lifelong invalid" (*SMBD* 252): with negative impact for a number of multiplicities, the collectivity vitality of family and national futures. When such risks were attributed to childhood conduct, the relevant responsibility of averting these multiple deaths may have been attributed to the parent, but, as a number of commentators have argued, differently so. For even if the strictures against masturbation and perverse sex belong to paternal (and expert) authority, the preventive parental conduct will fall more to the mother (who is also being alerted to the dangers of wet nurses, nursemaids, servants, older children, erotomanic aunts and uncles—none of whom can be fully trusted with the relevant surveillance, for they are frequently being refigured as the dangerous outside influence against which the mother must defend). Thus the mother takes on an additional role as figure of death, not just because of her dissipation or unhealthy physiology or character but also because her maternal failings might result in a failed defense of children against these influences.

In sum, a great deal of suspended capacity lurks in this conjunction of texts and of problems. Foucault turned toward the biopoliticization of sex and toward a biopolitics that could be differentiated from sovereign modes associated with the privative—at the extreme, the taking of life. He did not occlude biopolitical "powers of death." But, when he articulated the latter, he omitted a foregrounding of reproduction, parents, children, and mothers *as* the biopolitical *envers*: as the thresholds of death stimulated by biopolitical logics. Nonetheless, his work is a resource for showing how reproduction, parents, children, and mothers are made as powers of death—how biopoliticized reproduction and reproductive futurism becomes (to borrow the term not used by Foucault in this context) thanatopolitical. The perverse and the maternal come to be associated with the possibility of biopolitical harm, becoming forces and subjects obstructive of reproductive futurism. This phenomenon includes negligent maternities and the point to which I turn in the next section: the proliferation of phenomena (including legal regimes) stimulating a new kind of vulnerability associated with the specter of their maternal capacity to (according to an extreme imaginary) impose death. In fact, as I shall argue, a phenomenon emerges for which Puar's analysis of the "terrorist" of homonationalism is illuminating.[86] The attribution to some women of conducts of procreation deemed irresponsible and antilife becomes the pretext for harms to which women are subject. (Simply put, women are subject to new forms of harm insofar as they are associated with new forms of *doing* harm.)

REPRODUCTION, RACE DEFENSE, AND THE DEATH OF FUTURES

A number of commentators (Weinbaum, Bernasconi, McWhorter, Stoler, Dorlin) have suggested that the association between hereditary, reproductive truth, and the risk of degeneracy implies in Foucault's work a link between race hierarchy, the defense against forces understood as jeopardizing biological, or national integrity, the principles of divisions of populations, and the differential worth of life rights.[87]

As Stoler and Elsa Dorlin have shown, colonialism problematized exactly these overlapping bodies, and all the more strongly given its figuring of national wealth in terms of expanding white and healthy population. The paradoxes of colonialist expansion (a claim to expanding life intertwined with its new risks of death and degeneracy) are seen in images of France's spatial, security, physiological, and sexual exposure. Against bodies understood to transmit harm, the necessities of colonialism were associated with a sexual defense of the conjoined, corporeal multiplicities of child-mother-nation.

Thus Stoler adds, to Foucault's account of the simultaneously vulnerable and dangerous masturbating child, the colonial depiction of European children as sexually (as described by Foucault) but also *racially* vulnerable and dangerous, threatened by sexual desire in their new colonial locations, sexually vulnerable as compared to "precocious Indies youths." In an overlapping of the exposed bodies of child and empire, Europeans were said to be threatened by the lesser sexual discipline and sexual contamination of colonial contexts.[88] In drawing attention to the child as threshold of sexual transmission and risk (the European child said to acquire, with multiply disastrous results, premature sexual maturity in colonial climates), Stoler gives less attention to the mother, who becomes the vector (either through nondefensive child-rearing or through reproductive transmission) of the fear that degeneracy will impede the vitality and growth of colonial expansion.[89] For the dangers associated with sexual relations between colonizer and colonized are not just those of moral decay and sexual disease. As argued in Dorlin's *La matrice de la race*, exposed to such contaminants, the woman is also understood as the primary conduit *through which* this deadly transmission will then proliferate into the following generations.[90] Thus a vigilant hermeneutic practice could be included among her new responsibilities: to identify the signs of degeneracy in a real or prospective spouse as much as in the conduct of her children.[91]

Yet the passage from *Society Must Be Defended*, cited previously, concerning degeneracy and reproductive transmission continued into the well-known discussions of the paradoxes of biopolitics: its atomic power, its viruses, its capacity for self-destruction. That the following question forms no part of his rhetoric does not inhibit us from amplifying the point that connects these near paragraphs so immediately. And so we turn to the question: the murderous capacities of the biopolitical were, for Foucault, to be thought as potentially paradoxical at (as I will further argue in the next chapter) the point of their ungovernability. So what was the reproductive equivalent of this paradox? For Foucault, procreation was not, of course, a natural phenomenon.

It was a problem of conduct, of governmentality, of preemptive security. It delivered biopolitical life, but also the equivalent possibility of biopolitical catastrophe. Foucault cannot mention the concern about degeneracy's transmission into the "seventh generation" without gesturing toward this reproductive conduit and its problematized agents.[92] The fears for the "seventh generation" remind us that reproduction had become associated with the possibility of poor management, and the latter was seen as capable of delivering biopolitical catastrophe.

Space of overlap of the child's life, its futurity, and that of the population and nation, the family is, as Chow and Foucault both note, one of the sites where life and death enter "into history." Insofar as she has become principle of life (of both child and nation), the mother also becomes a potentially destructive figure. This is almost, yet not quite, Foucault's own conclusion: overlapping with the racial inflections of national life, health, and vitality, women's reproductive bodies are associated with the "society that must be defended": in a making of dangers understood as disastrously transmitted to entire generations, as principle of life they becomes the thanatopoliticized thresholds of possible harm, population decline, or race decline. Foucault's account of reproduction, procreation, and child raising as principles of biopolitical life is also an account of the proliferation of forms of antilife, with implications for women he left unexplored.

In other words, women can only be represented as the thanatopolitical threat to the future of a population or community insofar as their reproductive lives have come to count in new ways politically and biopolitically. Having emerged as a biopolitical resource (key, for example, to birthrate in a sense Malthus would not have recognized), as reproductive agents or else conduits of the problematized population impact, they occupy a redoubled role: objects and agents of biopolitical technics, potential for thanatopolitical threat they would relay and to which they can also be considered exposed.

POPULATION AND THE SOCIETY THAT MUST BE DEFENDED: RACE, RISK, REPRODUCTION

Thus, perhaps it is not quite, as Michelle Murphy formulates this, that Foucault's accounts of the biopolitical "largely foreclosed" not only colonialism and capitalism but also "reproduction, or even women."[93] Foucault is not entirely omitting from the discussion the problematization of women, their reproductive and maternal conduct, and their emergence as either categories of abnormality or vectors of harm emerging within the apparatuses he analyzed—though certainly he is not foregrounding them.[94] But, when he writes of the strategies that crossed through "and made use of the sex of women, children, and men" (HS I 105), he is clearly describing the *making* of those invested subjects and objects. It is a rigorous point for Foucault that strategies, problematizations, governmentalities, subjects, and objects form together. Thus the women his analysis remembers but does not foreground are those who (as responsibilized principles and thresholds) emerge within the biopolitical strategies he describes.

There certainly is not a comprehensive omission of reproduction and women, still less of the problematics with which they are intertwined in Foucault's work. So these questions prompt methodological choices for reading Foucault. It is an option to mark omissions as foreclosures—but these can also be read as suspensions. We might not want to accept that women have been—or can be—erased quite as thoroughly, as is sometimes taken to be the case.

We can't entirely separate the "Children" (in Edelman's sense) jeopardized by the antisocial and antilife factors deemed to impede their (and societal) futures, from the conjoined formations of masturbation, and perversion, Malthusianism, and the negligent, nervous, or neurotic mothers. These are all intertwined: imbricated in sovereign, disciplinary, pastoral, biopolitical, and security modes and techniques. But they are not addressed by just one kind of power, nor in a singular way.

This is also why we can challenge the supposition that a focus on the women, the children, or the reproduction returns us automatically to a more identity-based analysis of the disciplines or to a default heteronormativity of perspective. Instead, we should maximally foreground that we do not know what procreation is, by means of a genealogical making strange of its problems, politics, interests, identities, lives and deaths, vitalities and mortalities. This includes the emergence of "woman" as a segment of harm, impeded growth (of child and of people), mortality, death. Reproduction has become a conduct capable of rendering multiple kinds of death, and women have become agents of a simultaneous life and death. Foucault's account is never more focused on the intersection of bodies and populations as when he partially elaborated this making of death, its factors, agencies, and paradoxes.

Reproduction is, then, not just the principle of life against which perverse and race vilified subjects have been opposed, nor the interest to which they have been subordinated. Just as much is reproduction a principle of death and its protagonists those of antilife. This challenges the supposition that we can isolate, disaggregate, and speak on behalf of the interests of any of the overlapping forces described: whether that be reproduction or reproductive rights or "life," as opposed to the preoccupation with death attributed to necro- and thanatopolitical theory, or indeed "sex" as opposed to "maternity."

This is also to put pressure on the view that preexisting reproductive rights come under threat once reproduction becomes a saturated matter of biopolitical interest. That view must be exchanged for a different approach: an account of how the very possibility and concepts of reproductive rights have taken shape in tandem with these biopolitical formations.[95]

To proceed, I frame the next chapter with a definition of the thanatopolitical in eight parts:

1. With one exception, *thanatopolitics* is not a term used by Foucault—rather the term is increasingly used in post-Foucauldian biopolitical theory.[96] Yet its origins can be found in the following point. When Foucault defined the biopolitical as a form of political governmentality that endeavors to "administer" (*gérer*), increase (*majorer*), and multiply (*multiplier*) life (*HS I* 137), he also described the latter's "power of death," its capacity to be murderous and genocidal. As described by Foucault, "biopolitical" powers of death have a distinguishing characteristic: they are deaths or harm or what he calls "indirect murder," pursued *not* in an exertion of sovereign power (i.e., power to execute, to attack, to withhold, to capture) but rather *as* a part of overall biopolitical aims—in other words, to the (putative) ends of administrative optimization of a population's "life," quality of life, health, environment, flourishing, order, stability, etc.

2. Such powers of death take a wide range of forms, many of which are referred to by Foucault. For example: a) they may be seen in the differentials of biopolitical interest relating to wealth, class, national, political and media interest, visibility, sentiment. They are, as stressed by Judith Butler, dividing practices bearing the differentials of interest versus disinterest, valuable versus less valuable lives, legible versus socially invisible individuals, groups, bodies, populations, etc. b) They may be seen in (overt or tacit) suppositions or calculations concerning the acceptable margins and collateral damage of biopolitical aims. c) They may be seen in a caesura Foucault describes as directly cutting into the "domain of life that is under power's control" or "within the biological continuum addressed by biopower . . . between what must live and what must die" (*SMBD* 254–55), as when whole groups (ethnic, sexual, antiprocreative, etc.) are deemed to threaten or impede futures.

3. Confusingly, biopolitical powers of death may share capacities Foucault attributed to sovereign power: the power to imprison, to deprive, to deny the means of life, to expose, to kill. As sovereign, however, the latter would be understood as primarily privative (power over territory, power

to dispose of bodies, the power to deprive of freedom of movement, of land, possessions, life). Thus biopolitical powers of death can be differentiated from sovereign power in a number of ways: their telos, language, their overt and tacit justifications, their epistemic conditions, their technics and technologies, their administrative modes, the type of life and death with which they are concerned (biopolitics are primarily concerned with distributions of life and death in populations). Sovereign power to kill may be more individualizing. Since governmentalities and their objects form together, the "life" and "death," like the power, aims, and conduct of sovereign and biopolitical modes, would, technically, all be differentiable.

4. However, the overlap of such "powers of death" has led a number of prominent commentators to argue that biopolitics rearticulates, transforms, reshapes, and/or integrates sovereign power. Others have preferred to emphasize the thresholds Foucault sometimes asserts (distinguishable historically or "analytically"), for example, between sovereignty and biopower in *DP* and *HS I*. This ambiguity has also led to Esposito's elaboration of an immune relationship between biopolitical powers of life and death or other approaches to a seemingly paradoxical relationship, most obviously from Agamben.

5. A related term to have emerged in contemporary literature is *necropolitics*, introduced by Achille Mbembe. In secondary, post-Foucauldian literature, the terms *thanatopolitical* and *necropolitics* are sometimes used interchangeably.[97] But they should be distinguished: the latter term would be a management in populations of death and dying, of stimulated and proliferating disorder, chaos, insecurity. In particular, a reference to necropolitics rejects Foucault's characterization of modern biopolitics as managing death to the ends of "life" (however murderously). The dissemination of chaos, violence, disposability, and disorder understood as *necropolitical* is not necessarily subordinated to the putative "vital" ends associated with biopolitical direct and indirect murder. However the necropolitical may share (in its distribution of death) some of the proliferating and disseminating modes associated with biopower's governmentality of life.

6. By contrast, the term *thanatopolitics* refers to a problem introduced by Agamben and Esposito in their discussions of Foucauldian biopolitics. Esposito has characterized the "thanatopolitical drift" of biopolitical administration, seen when politics comes to "decid[e] what is a biologically better life, and also how to strengthen it through the use, the exploitation,

or, when necessary, the death of a 'worse' life."[98] As such, the extreme of this thanatopolitical drift would be seen when death's role in defending life is extended to the point where "the defense of life and the production of death truly meet at a point of absolute indistinction."[99] This means that the introduction of the term *thanatopolitics* also marks Esposito's disagreement with Foucault, for the former sees the thanatopolitical as demonstrating the very paradigm (he terms this the *immune paradigm*) of the biopolitical.

7. The term similarly marks an extended response to Foucault by Agamben. In a number of his references to Foucauldian biopolitics in his early *homo sacer* volumes, Agamben has placed sovereign interest in bare life (and so "biopolitics") at the origins of politics dating to ancient Greece, presenting both in terms of the sovereign exception. In other words, sovereignty institutes political life through the latter's self-constituting exclusion of those who are no more than bare human life or (as discussed in the next chapter) who are responsible for life. But there are modern formations Esposito, Foucault, and Agamben can all agree to call biopolitical. For Agamben, insofar as politics undertakes the management of life and attaches rights to basic human life, the space of this exception has yawned open, exposing humans to becoming life "not worth being lived." (Contentious in Agamben's work is the very wide scope he gives to this possibility.) Thus what Foucault would call modern biopolitics is reconceptualized by Agamben as, in this different sense, thanatopolitics. As we shall see in the following chapter, this phenomenon has also been associated by Agamben (fleetingly) and by Esposito (briefly) with forms of sexual and specifically reproductive violence.

8. In exploring the thanatopolitical counterpart of the biopolitics of reproduction, I will argue in chapter 4 that this includes modern figurations of women as the agents of reproductive decisions but also as the potential impediments of individual and collective futures. This takes shape through the attribution of a pseudosovereign power—as when women are attributed a seeming power of decision over life. Thus, to whatever extent there is an administration of reproduction, it may also include the administration of a phantasmatic reproductive agency both positively and negatively understood. These modern subjectivities, as I argue in chapter 5, can also be understood as a form of precarious life.

4

IMMUNITY, BARE LIFE, AND THE THANATOPOLITICS OF REPRODUCTION

Foucault, Esposito, Agamben

The womb, rather than Agamben's camp, is the most effective example of Foucault's biopolitical space.

—RUTH A. MILLER, *THE LIMITS OF BODILY INTEGRITY*

FOUCAULT AND BIOS: THANATOPOLITICS AND "FORESTALLED LIFE"

Arguing that there are unstable oscillations in Foucault's account of the relationship between sovereignty and biopower, the Italian philosopher Roberto Esposito has argued that they arise from a missing component or an "interval of meaning" in Foucault's work—and in a number of modern philosophers from Hobbes onward.[1] He has coined a term for this missing link between Foucault's account of the biopolitical and its tendency toward the thanatopolitical, naming this the "interpretive key" of immunization (*Bios* 44). It is described as eluding Foucault, yet also as emerging in all its analytic necessity within Foucault's own work. Making the argument, Esposito returns us to the point on which we have been concentrating: Foucault acknowledges that formidable powers of death (including execution, genocide, massacre, war) are biopower's underside (*l'envers; HS I* 137),[2] for they have been exercised in the "exigencies of a life-administering power" (*les exigences d'un pouvoir qui gère la vie;* HS I 136).

BOUCLER LE CERCLE

As we have seen, such powers of death are considered by Foucault as the end point or culmination (*l'aboutissement;* HS I 137) of biopower's process. If biopower has this power of death as its counterpart (*le complémentaire;* 137),[3] and if biopolitics distinctively administers life on the level of the population, then it does complete that circle (*boucler le cercle;* HS I 137) if its power of death could similarly impact whole populations, effecting an all-out destruction. The capacity to expose a whole population to death arises with the technologies and governmentalities oriented to comprehensively optimizing its biological life, and in this sense does not bear an accidental relation to the latter.

We saw that in *The History of Sexuality,* volume 1, and also in *Society Must Be Defended,* nuclear power is not only considered by Foucault as an extreme variant of the sovereign power to kill. Nuclear power has been comprehended in strategies of management of security and of collective well-being. Perhaps its threat of annihilation will present as serving an overall common interest such as stability. It may be said to defend peoples and nations against the possibility of attack or to maintain global military equilibriums. The biopolitical "underside" (the correlate capacity of all-out destruction of a population) would therefore be distinguishable from the destructive might—or right—of sovereign power.

However, in *Society Must Be Defended* Foucault presents a different version of this argument. Its final lecture discusses a deployment by state powers of biopolitical governmentalities through which the distinction between biopower and sovereign power can blur. Thus Foucault argues that there is *also* the possibility of a biopower that may come (as seen in state racism) to function through "the old sovereign power of right of death" (*SMBD* 258).[4] The latter may be said to modify (*modifier*) to "penetrate," or to "permeate (*traverser*)" the former (*SMBD* 241). As Esposito considers the emerging ambiguity: "If we consider the Nazi state, we can say indifferently, as Foucault himself does, that it was the old sovereign power that adopts biological racism for itself. . . . Or, on the contrary, that it is the new biopolitical power that made use of the sovereign right of death in order to give life to state racism. If we have recourse to the first interpretive model, biopolitics becomes an internal articulation of sovereignty; if we privilege the second, sovereignty is reduced to a formal schema of biopolitics" (*Bios* 41).

While these variants may not be easy to distinguish, they remain analytically distinguishable for Foucault. Yet, as Esposito points out, "Foucault never opts decisively for one or the other" (*Bios* 41). Foucault's account of sovereign power remains stable in his work: it is primarily privative, it is a power over territory, bodies, life, it is a right of seizure or domination, it is associated with legal mechanisms of enforcement. He claims that this mode of power is supplanted in importance by the biopolitical, yet it may coexist with, be imprinted by, or inflect the biopolitical. Even so, he does not relinquish the view that they retain different characteristics.

Not all the resulting coincidences are understood by Foucault as paradoxical. For example, it is *not*, finally, "a limit, a scandal, and a contradiction," for capital punishment to persist and be reconfigured as part of a biopolitical context *if* execution is pursued as part of a strategy of optimizing overall well-being (*HS I* 138). It is similarly not, for Foucault, a paradox that such biopolitical powers of life as the administration of subsidized medication or of health insurance may include a differential withholding from certain groups, where this is claimed to be necessary to ensuring the stability of health care. No more is it a paradox, for Foucault, that the biopolitical powers of death he distinguishes from the sovereign powers of life may come, as he argues in *Society*, to "function through" the latter. Even the fact that the entire biological existence of a population might come to be threatened by its own optimizing biopolitical strategies still is not deemed by Foucault a contradiction, but rather as continuous with the underside (powers of death) comprised in the very means of pursuing powers of life.

Yet Foucault does progress to several seeming or possible paradoxes, as follows. First, what if the powers of death of sovereign power and of biopower, though differentiable as modes and aims, coincide in the same phenomenon? Now Foucault offers a different consideration of biopoliticized nuclear power, this time suggesting that its use might be implicated in parallel but conflicting strategies. For example, one could imagine its deployment taking place *both* as an exercise of sovereign authority and as the putative assurance of a population's biopolitical interest, and he also proposes the possibility of the latter acting "through" the former, or vice versa. But what if such double strategies, playing out in the very same event (the threatened use of nuclear power), also challenge each other's interests or substance of operation? For example, what if the biopolitical exercise annihilates the life over which sovereign power would claim authority? Or what if the sovereign power annihilates the life that the biopolitical variant aims to optimize? Foucault most clearly refers to a paradoxical variant (using that term) to describe a possible outcome of the capacity to create and deploy viruses generated by biopolitical management of life at the level of population. Here the question might be: what if that virus mutates or becomes uncontrollable? What if it exceeds the possibilities of its biopolitical administration, taking on a destructive life of its own, so to speak? The fact that generating a virus could annihilate rather than contribute to the optimal administration of life would no longer be the "counterpart" or "underside" of the latter. Instead, it constitutes a limit to the corresponding administrative capacity, a disastrous excess to life's governability. In this it is like the variant of nuclear power that is "not simply the power to kill, in accordance with the rights that are granted to any sovereign," but "the power to kill life itself . . . power . . . exercised in such a way that is capable of suppressing itself" (*SMBD* 253). Therefore, says Foucault in a passage widely discussed by post-Foucauldian theorists who have foregrounded thanatopolitics, we can

> identify the paradoxes that appear at the points where the exercise of this biopower reaches its limits. The paradoxes become apparent if we look, on the one hand, at atomic power, which is not simply the power to kill. . . . The workings of contemporary political power are such that atomic power represents a paradox that is difficult, if not impossible, to get around. The power to manufacture and use the atomic bomb represents the deployment[5] of a sovereign power that kills, but it is also the power to kill life itself . . . And, therefore, to suppress itself insofar as it is the power that guarantees life. Either it is sovereign and uses the atom bomb, and therefore cannot be power, biopower, or the power to guarantee life. . . . Or, at the opposite extreme, you no longer have a sovereign

right that is in excess of biopower, but a biopower that is in excess of sovereign right. This excess of biopower appears when it becomes technologically and politically possible for man not only to manage life but to make it proliferate, to create living matter, to build the monster, and, ultimately, to build viruses that cannot be controlled and that are universally destructive. This formidable extension of biopower, unlike what I was just saying about atomic power, will put it beyond all human sovereignty.

(SMBD 253–54)

So, to reiterate, neither the seemingly conflicting aims of biopower and sovereign power, nor the fact that their aims and techniques can coincide in certain contexts, nor the fact that as modes they may temporally coincide, even be "co-present" despite Foucault's claim that the one is "on the retreat" (SMBD 254), supplanted in importance by the other ("on the advance," SMBD 254), nor the fact the biopolitical may sometimes function *through*, or "deploy," sovereign modes (or the reverse), earn, in Foucault's work, the term *paradox*. That term is used when biopolitical modes (whether pursued through powers of death or understood as supplanting, coinciding, working through, or conflicting with what he names sovereign modes) produce unmanageable powers of life and death which resist or exceed the governmental aims of biopower, threatening the latter's aims of equilibrium, stability, security, anticipatory management—if not threatening life itself (SMBD 249). For biopolitical strategies, even when they concern the management of death (or amount to direct or indirect powers of death) aim, in their optimization of life, for a form of administration so comprehensive as to be able to factor, adjust, and correct even for the random and unpredictable.

But where Foucault sees the biopolitical paradoxically reaching its own limit, Esposito will identify differently the limit in Foucault's parsing of biopolitics. Foucault draws no broader or systemic conclusions from the capacity of the biopolitical to terminate its own substance. For his part, Esposito loses from Foucault's discussion the coefficient of ungovernability that establishes the difference between biopolitical powers of death "completing their own circle" versus (where they result in an incapacity of governability) becoming paradoxical.

For Esposito, such phenomena can be understood otherwise. His question, "why does a politics of life always risk being reversed into a work of death?," (*Bios* 8) converts to an argument that the more defensive the political project, the more the latter delivers a destructiveness culminating in self-destructiveness. Esposito generalizes and attributes this tendency to the biopolitically life-optimizing aims of modernity. Foucault would have brilliantly identified the latter's tendency toward destructiveness, *and* autodestruction, and yet also failed to account for it[6]—opening the analytic gap Esposito undertakes to fill.

A number of times Foucault refers to the taking shape of new powers, and their new objects, when other powers may have become inadequate or inefficient or unviable under new conditions. Describing biopolitical governmental aims, he speculates: "it is as though power, which used to have sovereignty as its modality or organizing schema, found itself unable to govern the economic and political body of a society that was undergoing both a demographic explosion and industrialization . . . too many things were escaping the old mechanism of the power of sovereignty, both at the top and at the bottom, both at the level of detail and at the mass level" (*SMBD* 249). Not just new capacities for governance but also new *objects* of governance emerge to replace incapacities of governance. Foucault can describe this emergence, but without attributing to it an inevitability. At most: "it is as though."

Focusing on Foucault's account of a biopolitics producing the life that it administers, producing new subjects, new forms of death (*Bios* 32), and new forms and objects of governance, Esposito argues that an additional conceptual or theoretical level is required. This "missing" level would provide an alternative to an unwanted but persistent Foucauldian separation between the political and the life it takes "charge" of (*HS I* 89), which is "penetrated" or "transformed" (*HS I* 143) by power or comes under state control (*SMBD* 239–40). Esposito concludes that it is "as if biopolitics is missing something," a "more complex paradigm," whose necessity would impose itself within the problematically distinguished terms of Foucault's own work. There can be no biopolitics, no biopower, and no independently understood "power" prior to its "seizure" or "penetration" of life. So there is an analytic inadequacy in the Foucauldian formulations, for "it is as if the two terms from which biopolitics is formed (life and politics) cannot be articulated except through a modality that simultaneously juxtaposes them" (*Bios* 32). Yet Foucault avoids designating life as preexisting the biopolitics that seemingly seizes hold of it, considering that they emerge only together.[7] Esposito therefore proposes that Foucault's work contains a number of oscillations between references to a "life" and a "biopower" that could not precede each other and references to seizures or penetrations of the one by the other. These include life understood as somehow captured by politics and life understood as a problem whose management is somehow holding politics back.

This is where Esposito also eases the term thanatopolitics into the discussion. If Foucauldian powers of life can be pursued through powers of death, Foucault can indeed describe projects of national insurance as coinciding, without paradox, with projects of war. But why, asks Esposito, does the biopolitical proliferate a life "nourished by the deaths of others?" Doesn't this remain unexplained by Foucault? Adding this dilemma to the paradigm whose absence he has just articulated (the life and power of biopolitics should not have a prior separability), Esposito will then claim to have traced a missing interpretative key that eluded Foucault.

This is the immune paradigm. It fills the interval Esposito locates in Foucauldian biopolitics and then is widened out (*Bios* 43, 45). Power and life form an inseparable immune paradigm that accelerates into the thanatopolitical.

REPRODUCTIVE IMMUNITIES

Esposito discusses the "paroxysmal point" of play Foucault recognizes between the sovereign right to kill and the mechanisms of biopower, attributed at one point to "the workings of all States." While the theme of birth is going to be of particular interest to Esposito, it so happens that he doesn't identify birth as having a particular interest for Foucault in this respect.

Is it an accident, then, that *Bios*,[8] in which the development of Esposito's "immune paradigm" partially takes the route of responding to Foucault's biopolitics, begins with a particular group of seven vignettes, four of which discuss sex-selective abortion in China; pregnancies resulting from the ethnic rape of Tutsi and Bosnian women;[9] forced pregnancy; forced abortion, totalitarian eugenics; regimes of forced sterilization, some of which have incurred high death rates of women; the preemptive destruction of the possibility of birth pursued as a Nazi tactic; and a controversial French legal case in which damages were claimed following a diagnostic error leading to the carrying to term of a pregnancy with severe congenital disabilities, contrary to the mother's intent.

Characterizing the concerns of these vignettes, we might have supposed Esposito to be undertaking an account of the thanatopoliticization of reproduction. But they are grouped with other framing examples of *Bios* (including the killing of Chechen hostages as a means of defending their lives, the "humanitarian" bombing of Afghanistan, and infection by AIDS through negligent administration of blood collection in a Chinese province). Ought all these examples be grouped together, or is the first group I have mentioned linked by a more specific phenomenon for which we would need to develop its own conceptual language? Is Esposito right to characterize all these vignettes as "exactly the tragic paradox that Michel Foucault, in a series of writings dating back to the middle of the 1970s, examined" (*Bios* 8)? Their content seems far from the themes articulated by Foucault.

Moreover, they are grouped under the rubric of the "growing superimposition between the domain of power or of law [*diritto*] and that of life [and] an equally close implication that seems to have been derived with regard to death" (*Bios* 7–8). But, while Foucault describes a new status sometimes assumed in biopolitical contexts by the law (traditionally the expression of sovereign authority, but taking on new functions as the auxiliary of biopower),[10] he attributes no particular role to the law with respect to the merging of power and life.[11] Above all, when Esposito describes these vignettes as expressing the question asked by Foucault—"Why does a politics of life always risk being reversed into a work of death?" (*Bios* 8)—he could be said to miss a problem that also evaded Foucault.[12] First, despite embedding it in his framing vignettes, Esposito misses the opportunity to introduce thanatopoliticized reproductive biopolitics as a specific problematic. Similarly, he misses the opportunity to describe it as a problematic absent (and, for his own purposes, interestingly so) from Foucault's work. If the reversal of a politics of life into a politics of death also takes a more singular form as a mode of reproductive thanatopolitics, it calls for a conceptual approach adequate to that specificity. Esposito may undertake to account for what is missed by Foucault, yet that project omits in turn the Foucauldian omission of thanatopoliticized reproduction. Curiously, one might say, given Esposito's own interest in reconfiguring birth and given the themes of *Bios*'s prefatory material.

The emphasis on contingency of formation that is available from Foucault's work is replaced by Esposito with an analysis of inevitable and accelerating formations. This is one reason for his claim that the biopolitical "*always*" risks reversing into a politics of death (*Bios* 8). But such a claim would have a different status for Foucault. Foucault may describe a politics of death undergirding biopolitical strategies and aims,[13] but not with the structural necessity attributed by Esposito, understood by him as leading to catastrophic results.[14]

Returning to the opening vignettes, and the interval of meaning established by Esposito in Foucault's work, we can press the project further. The point is not that Esposito himself entirely neglects the thanatopoliticization of reproduction: to the contrary, as we saw. But he neglects its role within Foucault's projects. This is all the stranger, given that his opening vignettes lead into his analysis of Foucault. That transition includes an additional discussion by Esposito of oscillation in Foucault's work with respect to whether sovereign and biopolitical modes can be given a linear periodization. We should recognize, he answers, that such modes are *also* described by Foucault as coinciding, and so identify the more "ancient" genesis of biopolitics, "one that ultimately coincides with that of politics itself which has always in one way or another been devoted to life" (*Bios* 52). The examples which follow then include "the power of life and death exercised by the Roman paterfamilias," Plato's account of infanticide as a form of reproductive eugenics, and the latter's enlarging "of the scope of political authority to include the reproductive process" (*Bios* 52-3).

A thanatopoliticized reproductive biopolitics is circulating as a tacit theme in Esposito's work, contributing to his elaboration of the immune paradigm. Yet Esposito's problematics are different than those of Foucault. Much of what is specific to the latter—the focus on conduct of bodies, stimulation by space and architecture, capillary intensifications, the complex multiplicities of power-knowledge-bodies—are outside Esposito's interests. Articulating Foucault's missing link, Esposito establishes his paradigm, and leaves Foucault behind. Let's say that he does so just at the point where his own examples of a thanatopoliticized life—and reproduction—are prompting a discussion of the immune paradigm. This means he departs from Foucault's resources, just short of that point where he might have turned to them for the elements contributing to a possible articulation of a reproductive biopolitics.

In *HS I* Foucault does not hesitate to include reproduction, optimal child raising, birth, and birthrate among the long-standing biopolitical preoccupations. As I asked in chapter 3, why, then, do we hear of biopolitically justified execution, the atomic bomb, the uncontrollable virus, an order given for the suicide of a people, when Foucault turns to thematize biopolitical powers of death—but not of biopoliticized birth and birthrate under the rubric of the latter? Are there not formations of powers of death arising from a biopolitized reproductivity? What of that account of the biopolitical in *Society Must Be Defended*, as effecting the split in the biological continuum between what must live and what must die, for example in light of the discussion of eugenic strategies intended to deter certain women from reproductive transmission (deemed thanatopolitical by Esposito in the final chapters of *Bios*)?

I have argued that to see reproduction and parenting taking shape as technologies targeting the health and optimization of individual and population futures is to see them concurrently taking shape as parallel technologies of death, with corresponding conducts including averting, managing, gridding, stimulating, predicting, distributing, and proliferating.

Yet for all that *Psychiatric Power, Abnormal, HS I*, and the last lecture of *Society Must Be Defended* all mention biopoliticized formations of reproduction conceived as countering (and so managing) the corresponding (individualized and collective) mortal risks to peoples, Foucault does not overtly conclude that these are the reproductive variants of biopolitical powers of death. Esposito's immune paradigm might seem more promising in this respect, given that it both undertakes to explore Foucault's missing link and pays more attention to historical techniques of forced or deadly sterilization, forced or withheld abortions, projects to annihilate a people's reproductive possibility, and the suppression "not only of life but of its genesis" (*Bios* 143).

Esposito deems the *forestalling of life in advance* an extreme point of the thanatopolitical. But this discussion occurs under the general rubric of a thanatopoliticization of "life." In consequence, a more specific attention would need to be directed at how reproduction, in particular, takes shape as the threshold of concurrent protection and destruction, prospect of life and death—this is not developed in his work.

My suggestion is that Esposito's project of identifying Foucault's oscillations can therefore be refracted back to his own work. Esposito oscillates between a thanatopoliticization of "life" and a more specific phenomenon, the thanatopoliticization of reproduction and maternity. Just as Esposito describes a missing interval in the Foucauldian account, a missing interval can similarly be identified in his own.

For we can ask: what are the conditions for maternity becoming a plausible candidate for a thanatopolitical biopoliticization of life? Esposito takes this possibility for granted, not considering that it requires its own genealogy. It is included in the immune (bio)politization of "life." But women and reproduction are only available for biopoliticization (and so thanatopoliticization) in the terms described (through which they appear as "principle of life," vector of life, vector of concurrently individual and collective life) by virtue of contingent formations of reproduction for which he does not account.

Consider also how, with one swing of the oscillation, the thanatopoliticized mother is supposed when Esposito describes the sterilization of women and the impact of selective antinatalism on "pregnant women" as leading to large numbers of deaths of *women* (*Bios* 144). We saw an oscillation to the other pole when Esposito also describes something else—sex-selective abortion in China, "the abortion of all those who *would have become* future women" (*Bios* 6, my emphasis). Esposito swings between the deaths of women and the suppression of birth,[15] the "nullif[ied] life in advance," (*Bios* 145) as if these can similarly be grouped under the rubric of suppression of "life." Here what ought to be given close scrutiny: the very plausibility of an interchangeable reference to a biopoliticized woman-as-reproductive, her subsumption as principle of "life," and that of a biopoliticized potential fetus is exempted by Esposito from critique and genealogical analysis.

ESPOSITO AND FOUCAULT: SUSPENSIONS

This is an encounter between the work of Foucault and Esposito in which the resources of each are retaining good potential to resist and stimulate those of the other. On these questions, it is Foucault, not Esposito, who broached the emergent status of reproduction as a biopoliticized responsibility for staving off new forms of lurking death. Yet it is Esposito, not Foucault, whose immune paradigm has, and in conversation with the latter, linked the biopoliticization and thanatopoliticization of women as reproductive. We can turn back to Esposito (citing Gisela Bock) for the corresponding reminder that women have been exposed,[16] accordingly, to greater possibilities of their own injury and death, partly in association with the perception of their biopolitically promising or harmful impact. But we would need to turn to Foucault for a genealogical perspective on any of the forms of life (reproductive, infant, maternal, individual, that of populations) Esposito takes to be available for thanatopolitical forestalling. The resulting articulation is offered by neither Foucault nor Esposito, but it can be productively dislodged from the confrontation not only of their respective interests but also of their respective omissions.

Of Foucault, I had asked how we might theorize women's comportment in reproduction insofar as it comes to be deemed, for example, obstructive to the interests of family, population, or nation, religion, ethnicity, the law or the state? How should we understand the sanctions sometimes emerging in this context—as stimulating new understandings of resistance and civil disobedience? As the new legal auxiliaries of biopolitical interest? The residual capacities of otherwise weakened sovereignties, lashing out in an exercise of phantom powers and so challenging what seems to represent a competing sovereign authority over life? A new division in a biological continuum since groups of women will, accordingly, by virtue of wealth, race, age, or immigration status be differentially exposed to such legal and social sanctions, prohibitions, harm, and death?

Or could it be, to recall the earlier discussion of Foucault's paradoxical alternatives, that either the state imposes itself as sovereign over the woman's capacities to reproduce—and then this is not "biopolitical"—or that reproductive women become a biopolitical technology of the health and life of the nation or the abstractions of collective "birthrate." But, as such, they have reformed as the corresponding risk of harm to futures, collectivities, population. In the administration of this counterpossibility, we see what Foucault might have called the corresponding *envers* of (reproductive) biopolitics. We see the making of the possibility of excess, uncontrollability, unregulatability, located in reproduction-as-threat. We see, as Foucault might have said, the formation of a biopolitical excess to sovereign powers—or else the paradoxical limit, a kind of self-cancellation in the harm to or destruction of what was to be administered and in the capacities of such administration—in the very biopolitical interest in reproduction.

Exploring this, we could similarly ask if this point of excess and paradox (a lurking ungovernability) stimulates or marks the emergence of new objects and new governmentalities?

To return to Foucault's "it is as though" (*SMBD* 249), he speculates about the "living on" or survival of a tiring or increasingly incapacitated sovereignty in new, biopolitical forms. This is a possibility explored (though not more specifically about thanatopolitical reproduction) by Esposito, for whom Foucault returns to "a logic of copresence.... On the one hand, he hypothesizes something like a return to the sovereign paradigm within a biopolitical horizon. In that case, we would be dealing with a literally phantasmal event, in the technical sense of a reappearance of death—of the destitute sovereign decapitated by the grand revolution—on the scene of life" (*Bios* 40–41). But it is also a possibility briefly broached by Wendy Brown, whose *Walled States* adds to reflections of the effects of nostalgic or phantasmatic sovereignty. She describes the exaggerated expression of sovereign authority in contemporary contexts where it otherwise,[17] and simultaneously, can be understood to have weakened: in legitimacy, authority, field of influence, capacity for due process. Her discussions of more aggressive border and immigration control, walled states, military actions and rhetoric briefly mentions the resurgence of interest in controlling and restricting access to abortion.[18]

Brown and Esposito belong to a widespread trend among post-Foucauldian theorists who have interrogated the status of sovereignty in Foucault's work through an exploration of more adequate models. Brown adds the compensatory efforts of phantom, nostalgic, or voided sovereignty, giving greater attention to contemporary crises in political legitimacy. Esposito locates the thanatopolitical extremes of an immune paradigm precisely in the "complex relationship, which [Foucault] instituted, between the biopolitical regime and sovereign power" (*Bios* 8). But the most extensive reconfiguration of Foucauldian sovereignty and biopolitics has been offered by Giorgio Agamben's *homo sacer* project. For Agamben, by contrast, the contemporary status of the biopolitical would in no way indicate a weakening in the contemporary capacity of sovereign power.

The question I explore in tandem with Agamben's response to Foucault is, however, an unusual one. Again it concerns the relationship between these reconfigurations of the sovereign-biopolitical relationship and reproductive politics.

FOUCAULT AND AGAMBEN ON SOVEREIGNTY

Prior to Esposito, Agamben had modified Foucault's understanding of both biopolitics and sovereignty, revising Foucault's deemphasis of the role of the law in contemporary biopolitics. Foucault primarily associates legal institutions, judgment, and enforcement with the appropriative and privative aspects of sovereign power, overlooking the significance of a sovereign capacity to suspend the law. Adopting the understanding of that power of suspension as definitively sovereign,[19] Agamben gives his attention to phenomena overlooked by Foucault: in modern biopolitical contexts, and by virtue of the capacity to suspend a subject's legal status and legal rights: "sovereign is he who decides on the value or the non-value of life as such" (*HS* 142). Both Foucault and Agamben explore sovereign power to take life. But Agamben's variant is able to include the particularly lethal variant seen in the capacity to cancel the status of what is put to death, so that it will not have had value or counted as human life, rights-protected life, or life worth living.[20]

Sovereign power will be seen in techniques, legal and otherwise, exposing to death what is considered to be not fully human or rights entitled, and in particular *rendering* less than human what it exposes, so that a death will count as neither murder nor sacrifice.

We saw that, for Foucault, the status of the "life" (and so the lives) that are grasped (or left to die) by biopolitics or exposed to possible termination in an exercise of sovereign power are not clearly distinguished. It is, however a defining point of his work that these would not be considered the same "life," nor the same death.[21] Agamben develops this problem. Foucault, he argues, lacks a distinction between bare human life (that of a human reduced to its merely being alive) and the life of humans understood as rights bearing, as citizens, or as qualified life "worth living." The missing distinction is the difference between *zoe* and *bios*. With it, Agamben can redefine sovereign power as the power to reduce *bios* to *zoe*, or bare life. This is seen in forms of political exclusion, in forms of exposure or putting to death that do not count as homicidal. Thus Agamben is able to respond to Foucault on the problem deemed underdeveloped in his work: "when life becomes the supreme political value, not only is the problem of life's nonvalue thereby posed, as Schmitt suggests but further, it is as if the problem of sovereign power were at stake in this decision" (*HS* 142).

Foucault acknowledges that mechanisms including the deprivation of resources, "increasing the risk of death for some people, or, quite simply, political death, expulsion, rejection" amount to indirect forms of murder he associates a) with the powers of death of biopolitics, b) their overlap with formations of racism and modern modes of normalization of biopower, and c) with a survival of the "old sovereign right to kill" (*SMBD* 256). But Foucault never deems a specific capacity to transform the *status* of human life to "less than human" life, the extreme or paradigmatic capacity of sovereign powers of death. One of the significant points of divergence, even in their closest point of proximity, therefore concerns the different capacity Agamben attributes to sovereignty.

Their definitions of biopolitics are correspondingly different as well. For Agamben, the Nazi camp is the most absolute biopolitical space, as an anomic extreme in which internees are stripped of political rights and human status and wholly reduced to bare life (*HS* 170–71). This is not the case for Foucault. We have returned multiple times to Foucault's own reminder that "wars were never as bloody" (*HS I* 136) as in biopolitical regimes (though always to the ends of the putative collective good and the collective future) and to his identification of the "formidable power of death" as the counterpart of biopolitics (*HS I* 137), even an end point or culmination. Yet there is no reason to think he considered this the most absolute form of biopolitics.

Also, in the "camp" analyzed by Agamben in these terms, the law functions to demarcate a space of anomie, a space of exception from its general application. This paradigmatic use of the term *camp* would refer to that legal space within which the law can be set aside: the space in which rights are deprived as an exception from what the law encompasses.[22]

Agamben generalizes both this possibility and the conjoinedly biopolitical and sovereign capacity to unmake human life, to deprive it of legal or ontological status. It is at once the paradigmatic space of the "camp," the fundamental sovereign capacity *and* characteristic of Agamben's understanding of the biopolitical. Thus it becomes the thanatopolitical quality of the biopolitical Agamben sees exemplified in the Nazi regime (*HS* 153, 122). In *Remnants of Auschwitz* Agamben revisits Foucault's treatment of this relationship in *Society Must Be Defended*. As Esposito would later, Agamben deems erroneous Foucault's identification of biopolitical paradox in the Nazi regime's combination of "an unprecedented absolutization of the biopower to *make live* [intersecting] with an equally absolute generalization of the sovereign power to make die . . . [this] represents a genuine paradox."[23] By comparison, this combination is entirely consistent with the alternative definitions of sovereignty and biopolitics Agamben has proposed.[24] Agamben gives greater attention than Foucault to the capacity of the law to effect anomic spaces, to revoke humanity and rights entitlement. Building on this response, I propose an additional layer be added that can take into consideration what may at first seem, by contrast, a very specific phenomenon: the form of legal mechanisms in place to make precarious women's legal access to abortion. This is not a revocability of human rights in general, nor of the status of the "human," but of abortion's legality. I will argue that the phenomenon depicted by Agamben, the potential for political and legal reduction to bare life, assumes a distinctively redoubled quality for women in modern biopolitical contexts. As we will see, it is characteristic of a phenomenon one might term thanatopoliticized reproduction, and it can be understood in terms of a threefold revocability. This comprises, first, a combination of reversibility and exceptionality belonging to legal regimes governing abortion. (This is seen when the latter's legality is an exception to its ongoing illegality. Legal access or legality carries a practically fluctuating, unstable, or historically reversible status.). Second, the malleability of embryonic life cannot be disconnected from the rescindable status of women as rights-bearing in a reproductive rights context. Third, a pseudosovereignty over fetal life is both attributed to the woman associated with reproductive rights and concurrently undermined.

BIOPOLITICS AND SOVEREIGNTY

This complex malleability is seen not just in a choice about a fetus or the variable meanings of a pregnancy. It is seen also in the intermittent appearing and dissolving of a woman's possible subjectivity as "decision maker." Insofar as reproductive decisions emphasize the malleability of both the object and the subject of the decision, there is a conjoined malleability in the status of the contemporary fetus or pregnancy and of the woman attributed with decision making. This may be a factor distinguishing populations (most obviously according to their legal regimes of reproductive rights) or groups within populations (for whom reproductive choice might be more, or less, available). Thus decisions may manifest as plausible or implausible in relation to the contextual malleability of the fetus and of the woman as "chooser." In some contexts, pregnancy might never present as plausibly prompting decision-making conduct. Or a number of social, cultural, and religious factors might divide such conduct as either appropriate or inappropriate for some versus others, including and excluding subjects, producing and deconstituting them. Or reproduction might present as a giving rise to contests between competing "claimants." Or reproduction might manifest as a problem of biopolitical "trends," sometimes depicted as demographic crisis. Or it might associate with diverse political aspirations: not just to manage individual conduct, but to modify overall patterns of behavior. Reproduction's stimulated subjectivities might involve interfaces with nature, politics, religion, technology, medical protocols, the law, or illegal or ad hoc measures. The emerging protagonists might include the activist, the criminal, the moral philosopher, the good or covert citizen, the problematic population trend.

Thus women may come to redouble the legal regimes interpellating them. In other words, women may be deemed capable of impeding life (variously understood) or revoking life or reversing its status. And regimes concerning abortion can be highly revocable, so that the one revocability comes to mirror the other. My suggestion is that this generalized rescindability (of fetus, of decision, decision making, of decision maker, of the phantom decision maker, of legal contexts for such decisions) be understood as a general field in which reproductive rights, abortion, and abortion law are negotiated. I turn next to the latter: the chronic revocability of abortion law.

INVERTED EXCEPTIONALITY

Access to abortion has repeatedly been made available through structures that might best be described as inverted states of exception. This form of exceptionality is unlike a general state of exception—it is not that the laws of a nation are set aside under such pretexts as a state of emergency. Instead a general practice—in this case regular and nonillegal abortion—takes shape through the granting of a general exception to an ongoing law that, in fact (except for the exception), continues to render abortion illegal. So we could ask what kind of sovereignty is produced when reproductive practice intertwines with a structure of exception to laws instigating, organizing, criminalizing abortion,[25] in relation to which the exception becomes regularized and regulative, yet unreliable?

From the 1820s and throughout the nineteenth century in the United States, abortion past the fourth month was increasingly banned by individual states. Though this was reinforced by the passage in 1873 of the Comstock Law "for the Suppression of Trade in, and Circulation of, Obscene Literature and Articles for Immoral Use," which was applied to bans on obscene literature, information about birth control, and the practice of abortion, abortion remained a matter of state rather than federal law. It had become illegal in all fifty states by the 1960s until, in 1973, *Roe v. Wade* newly established the grounds for its legality under the right to privacy protected by the Fourteenth Amendment so long as the fetus is not viable (meaning it cannot survive outside of the mother's uterus). According to this judgment: "State criminal abortion laws, like those involved here, that except from criminality only a life-saving procedure on the mother's behalf without regard to the stage of her pregnancy and other interests involved violate the Due Process Clause of the Fourteenth Amendment, which protects against state action the right to privacy, including a woman's qualified right to terminate her pregnancy."

Such legal configurations have frequently been entangled with the language of exception. Throughout the nineteenth and twentieth century, increasingly entrenched state-based criminalization of abortion had usually allowed for exceptions on grounds such as rape or concern for the woman's life, health, or well-being. The bans therefore included exceptions that could, according to the contingencies of individual states, doctors, judges, contexts, and cases, allow for considerable variation in the actual liberality of access to abortion. And, though *Roe v. Wade* is widely considered to have decriminalized abortion, Mary Poovey has noted how it simultaneously reconfirmed the state's readiness to intervene. Demarcating a woman's right to terminate her pregnancy as limited by the state's interests in safeguarding women's health, in maintaining proper medical standards and in protecting "potential human life,"[26] *Roe v. Wade* specified that although the state cannot override that right, it did have legitimate interests in protecting *both* the pregnant woman's health and the potentiality of human life increasing with the woman's approach to term.[27]

Challenges to *Roe* by individual states have included pressure on the point of pregnancy after which abortion becomes illegal. At state level, abortions have been banned from the point of heartbeat detection through abdominal ultrasound (Arkansas in 2013),[28] thus at about twelve weeks, or through transvaginal ultrasound (North Dakota, also in 2013), thus at about six weeks.[29] As women would rarely identify their pregnancy before five weeks, then having to meet abortion's procedural requirements, "heartbeat bans" can render most abortions effectively illegal without challenging their technical legality. State by state, the pro-life movement has found these and other legislative means to obstruct abortion. Another means has been the attribution of personhood rights to fetuses or court appointed legal representation for unborn fetuses who testify against women seeking abortions (under Alabama's HB 494). Case by case, such laws have been challenged. But, even when destined to be struck down by the Supreme Court—as the "heartbeat bans" were in 2016—abortion's obstruction has been accomplished by the need to seek injunctions, by legal battles, procedural uncertainty, and disruption of access.

Moreover, *Roe* has not guaranteed practical access to abortion,[30] nor redressed economic inequality in the ability to access abortion. Frequently abortion has been legal yet inaccessible. Thus there are currently states with only one abortion clinic (South Dakota and Mississipi), and a number of states with five or less clinics (Idaho—two, Utah—two, Louisiana—two, Kansas—three, Alabama—five), limiting access and imposing travel requirements. There are states requiring a seventy-two-hour waiting period and consultation with an accredited antichoice counseling center (South Dakota, Missouri, North Carolina, Oklahoma and Utah). In addition to bans and new legislation, access can be impeded through bureaucratic obstruction regulating how abortion clinics are located or run (Louisiana, Virginia). Thus abortion clinics may be closed for minor violations, held to hospital standards, or unable to access doctors because of requirements that physicians possess hospital admission privileges.[31] Poverty and youth might exclude abortions available only at a distance or interstate, particularly at clinics requiring waiting or "reflection" periods, periods of counseling, or local residency.

An effective and expanding practical illegality can be accomplished through bureaucratic pockets of anomie within the national regime of an ongoing federal right to abortion. The latter can enfold widening spaces in which it is illegal or inaccessible. There is a corresponding distribution of precariousness within the population among those who would seek it, with greatest impact falling on those who are least visible or consequential politically. Given the resulting hardship and danger for the young and the poor, such variabilities effect their differential disposability and grievability.[32]

The fact that *Roe* made mention of state interest in "life," while exempting women from that interest under their right to privacy, had already instituted abortion's legality as a set of exceptions from the persisting conditions of its illegality: the point at which fetal or state interests were deemed to become overriding. In fact, the decriminalizing of abortion has often followed a repeating pattern of dispensation, exemption, or exception from an established and persisting illegality—without repealing earlier laws rendering abortion illegal. For example, the "privacy" and "individuality" of the American version is often contrasted with the more "communitarian" values of abortion's post-1949 legal trajectory in Germany. Abortion in Germany was outlawed in 1871, an illegality that persisted under the Weimar constitution, yet with exceptions liberally granted on medical grounds. It was illegal under the Third Reich while also being forced on women on eugenic pretexts or to genocidal ends. It was again illegal after German defeat, with exceptions liberally granted on medical grounds. It was legalized for the first three months under the 1974 Reform Act, but the latter still mandated preliminary counseling (without which it remained illegal). It was illegal in 1975 when the Reform Act was struck down by virtue of a judgment that there was a fetal "right to life." Abortion is considered legal under current German law. In fact, this amounts to a suspension of the legal prosecution of abortion under stated conditions (if the abortion takes place during the first twelve weeks of pregnancy, and in conjunction with appropriate—pro-life inflected[33]—counseling, and after twenty-two weeks of pregnancy only on medical grounds). Given that exceptions can apply throughout the entire term of the pregnancy, every abortion could (hypothetically speaking) be allowed, with every abortion nonetheless remaining an exception to its own illegality.

Without discounting the important differences, one will find that a large number of those countries who decriminalized abortion in the twentieth century did so by instituting categories of exception to its illegality.[34] Describing this trajectory in France, Michèle Le Doeuff has argued that the so-called Veil law, decriminalizing abortion in 1975, also reconfirmed its criminalization. On her view, the Veil law amounted to an exception reconfirming that abortion is illegal (except under the specified circumstances), however broadly the scope of exception had become the norm. Under the French legal regime she considers, abortion was made illegal under the 1810 French Penal Code and was redeclared punishable in 1920 by the Cour d'Assises. The 1975 modification was in some respects, she claimed, misinterpreted:

Under the law passed in 1920 . . . abortion, information on abortion and . . . [about] contraceptive products [were] . . . offences under the law. . . . The Veil law which permit[ted] abortion in certain circumstances, [was] simply [a] dispensation . . . in relation to the law of 1920. This [meant] that the right of women freely to control their own fertility [was] still not legally recognized. Together, the underlying principle of a penalizing prohibition and two dispensations posit a non-right combined with minimal concessions . . .

We should also recall here the correct formulation of an old legal adage:

"The exception proves the rule for non-excepted cases."

From this point of view, the dispensations provided for by the Neuwirth and Veil laws correspond[ed] to a reproclamation of the 1920 law . . .

The legalization of an exception amounts to letting go of one element in order to uphold the fundamental point.[35]

This form of legality and exceptionality has been a primary form of investment in and incitement, stimulation, production, and regulation of women's bodies as bearing reproductive biopolitical interest. Irrespective of how readily women can, as a result, access abortion, the law marks that access as conditional. Its status as an exception to illegality reinscribes the possibility of its unavailability, administering states of unease, and enshrining if not administering the possibility of revoked access.

Broadly, Agamben has argued that "the voluntary creation of a permanent state of emergency . . . has become one of the essential practices of contemporary states." The state of exception has become not only a "constitutive paradigm of the juridical order,"[36] but a ubiquitous technique of government. The phenomenon described with respect to abortion law is a different phenomenon. Whereas Agamben pursues understandings of contemporary sovereignty by virtue of a setting aside of the law and the institution of spaces of anomie, a different variation of sovereignty is seen in the inverted exceptionalities of abortion law: the legal regimes in which even where (in the optimal case) there is almost never an illegal abortion there is almost never a legal abortion that is not an exception to its own illegality.

A language would need to be developed to register the significance of the forms, juridical and otherwise, through which women's reproductivity is produced as concurrent target and result of such forms. One could adopt Agamben's reminder that "there is not *first* life as a natural biological given and anomie as the state of nature, and *then* their implication in law through the state of exception. On the contrary, the very possibility of distinguishing life and law, anomie and *nomos*, coincides with their articulation in the biopolitical machine" and the phenomena produced by reproductive biopolitics: effects of freedom, fetal life, potential personhood, right to life, rights over one's body, autonomy, privacy, etc.[37] With respect to the widespread legality, in a number of countries, of abortions taking place as exceptions to their own illegality, we can add the reverse phenomenon, seen in challenges to reproductive rights in the United States, in which increasingly wide states of illegality have taken shape within the space of a legality which itself is instituted provisionally.

THE PSEUDO HOMO SACER AND THE BIOPOLITICIZATION OF WOMEN'S REPRODUCTIVITY

What consequences would arise from an interrogation of the biopoliticization of women's reproductivity from the perspective of Agamben's work? When he mentions the replacement of the historical political distinction between one's status as "man" and one's status as "citizen," by the modern category of bare life to which both can be reduced, he mentions as candidates a curious series in which not only the "voter," and the "worker" figure as the social or political entities "resting on" and vulnerable to being reduced to bare life: "The Marxist scission between man and citizen is thus superseded by the division between naked life [ultimate and opaque bearer of sovereignty] and the multifarious forms of life abstractly recodifed as social-juridical entities (the voter, the worker, the journalist, the student, but also the HIV-positive, the transvestite, the porno star, the elderly, the parent, the woman) that all rest on naked life."[38] So we should ask: who are those women whose social-juridical status rests on a division from the bare life to which they can readily be reduced? Women in general? Why? My suggestion is that this be redefined as applying to those women who bear a redoubled and additional status as potentially reducible to bare life—by virtue of their potential or actual, symbolic and historical relation to reproductivity. For that relation has historically been the grounds for their liminal or excluded political status. Modern political humans bear the capacity to be reduced to bare life. But some also have a redoubled (and more specific) exposure to this reduction by virtue of belonging to a sex, a race, or a category traditionally excluded from political rights.

For this reason, there is an additional paradox at work when women are figured as a threatening and competing sovereign power over the fetus, the latter sometimes acquiring (as seen in antiabortion rhetoric) the status of a pseudo homo sacer. For (as seen in even *Roe*'s language of competing interests) this very association particularly exposes the woman to a barer reproductive life: it is the point at which her rights are likely to be challenged or deprived. It is precisely insofar as she is figured as the pseudosovereign whose body seems to offer a fetus the pseudoanomie of a pseudocamp (and precisely insofar as she is concurrently understood in biopolitical terms as a capacity to optimize life) that she is all the more produced as a form of political life bearing correspondingly unstable and rescindable rights.

FEMINISM AND AGAMBEN

A number of feminist readings have criticized Agamben's work for his neglect of sexual difference in the discussion of infancy, possibility, potentiality, the happy life, community after identity, the human beyond metaphysics.[39] It is widely recognized that this work is inhospitable to an interrogation of gender and sexual difference.[40] In the words of an early assessment by Astrid Deuber-Mankowsky: "As in all of *Homo Sacer*, which turns centrally upon bare life, neither natality nor gender, neither sexuality nor the relations of the sexes, neither the heterosexual character of the symbolic order and of political culture nor the interest of women in the reproduction of life is thematized. The entire sphere of the question of sexual difference . . . is banned from Agamben's horizon."[41]

Alex Weheliye points out that Agamben's bare life would, formally, be "prior" to race and sex difference,[42] rendering complicated a sex- and race-based critique. In recent years a cluster of feminist and critical race theory responses to Agamben have nonetheless emerged,[43] ranging from analyses of productions of bare life in specific spaces of slavery, such as the colony and plantation,[44] to at least one feminist speculation that the fetus would, in Agamben's terms, be considered a form of bare life.[45] Ewa Ziarek notes that feminist and race-inflected readings will be more interested in "the negative differentiation of bare life with respect to racial and gender differences" and in "the way bare life is implicated in the gendered, sexist, colonial, and racist configurations of the political and, because of this implication, how it suffers different forms of violence."[46] She is also one of a number of readers to have questioned Agamben's neglect of the political and revolutionary resistance that can be sparked by the relegation of some humans to the status of bare life. A perspective inflected by gender and critical race studies is less likely to omit such phenomena (as seen in her own analyses and those of Weheliye of the phenomenon of hunger striking). These analyses both challenge and enrich Agamben's project, showing how variants of reduction to bare life *become* political resistance.[47] Exploring how the sexuality and reproductivity of some groups of women and children, whose marginal status constitutes a social or political vulnerability, also amounts to a social and political threat,[48] Stoler has also argued this may give an additional or differently specific relationship to suspended rights generally discussed by Agamben. Of course, women occupy such zones in many capacities— as illegal immigrants, as stateless, as objects of incarceration, enslavement, or genocide. But women are also vulnerable in a way specifically inflected by the association with actual or potential reproduction. This association may lead them to being seen as all the more a resource of slavery, or, in the instance mentioned by Stoler, a biopolitical threat: as when illegal immigrant mothers and "those who care for children are potential [national or border control] dangers."[49]

Agamben's concept of bare life and his multivolume homo sacer project more generally, (particularly its first volume) has been the focus of most feminist responses to his work. There is no doubt that the homo sacer project overlooks sexual difference and questions relevant to a feminist reading. But a reading for suspended potential allows an exploration of women's reproductive life as a distinctive, phantasmatic form of homo sacer: one almost but not quite addressed by Agamben. This form connects with the peculiar status taken on by those whose citizenship (acknowledged or denied) is both traditionally, and biopolitically, associated with the capacity for maternity. Among the many possibilities for this critique, I have concentrated on two specific points: first, by adding to the analysis of bare life (the human bearing the possibility of being rendered less than human in an anomic space or status for which Agamben has offered the camp as paradigm) a redoubled level (through which the woman attributed reproductive rights is produced as bearing the possibility of their loss). Here I have suggested attention to the legal regime of abortion as a persistent, inverted exceptionality, producing a special form of precariousness for some women. The second point concerns the political status assumed by women insofar as they are traditionally excluded from political life by virtue of their association with reproductivity. My argument is that the curious status assumed by women in this respect lends itself well to the intersection of a Foucauldian understanding of biopolitics and that developed by Agamben.

Responding to Foucault, Agamben argued that politics had always been concerned with life and had always placed life in question. An ancient Greek context established political life as more than mere human life, including the latter's exclusion as extra- or prepolitical. Insofar as politics variously makes and demarcates categories of life, one could say it always has been (in this sense) "biopolitical." Thus Agamben's recoins the term used by Foucault, offering a different understanding of biopolitics to new ends.[50] I next consider an element of this argument that has seized the attention of a number of feminist readers: the ambiguous status of reproductive life to which Agamben refers in the homo sacer projects.

These fleeting references prompt the question of how the changing status of a biopoliticized reproduction accompanies the transformations in the status of politics, law, and life he describes. I will argue here for a *possible* reading which retakes the text's treatment of bare life from the perspective of prepoliticized, politicized, and depoliticized reproductive life.

HOMO SACER

When Agamben reminds us that "the Greeks had no single term to express what we mean by the word 'life'" (*HS* 1), distinguishing between *zoe* and *bios*, the following remark has received considerable feminist commentary: "Simple natural life is excluded from the *polis* in the strict sense, and remains confined—as merely reproductive life—to the sphere of the *oikos*, 'home'" (*HS* 2). Catherine Mills, for example, describes this as silence "on issues of gender in his reference to Aristotle's distinction between the life of the *oikos* and politics, even though gender is insistently present in the designation of the *oikos* as the domain of reproduction that necessarily precedes and supports the life of politics."[51]

How does this exclusion relate to the included illusions of the political life of the citizen? This reference concerns the status of the domestic domain, where one finds those beings responsible for basic life processes (including matters of reproduction) whose proper sphere is restricted to the household: women and, differently, slaves. When Agamben reminds us that the status of the citizen as *bios* (as qualified political life) can be distinguished from the latter's status as *zoe* (mere life processes), this distinction will not capture those who are associated with domestic life and reproduction. We see the moment of suspended potential when Agamben does refer to those of the household, those responsible for the reproduction of life, and the somehow related categories of exclusion, without asking what is needed here analytically. So Agamben's reference reminds us, even if this is not his intention, that the political citizen also has a status as *not* those entities primarily responsible for merely reproductive processes taking place in the *oikos* (women, servants, and slaves). Reworking Johanna Oksala's description of bare life, reproductive life, "through its exclusion, is [another] hidden foundation of politics."[52] Agamben must be deemed insensitive to the gendered dimension of exclusion of natural life from the realm of the political, Mills adds, given the many feminist analyses of femininity's association with natural biological life.[53]

A similar elision is seen in Agamben's subsequent discussion of ancient Rome. Here we find a discussion of the father who, as head of the household (*domus*) has a kind of power of life and death over his son. It is *unlike* that "which lies within the competence of the father or the husband who catches his wife or daughter in the act of adultery, or even less with the power of the *dominus* over his servants" (HS 88). Agamben continues as follows: "both of these powers concern the domestic jurisdiction of the head of the family and therefore remain, in some way, within the sphere of the *domus*."[54] This exposure of the son or citizen's life to father or sovereign is identified by Agamben as the "originary political element" (HS 90).[55] The wife and daughter would be differently exposed, let's extrapolate, insofar as they are already politically excluded, or politically liminal, in the domestic domain.

Wife and daughter on the one hand, son and political citizen on the other—Agamben has again embedded in his text the difference between these figures as exposed forms of life. Agamben marks the relevance of sexual difference with respect to forms of exposure of life, we might say,[56] but there is no elaboration of this point. Later even Agamben mentions reproductivity as associating women with biological and national futures in a way exposing them to attack.[57] He specifically mentions this phenomenon in *Homo Sacer* in referring to procreatively oriented ethnic rape, naming it a "perfect threshold of indistinction between biology and politics" (*HS* 176, 187). However incoherent its objectives,[58] this is a form of deprivation of rights and reduction to the homo sacer that is unique to women.

AGAMBEN AND THE BIOPOLITICS OF MODERNITY

Having offered an alternative sense in which "Western politics is a biopolitics from the very beginning" (HS 181), Agamben develops the consequences for a problematic of included exclusion. The modern variant of biopolitics is that (as Foucault also has it) *as* biological life, those governed are now of political interest. But the consequence identified by Agamben is as follows: when political interest is directed at the collective biological life of a population, the latter redivides into fully human lives and new forms of excluded life. Those who have a reduced status as mere bare life are not excluded "outside the city" as against the included rights bearers. Rather, all the rights bearers acquire a new status as easily reducible to the status of mere life, a phenomenon that occurs increasingly in internal spaces of anomie in which one is alive but not rights bearing: not just the camp and the blackbox, but also statelessness, collateral damage, acceptable margins, permissible killing, even the overcoma. For there may well be a comprehensive biopolitical interest in taking charge of our biological life, but that administrative interest is not the domain of legal protection and political rights. It is the technics of management, at best pastoral care, and it is the space where the law easily withdraws or is set aside. To occupy its administrative space is to approach anomie, rather than the basis for political claims, and as such to be highly vulnerable. In this modern variant, with the rise of post-eighteenth-century biopolitics (as described by Foucault), we all become (according to Agamben's modification) the virtual homo sacer, exposed to the ways in which the law can abandon life. Agamben includes here the deprivation of citizenship, the interning of refugees, border detentions, those interned without due process, those interned as lesser forms of life, or those possessing lesser (or no) rights.

On this argument, the growth of modern biopolitics has been accompanied by a growth of such states of exception: settings aside of the law, or specific laws, for designated reasons. "Emergency powers" become exemplary of an increasingly banal structure. Legality becomes a domain enveloping its ever expanding space of anomie—the included exclusion—so extensive in its application and frequency as to become the new biopolitical norm. The space of anomie expands to exceed the space of the law and yet remains encompassed within it as exception so that the anomie never quite counts as illegality. We can have a strong sense of human rights, and of the fundamental importance of habeas corpus, and yet accept or tolerate concurrently with these commitments an ever increasing set of contemporary exceptions: the conditions under which surveillance and detention on suspicion are deemed acceptable, the internship of "enemy combatants," the exceptional use of torture, exceptions to the rights of detained prisoners, illegal refugees, those suspected of terrorism or of terrorist sympathy, or the targeting of particular races, ethnicities, or nationalities as security measures. This offers a new variant on the concept of the homo sacer as the included exclusion: the camp as the "biopolitical paradigm of the modern" (*HS* 117).

REPRODUCTIVE MODERNITY: AGAMBEN ON THE PASSIVE CITIZEN

I situated Agamben's brief mention of reproductive life in the initial account of the homo sacer of antiquity and turn now to the second variation attributed to biopolitical modernity. Again my question is how reproductive life either is, or could, be situated in this context.

When Agamben discusses the 1789 French Declaration of Rights of Man and Citizen, he identifies the distinctive fact that "it is precisely bare natural life—which is to say, the pure fact of birth—that appears here as the source and bearer of rights. "Men," the first article declares, "are born and remain free and equal in rights" (*HS* 127). Agamben emphasizes the consequences of this overlap between birth and the rights of the citizen indicated by the declaration. He claims that it is not possible to understand the "'national' and biopolitical development and vocation of the modern state in the nineteenth and twentieth centuries if one forgets that what lies at its basis is not man as a free and conscious political subject, but, above all, man's bare life.... The fiction implicit here is that *birth* immediately becomes *nation* . . . rights are attributed *to man* . . . solely to the extent that man is the immediately vanishing ground (who must never come to light as such) of the citizen" (*HS* 128).

But Agamben emphasizes that another fiction is also at work. He recalls that in the first version of the French constitution a number of individuals born on French soil did not automatically become full citizens, but were so-called passive citizens.[59] That legal tradition persisted, particularly in its inclusion of women. It is exemplified in Agamben's argument that modern political interest in life (also seen in claims to political rights by virtue of one's status as human life, or one's birth) in fact stimulates new divisions at the heart of civic space between included and excluded humans: "Hence too . . . the rapid growth in the course of the French Revolution of regulatory provisions specifying which *man* was a *citizen* and which one not, and articulating and gradually restricting the area of the *ius soli* and the *ius sanguinis*" (HS 129-30).[60] Discussing the division between active and passive rights, Agamben cites two passages, one from Emmanuel-Joseph Sieyès and one from Jean-Denis Lanjuinais,[61] which outline the exclusion of women from this newly defined citizenship, the first grouping them in this regard with children and foreigners and the second grouping them with children, minors, the insane, and some categories of criminals.

What does this mean for women's relationship to bare life? For all that his attention is not especially on the status of women, Agamben makes the illuminating point that their exclusion is *coherent* and not in contradiction with the Declaration of Rights and its principle that "Les hommes naissent et demeurent libres et égaux en droits." This coherence manifests through its biopolitical prism. Where "mere" birth coincides with the claims of political life, human *zoe* has passed over from the exterior to the interior of the political sphere. In consequence, the threshold of inside and outside will now be constantly redrawn at the interior of this political space.

Again we can identify suspended potential for an elaboration not undertaken by Agamben. The form and logic of the exclusion of women from the 1789 Declaration of Rights has been of interest to many feminist readers and historians of women's rights.[62] We can add to Agamben's elaboration a) that the exclusion of women from political life is not in contradiction with the newly internally dividing status of biopolitics and that b) to the contrary it manifests the very form and function of the new biopoliticization of the polis.

Agamben proposes we identify a new political entity: the living dead human (HS 131), a category that includes the traditional passive citizenship assumed by women in France in the wake of 1789. Grouped with others who do not vote (including children, the mad and criminal), they are deprived of the rights otherwise belonging to the French born. A point Agamben does not make is that it is as potentially or metonymically *procreative* that women take on this status. They are passive citizens because their natural function is deemed to be the reproduction and nurture of citizens.[63] At the point where mere birth can be a qualification for eventual political rights, women become a political exception. They were, in this sense, abandoned by France's political institutions, deemed excluded from the definitionally broad inclusions of universal rights on the pretext of their naturally maternal role, if not their traditional status as *feme covert*.

This is a tradition of included exclusion in which the alternative possibility of women's political life (real or hypothetical) is excluded by virtue of their association with reproductive life. Their traditional exclusion from the political space certainly provides early examples (insofar as women are noncitizens in ancient Greece and citizens without voting rights in ancient Rome). So does their special inclusion within the political space in the guise of a specific exclusion from franchise, as the— effectively—passive French citizens of the period 1789–1945. I turn now to a third variation: as full political citizens, women may suffer an attack on or preclusion of their political status that is overridden by politically or nationally or ethnically oriented interest in women as reproductive life. This produces another possible variation on living dead humanity or the homo sacer—the moments of production of women's procreation as nationally or ethically significant, vital to peoples, populations, and futures. This is a thanatopolitical moment in their political life in which their reproductivity would survive their political rights.[64]

LIVING DEAD REPRODUCTIVE LIFE

If women's marginal political status has historically been associated with their reproductive role, what is the significance of the following two overlapping phenomena? First, the management of biological life has come to be one of the projects of political governmentality. Second, throughout the twentieth century, women progressively gained full citizenship in European and Anglo-American countries. What has been the interconnection between their traditional status as primarily responsible for reproductive life and their concurrent status as formally equal political agents whose rights were previously precluded on the basis of their reproductive role? As modernity has produced political contexts increasingly oriented toward the administration of biological life, women's traditionally "apolitical" status has changed accordingly. As reproductive women have been represented as making a vital national contribution while also being newly problematized as a threshold of possible risk to the political future—and, as we have seen, associable with new concepts of choice, agency, autonomy, impact, volition, recalcitrance, and competing interests.

Thus, even as women have achieved full citizenship and voting rights, they have continued to be associated with a biopoliticized reproductivity. In addition to abortion laws, they have been the targets of a number of forms of public policy and new senses of "responsibility" aimed at promoting a milieu in which women are the primary locus of moralized choice with respect to reproduction (where duty may be given both individual and collective or public inflections).[65] They may also be objects of policy aimed in some countries at modifying national birthrate.[66] The point is that when women's capacity to reproduce has, as a matter of biopolitical concern, been variously targeted for stimulation, regulation, control, or destruction—sometimes with the deadly results mentioned by Esposito, this reproductivity does not preclude them from political interest or status. It can no longer be the case that they are, *as* reproductive, rendered pre- or apolitical. Another way of putting this (we would turn to Foucault for this insight) is that, all appearances to the contrary, this is not a *privative or reductive* function. Women's association with reproductivity is consistent with Agamben's account of a category of "mere life" *produced* as the concern of politics, creating new internal divisions as a result. It has manufactured a new kind of thanatopolitics in two forms. First, it produces women's rights as more precarious (for reproductive rights are precarious rights), and the precariousness of such rights (or their deprivation), in many cases, exposes their health, if not their lives, and causes states of structural unease. Second, this can also amount to a conversion of women's political significance to a teleologized or controversial biopolitical reproductive significance. Here the very association with the principle of life produces results ranging from the coercive, punished, sanctioned, violent, or deadly.

THE DIFFERENTIAL POLITICAL RELEVANCE OF WOMEN'S REPRODUCTIVE LIVES

Agamben does not refer to the biopoliticized reproductive life of women in such terms. Yet we can amplify the brief moments in which such a path of inquiry is averted. Similarly, Ziarek sees Agamben as strangely *including*, while failing to follow, the implications of the race, ethnic, and historical diversity of his own examples: "Although Agamben's heterogeneous examples of bare life—for instance, the father-son relation in antiquity, Nazi euthanasia programs for the mentally ill, the destruction of the Romany, ethnic rape camps in the former Yugoslavia, Karen Quinlan's comatose body, and especially the most important case of the *Muselmann*—are always diversified along racial, gender, and ethnic and historical lines, his conceptual analysis does not follow the implications of such heterogeneity."[67] A text neglecting difference, including sexual difference,[68] rarely does so comprehensively. More typically, it intermittently gestures toward these omissions. To bring the challenge of sexual difference to Agamben's homo sacer project is to look for those moments where such questions are broached, to reread the text through this prism and refract it back accordingly, disturbing the limits it sets.

But this is not to say that the sheer biopolitical interest in the management and administration of reproductive life amounts to the setting aside of women's political life. To the extent that there is a consensual expectation that governments and public health campaigns will be interested in healthy pregnancies, there is not necessarily a corresponding reduction of women's political life to their reproductive life. (Similarly, health campaigns concerned with reducing rates of colon cancer will not necessarily be considered the reduction of political life to combatting disease.) Instead, biopoliticized reproduction moves toward the thanatopolitical insofar as it belongs not just to legality but to the institution of anomic spaces within the law and their associated precariousness. One way of understanding this is as follows: as equal rights-bearing citizens, women are legally and politically within the law. But they concurrently enfold a reproductive space, which was traditionally the pretext of exclusion from political rights, only to become the object of particular biopolitical interest. That space has a more specific capacity to become anomic. I've suggested abortion law as a particularly good example, since the annulment of a previously established legality is not a simple "privation": it is, for example, a stimulation of the woman's status as that of contest, challenge, significance, unease, disorder, uncertainty, persistent reversibility or rescindability, criminality, resistance, rights polemics, the dividing point of wealth, medical insurance, mobility, and privilege.

In this chapter I have argued for a more specific factoring of (bio)politicized reproduction as a depoliticization, and one that accompanies the political history of women's entry into the history of rights bearing. Such an exploration is not available from Agamben, but, I have argued, it is not irrelevant to his account, nor even entirely absent from it. For this reason, reiterating a methodological gesture proposed throughout this book, I have proposed it be seen as a suspended capacity of Agamben's account of the making of anomic bare life.

Pursuing this account, I have suggested an analysis of women's redoubled political status in these terms. The exclusion of women from full political status by virtue of their role as wives and mothers has carried over and survived their attaining full citizenship. This association can take place under the rubric of biopolitical interest in and care about the good conduct and administration of reproduction in populations. Thus there is a supplementary paradox to be added to the dissensus between Esposito, Agamben, and Foucault concerning biopolitical paradox. In fact it manifests particularly clearly when their different accounts of the relation between sovereign power and biopolitics are read together. This additional paradox circulates through their own pages: all of them are referring intermittently to women and to the forms of biopolitical interest that come to include reproduction and the conduct of real or hypothetical maternity.

Thus we would add to Agamben's sex- and race-neutral account that we are all the virtual homo sacer, an additional production of a form of bare life that takes place in relation to the management of women's reproductive lives. Its more specific inflections relate to the long history of women's exclusion from political status because of their (attributed) responsibility for reproduction and persists with the more generalized mode of biopower associated with modernity.

REPRODUCTIVE RIGHTS

Reviewing the 2011–2012 war of prominent Republicans against Planned Parenthood and reproductive rights more generally, Jill Lepore commented in the *New Yorker*, "if a fertilized egg has constitutional rights, women cannot have equal rights with men."[69] This remark identifies the association of Western women with a heavily regulated and politicized reproductive life concurrent with the time in which they are assumed to have equal political rights. It assumes that the former amounts to a preclusion, or inhibition, of the latter. The problem can be formulated differently: the women to whom Lepore refers *do* have equal rights with men, *and* they are associated with forms of stimulated biopolitical interest in their fertilized eggs, an interest that *also* produces them as accordingly extrapolitical figures. But biopolitical interest itself is newly politicizing rather than depoliticizing. At the same time it is productive of a category whose traditional associations do bear a prepolitical connotation. Women have long been understood as enfolding the space of the potential "child" that is itself the space of potential futures. Today, this is also to enfold the space by virtue of which, in a more specific sense than the concurrent, general possibility described by Agamben, the woman's body contains the possibility of becoming anomie. She becomes at least three modes: the phantom sovereign deemed capable of a revoking of life, the principle of life (and of its potential undermining: whether with respect to individuals or collectivities such as nations, populations, or the general good or community interest) and a bodily space enfolding more intense instability and revocability of the corresponding legal regimes.

Since reproductive rights have been formulated only in the context of modern biopolitical contexts, it cannot be said that this biopoliticization itself infringes "prior" or preestablished reproductive rights.[70] We can turn here to a recent argument by Ruth A. Miller, who has proposed that the womb, not the camp, is the paradigmatic biopolitical space. Her argument is not that the womb is like Agamben's camp: a space in which legal rights are set aside. It is also not a space (as an antiabortionist might want to argue) in which "fetal rights" will not count as such. Instead, as a biopolitical governmentality, this is a space of particular political-administrative interest for "taking care of life" rather than a rights-bearing space.[71] Paradoxes will then emerge where rights claims are made on behalf of this space.

As compared to traditional forms of political inclusion (excluding mere human bodily existence as non rights bearing), Miller agrees that once politics gives itself the task of governing human bodily existence, political existence becomes more precarious. One is administered politically *as* a category whose very status equates with an absence of rights, for all that that status (the paradigmatic camp) may be replaced by biopolitical administration, care, and the optimization of life. Reproductive rights are, therefore, claimed *as* political rights even though reproduction is the bodily space of the absence of rights. This offers a new challenge to a long-standing feminist argument that the male subject was paradigmatic of the political rights bearer. The problem had been that women were relegated to a private, domestic sphere considered extrapolitical. Miller proposes a feminist revision of this received narrative, for, in a modern biopolitical context, this is decreasingly correct. In fact, the woman (in all her stimulated revocability and enfolding of potential states of anomie) has become paradigmatic of the paradoxical status of the modern political citizen.

It is unsurprising, in consequence—this is to add to Miller's argument—that reproductive rights are established and persist in states of extreme revocability. One might say: reproduction compresses multiple states of revocability. It fits particularly well the definition of sovereignty as the demarcation of life denied political rights (Agamben's definition of the biopolitical). Perhaps the woman is a figure one can also understand as biopolitically "thanatopolitized" in the sense that (because of her traditional association with a reproductive role) the forms of death to which this also exposes many women systematically are less likely to "count" as political forms of death or as politically consequential forms of death. Moreover, could it not be said, *both* in the senses available from Foucault, and from Agamben, that these are, quintessentially, biopolitical deaths? They are a biopolitical making of women as figures of death, a making of women as enfolding the space of legal anomie and challenged political status. They make states of political and biopolitical unease. Not infrequently, they have been sovereign *and* biopolitical makings of women's deaths.

OVERLAPS

In fact, one might see Agamben as effectively describing the overlapping of regimes, modes, and techniques Foucault proposed. True, he redefines biopolitics and sovereignty: both take on senses they do not possess for Foucault. But these recoinings also become means of offering a new understanding of biopolitics and sovereignty as enmeshed and as coinciding. Agamben adopts and expands the definition of sovereignty as power over and power to dispose of, adding the power to set the law aside, to create the widening state of anomie, rescindability, and exception. Foucault retains a definition of sovereignty as power over (territory, bodies) and the power to deprive (taxes, property, freedom of movement, life), and, at the extreme power to kill. He defines biopolitics as the power to administer, enhance, and optimize life and describes the administration and optimization of life as a primary political project. Agamben defines the originary political gesture as the division between forms of political life and forms of life excluded from political existence and its associated rights claims. But these are different definitions allowing us to revisit the Foucauldian definition of both biopolitics and sovereignty.

Thus we find new means in which, from Foucault's perspective, the administration of life could be said (with Agamben's addition) to a) include the thanatopolitical-"sovereign" capacity to "let die" (to produce life as not worth being lived); and b) by the same means to have a thanatopolitical-sovereign capacity to expose (to harm or death) as a means of administering life; and c) this is a production of forms of life and governmentality that are not best understood as privative—irrespective of whether they are understood as biopolitical in Foucault's sense or that of Agamben.

Agamben's focus on the camp and on the more specific forms of sovereignty required and produced by the camp's state of exception certainly move into a domain of the administration of life, death, of sovereignty and of thanatopolitical biopolitics neglected by Foucault. Similarly, the administrative, juridical, and sovereign mode of setting the law aside allows a different understanding of the overlap of biopolitical modes and sovereign modes and of how the sovereign acts as biopolitical and vice versa. These understandings can be parsed through Agamben's definition (sovereignty producing anomic spaces of rights deprivation and forms of exposure and death not counting as murder) or through Foucault's definitions (biopolitical administration of life may include a deadly effect understood as part of the management of life). For all that Agamben's definitions should be held distinct from those of Foucault, they offer new options for conceptualizing the overlapping of sovereignty and biopolitics also explored by Foucault.

If we explore the connected argument that revocability is the "pre-eminent modern political space" and that (as Miller proposes) reproductive space has become the pre-eminent modern political space,[72] we would also return to the possible consequence, that (as I suggested in chapter 3 in the company of Foucault) reproductive life particularly emerges as the coalescing of dehiscent modes of power. This is exactly the possibility explored by Miller: "Rather than a progression or movement from a traditional focus on marital status to a liberal focus on individual freedom or privacy to a post-liberal focus on bodily integrity . . . the situation that I will be describing involves an overlap of all three,"[73] giving rise to her conclusion: "it is in the arena of this overlap that the biopolitical subject is formed— . . . it is, in other words, the blurring of these political boundaries that allows for reproductive space to become the pre-eminent modern political space."[74]

Again considering collective administrative interest and the interest in optimizing health, I will, finally, consider the conjoined production of new kinds of responsibilized subjects and new kinds of responsibilities:

as when sovereign powers "over life" long associated in France with illegal abortion, were then associated with its legalization: in new conducts of responsibilization that could not be declined, and in a stimulation of new kinds of illegibility. In visiting these recent effects of subjectivation, I will explore one final sense of the thanatopolitical, seen in the divisions between those who are considered to exercise reproductive choice appropriately or inappropriately. Abortion controversies have been contexts in which women may find themselves associated with agencies of death (fetal, individual, collective, population, and futural), and I have argued that these associations and their conjoined revocability be understood as one of the senses of thanatopoliticized reproduction. But another sense of thanatopolitics can also be seen in the capacity of these very associations, and regimes governing abortion, to divide groups of women and their biopolitical and sovereign decision making into the more and less visible or legible or appropriate or individualized decision makers: producing some as "less than subjects."[75] As such they manifest one more variant of Foucault's biopolitical caesura dividing populations. A thanatopoliticized reproduction can expose women in the following way: insofar as they become figures of impediment, thresholds of harm, or responsibility for procreative and population harm or death, they have a conjoined exposure to harm and death.

5

JUDITH BUTLER, PRECARIOUS LIFE, AND REPRODUCTION

From Social Ontology to Ontological Tact

These norms draw upon shifting scenes of intelligibility, so that we can and do have, for example, histories of life and histories of death. Indeed we have ongoing debates about whether the fetus should count as life, or a life, or a human life; we have further debates about conception and what constitutes the first moments of a living organism; we have debates also about what constitutes death, whether it is the death of the brain, or of the heart, whether it is the effect of a legal declaration or a set of medical and legal certificates. . . . The fact that these debates exist . . . implies that there is no life and no death without a relation to some frame.

—JUDITH BUTLER, *FRAMES OF WAR*

The central ethical question analyzed by Gilligan is precisely the decision whether to have, or not to have, an abortion. The first time I read the book, this struck me as strange.

—BARBARA JOHNSON, "APOSTROPHE, ANIMATION, AND ABORTION"

This chapter returns to a philosopher for whom biopolitics has not been a dominant theme, Judith Butler. As we will see, it is interesting that her engagement with the concept has been brief, particularly insofar as related terrain in her work has brought her into debate with Foucault and Agamben. She has made intermittent responses to both, in the course of developing an understanding of life as always framed by social mechanisms through which life, or lives, emerge as differentially grievable.

My argument is not that Butler herself introduces a Foucauldian approach to life, nor is the object of the following discussion the interested and critical responses to Foucault to be found in Butler's work, dating back to *Subjects of Desire*. Instead, recalling a form of critical encounter also pursued in previous chapters, particularly between Foucault and Derrida, I pursue an alternative means of understanding the possible dialogue between their interests.

Foucault has encouraged interrogation by means of the questions— "*what* life?" "*what* death?"—in contexts ranging from *The Birth of the Clinic* through *The Punitive Society* and beyond. But in a great number of ways he has also encouraged interrogation of what the problematizations of life and death "do." When the making of lives and deaths (most obviously, as differently mattering) play an important role in Butler's social ontology, this is in part because she is asking a similar question. Her own answer uses the language of subjectivation and desubjectivation: subjects are made and unmade as differentially grievable.

Thus one possible approach would be to interrogate the seemingly different understandings of life in Foucault and Butler's works, her early attribution to Foucault of a form of vitalism, or her critique of the role he seems to attribute to death in the biopolitics of *The History of Sexuality*. Chapter 5 takes a different route, however, redirecting to another interrogation: what kind of reading is facilitated by the encounter *between* Butler and Foucault. In chapter 1 I suggested (of the working space which opens up between Foucault and Derrida) that the results of such encounters ought to be surprising. The best way of understanding the resources that thereby emerge is not always through asking how the one characterized the other—to the contrary, we might sometimes conclude. Having discussed a number of alternatives, in this chapter I return, accordingly, not only to the interests Foucault and Butler have certainly shared (genealogy, Nietzsche, the making of life, death, sexuality, the stimulations of power . . .) but to a figure whose role is marginal in the work of both. This is an implausible figure, one might be tempted to say, almost un-Butlerian, un-Foucauldian. In chapter 1 I considered themes that were, in a sense, similarly implausible—biopolitics for Derrida, sexual difference for Foucault, terms with which they certainly could have spent more analytic time, but which were also bad, jarring fits, and I pursued a reading arising from that working space. In this chapter the "fetus" is also proposed as a jarring figure.

This figure will not prompt an evaluation of Butler *on* Foucault, nor of their likenesses or differences, rather it will lead us to something different. Within a working space opened up between the Butlerian and Foucauldian projects, I am going to reroute their common interest in contingent formations of life toward an interrogation not just of precarious life but also of subjects understood as newly responsible for contingent formations of life: the conjoined making of new forms of ethical subjects. And where Butler has developed the concept of social ontology, in the space between Foucault and Butler I am going to explore the recent emergence of a phenomenon we might instead call ontological tact.

PRECARIOUS LIFE

Among the many quarters in which biopolitical theory has provoked caution, Judith Butler has, in her preface to *Frames of War*, characterized the following nervousness on the left: "It is difficult for those on the Left to think about a discourse of 'life,' since we are used to thinking of those who favor increased reproductive freedoms as 'pro-choice' and those who oppose them as 'pro-life.'"[1] The context for these remarks is Butler's development of the concept of precarious life. Only rarely has she used the terms *biopower* and *biopolitics*.[2] Although related problems are considered in her work, she has contrasted her approach to studies that "situate the discourse of life within the sphere of biopolitics and of biomedicalization more specifically." Rather than grouping herself with post-Foucauldian biopolitical theorists, she has identified herself more as a *compagnon de route*.[3] Differentiating her own interest from genealogies of life or death, she sees "precariousness as something both presupposed and managed by" biopolitical administrations of life which not only rely on but also contribute to the framing and apprehension of life (*FW* 17–18). Speaking to the further level of precariousness embedded in the very availability of 'life" to be managed (or reduced or precluded) by biopolitics, she has asked:

> Can life ever be considered "bare"? And has not life been already entered into the political field in ways that are clearly irreversible? The question of when and where life begins and ends, the means and legitimate uses of reproductive technology, the quarrels over whether life should be conceived as cell or tissue, all these are clearly questions of life and questions of power—extensions of biopower in ways that suggest that no simple exclusionary logic can be set up between life and politics. Or, rather, any effort to establish such an exclusionary logic depends upon the depoliticization of life and, once again, writes out the matters of gender, menial labor, and reproduction from the field of the political.[4]

Precariousness adds to an earlier and extensive use of the term *vulnerability* (*Excitable Speech*, *The Psychic Life of Power*, *Giving an Account of Oneself*) to describe subjects as originally dependent on others in a number of ways (for example, for the language that installs us as speaking subjects concurrently vulnerable to one another,[5] including the vulnerability to being named in injurious ways by the very language which brings us into being,[6]—thus language can simultaneously install subjects as human while embodying the terms and names that render some humans less than human). *The Psychic Life of Power* uses vulnerability to characterize "terms of power that one never made but . . . on which one depends in order to be."[7] Here Butler favors the terms *power* and *recognition* to characterize the formative dilemma of the subject. A subject seeks—may passionately seek (*PLP* 113)—a necessary recognition (by individual and collective others) that simultaneously confers its subordination. This is true of processes of recognition of individual subjects and true also of the ways in which we belong to collective, social categories: for "social categories signify subordination and existence at once" (*PLP* 20). The result is that subjects seeking their own persistence can be characterized as necessarily "desir[ing] the conditions of one's own subordination . . . the very form of power-regulation, prohibition, suppression—that threatens one with dissolution" (*PLP* 9). Across a number of projects, then, Butler refers to formational and ongoing affective, intersubjective, linguistic, psychic, and social existence in terms of an unavoidable exposure and dependency on what formatively and continuously comes from the other (desire, language, recognition, norms),[8] whose role is to constitute and simultaneously deconstitute. A Foucauldian inflection is also seen in the account of paradoxical subjects as effects of the productivities of power even in their very hopes to resist the latter.[9]

An early focus on precariousness is evident in *Gender Trouble*, whose connection of gender normativity with questions of survival was amplified in later essays. Gender's dependence on its iteration contains the possibility of surprising and transformative versions. But Butler does not minimize the fact that gender illegibility may be unlivable[10] or deadly.[11] *Psychic Life's* account of subjection (being made as subjects by the forces, which concurrently, in a number of senses, also undo us) connects this to a problematics of death and survival. Norms and constituting forces are depicted as vulnerable, just like the subjects they bring into effect and deconstitute: "social categorizations that establish the vulnerability of the subject to language are themselves vulnerable to both psychic and historical change" (*PLP* 21). But these comments also lead to the different inflection of vulnerability: to be differentiated in terms of social categories for the fully human concurrently produces and maintains the "socially dead." The normative categories interpellating some as socially legible relegate others to social marginality or invisibility. Some are produced as belonging (by virtue of legal inequality, lesser social resources, misrecognition, social or political disinterest, exposure to prejudice and violence) to categories exposing them to harm or death (*PLP* 27). And in a different sense norms are also vulnerable. Insofar as they must be reiterated, Butler has consistently emphasized that they are exposed to change and unpredictability.

Butler's work engages a Foucauldian conceptualization of biopolitics more than may appear. Much of her work concerns the formation of subjects rather than the focal point of Foucauldian biopolitics: the (differential, life-enhancing, and death-delivering) management of populations. Her articulation of precariousness certainly gives attention to individual formations of subjectivity, from those of gender, to the neonate overwhelmed by an incomprehensible adult presence discussed in *Giving an Account of Oneself*.[12] But, from her early work, Butler has argued that the cost of normalization, of subjectivity, of one's intelligibility as human is the concurrent rendering of certain humans as less than human, less than intelligible, and as vulnerable and exposed to abjection and violence as such. This argument straddles an interest in individual subject formation, with an approach which is just as concerned with the divisions of populations into groups framed as more or less human, groups whose abjection contributes to the centering of others.[13] She acknowledges that there are multiple meanings and formations of life available for archaeological, genealogical and biopolitical analysis. Affirming the importance of such projects, the aspect on which she particularly focuses is the unmaking of life and of lives (in the sense of some lives versus those of others) as less "worth living," less valuable, less livable,[14] less human: with the consequence that the making of the human dehumanizes some. This countering production of the risks and conditions of dehumanization concerns both the formation of the conditional terms in which as human one *could* otherwise be apprehended as less than human. It also includes the formation of categories of humans who are, sometimes tacitly, sometimes overtly, ascribed a status as less than human by contrast to those whose lives will have mattered. These differentials, centerings, and concurrent marginalizations, inclusions, exclusions, and "included" exclusions hold Butler's main focus, rather than—more generally—the many ways in which one could describe the making of categories, epistemologies, forms, modes, materialities, norms, errors, errings, and contingencies of life.

More recently, in *Precarious Life* and in *Frames of War*, Butler has described how tacit or overt perceptions of the differential value of lost lives relate to interpretative schemas and epistemological frames. This might manifest in phenomena such as moral repulsion in response to some forms of killing, deaths, imprisonment, and torture but not others (*FW* 25). Thus, when she comments "If certain lives do not qualify as lives or are, from the start, not conceivable as lives within certain epistemological frames, then these lives are never lived nor lost in the full sense," she qualifies that "the frames through which we apprehend or, indeed, fail to apprehend the lives of others as lost or injured (lose-able or injurable) are politically saturated. They are themselves operations of power" (*FW* 1). In describing subdivisions within groups or populations into those more likely to be apprehended as threatened lives or as "threat to life" (*FW* 42), and into the more or less grievable, she is describing forms of power that can be understood as biopolitical. Butler will characterize this as "population management" (*PL* 96) not just by states but also by the capillary and retroactive effects of "petty" sovereigns (*PL* 56, 65), local administrators, bureaucratic measures, expert knowledges, forms of media, and other modes of diffusion and relay of power.

Precarious Life suggests that the biopolitical account of the optimization and administration of life ought to provoke at least two types of critical interrogation: a) Whose lives are *not* optimized to the ends of the management of the life of some? About which peoples or populations does a lesser interest (or thorough disinterest) in their being governed "well" manifest? b) How, moreover, do some populations or groups come to be managed precisely by being constituted as less than human or attributed some lesser status—such that these lives and their administration are apprehended as of lesser consequence? How can we understand dehumanization itself, or the production of subjects with lesser rights, or no rights, as a form of governmentality? (*PL* 97–98).[15]

Butler's interest in biopolitical questions of population governmentality can be identified even in her interest in the conditions of subjectivity. Thus she similarly relates the management of dispossession, expulsion, social invisibility, reterritorialization, statelessness, and those deprived of legal protection to an individuation of subjects as belonging to more or less valued groups (within or external to populations) and their differentials of grievability.[16] This precariousness is both made and presupposed by state powers, by powers with "state-like features,", and by the lateral, diffused processes characteristically described by Foucault's biopower.

This is to review the very long trajectory seen in Butler's work concerning the framing of human life by virtue of (included) exclusions of differential value and intelligibility.

We can also add Butler to a trajectory of theorists for whose projects the critical diagnosis of Foucault's occlusions, gaps, intervals, and blind spots has played a significant role. Sometimes, I have argued, this gesture can be refracted back to include the critic in a similar interrogation. For there is often an additional reserve of suspended resources identifiable in the contours of critique. Critique delimits, so it also allows us to think just beyond its limit points—to adjust its terrain a little or to reverse the relationship between the foregrounded and the overshadowed. Butler's responses to Foucault on a number of points are well-known: her discussions of his relationship to vitalism in *Subjects of Desire*, gender trouble, and the psychic life of power; her location of Foucault's limitations concerning Herculine Barbin, sexual difference, the modern relationship between biopolitics, death, and sex; the effects (both retroactive and nostalgic) of contemporary sovereignty (including the capillary "petty" sovereign); and her focus on the *de*constitutive roles of discipline and governmentality. There is also an important dialogue between Butler and Foucault's respective definitions of critique.

But in this project I have pursued a particular occlusion reiterating in the work of the theorists under discussion. This is not to assume that such occlusions have the same status when considered in the work of Derrida, Edelman, Foucault, Esposito, Agamben, or Butler. Also, the engagement of each with Foucault has been characteristically different. Perhaps Butler's has been the most sustained and ongoing. Yet, if they have shared one feature, it is that the biopolitics of procreation have tended to strike a jarring note in their work.

Butler is a surprising inclusion—in a number of essays she has considered the politics of reproduction far more directly than theorists considered in earlier chapters.[17] Yet one awkward reproductive figure can be located in her work, although its advent will barely be recalled. Again it is a liminal figure. Little discussed by Butler, and still less by Foucault: it is the figure of the fetus.

PRECARIOUSNESS AND FETAL LIFE

Addressing the relationship between the epistemological framing and differential grievability of life in a work entitled *Frames of War*, we are not surprised to see Butler direct attention to the framing conditions of prisoner detention and abuse, state-sanctioned torture, and military strike attacks. More surprisingly, because it is unclear that the theme could be productively pursued as a part of this project, Butler, at the outset, also evokes the status of embryonic life.[18]

Broaching the issue in the margins of *Frames of War* provides another occasion for her to differentiate her project from the foci of biopolitical inquiry: the focus on the administration of life and its technics and on new modes of knowledge/power for defining, managing, and/or regenerating life.[19] She clarifies that although she will be focusing most directly on war as a means of thinking life's epistemological framing and differential grievability, this is not to deny the potential for analysis of "the biopolitics of both war and reproductive freedom" (*FW* 17). But that possibility, particularly with respect to the latter, is set aside in being raised.

In fact, we have seen that reproduction has long been a concern of biopolitics, but has not always been emphasized as such. Moreover, I have argued that it presents an intriguing and undertheorized problem for those who have foregrounded the deadly and thanatopolitical aspects of biopolitics. What then of the variant we can attribute to Butler: the account of precarious life? It is not implausible to imagine a reproductive variant of the precariousness she understands to be both presupposed and managed by biopolitics (*FW* 18). But we might first consider some reasons mentioned by Butler for caution.

For there is a more specific variant of that nervous reaction on the left she had mentioned, evoked both in *Frames* and in an interview with Nina Power, who asks:

> You touch upon the question of abortion in your discussion of how we value "precarious" or "grievable" lives. "Life" is an extremely contested term, as you say. How do you understand some of the difficulties attached to this word in the context of the way it has been mobilized, for example by the Christian right in America?
>
> JUDITH BUTLER: Yes, of course. But my sense is that the Left has to "reclaim" the discourse of life, especially if we hope to come up with significant analyses of biopolitics, and if we are to be able to clarify under what conditions the loss of life is unjustifiable. This means arguing against those who oppose abortion and making clear in what sense the "life" we defend against war is not the same as the "life" of the foetus.[20]

Of course a "pro-life" politics has tended to conceptualize fetal life as exposed to the mother's seeming sovereign right to "make live or reject into death."[21] But this is to assume that the precariousness in question would be that of ambiguous embryonic life.[22] I have promoted an alternative in the previous chapters.

With respect to the recent trend toward a post-Foucauldian biopolitics foregrounding necro- and thanatopolitics, its making and management of biopoliticized forms of death and of precarious life, I have, in this book, offered three arguments. First, as one of the major concerns of the biopolitical, reproduction can also be thought in terms of its thanatopolitical variants. Second, the hesitation in developing this question may relate to the phantom fetus that tends to pull focus as the possible precariousness in question. Third, I have argued instead that the relevant thanatopolitics is seen in the attribution of a fetus's (or a people's) phantom vulnerability to the seemingly life-death decision-making capacity of the woman become pseudosovereign. That in itself is thanatopolitical insofar as it renders the woman the "agent of life-death decision making" (or, more extremely, in the tradition of antiabortion politics, "agent of death" and obstructor of futures). In other words, just as a biopolitics makes the forms of managed life and the corresponding agencies, a thanatopolitics makes its forms of death and the corresponding agencies. We have seen the long history in which women become biopolitical agents of life (of three enfolded types of life: potential pregnancies, actual pregnancies brought to term, and children's lives considered to enfold the futures of family, population, and nation). The counterpart is their intensified counter-role as impediment to these futures. Thus we have also seen the imbrication of these formations of women as "principles of life" in their counterpart: if they can deliver life, they can withhold, harm, or impede it and they can deliver "death" in all the corresponding variants. We can also use the term *thanatopolitics* in a further sense. The very association of reproduction with threat to "future" life has stimulated new forms of women's precariousness and precarity, vulnerability, illegality, and sometimes literal death to which they are exposed by legal and extralegal regimes of biopoliticized reproduction. While the fetus is a form of life whose malleability can be seen in its hovering between "desired future life," "biological life," and "biological waste," it is not, as such, independent of the technologies that render it,[23] nor from the female bodies who would carry it. An embryo, thanatopoliticized or otherwise, is not an independent entity. But insofar as it is understood as precarious life, the woman has become a redoubled form of precarious life. The woman is particularly precarious insofar as she has been attributed with both a sovereignlike and a biopolitically inflected power of decision or impact on the futures (individual, population, biopolitical, collective, the social good) her conduct is considered to unfold.

I begin with an example closest to the definition of precariousness considered so far, the differentiation of populations and parts of populations into greater or less value. Abortion was illegal under Ceaușescu's Romania, and (we will return to this later in the chapter) some nine thousand women are considered to have died from illegal abortion during this period. Gail Kligman has pointed out that, under this same regime, Romany women in Romania, whose reproduction was associated with an excessive and devalued population impact, could access abortion far more easily in a regime notorious for enforcing abortion's illegality.[24] Here the differences in access to abortion relate not only to power, wealth, and networking but also to differential valuations of women's biopolitical impact (here, by virtue of ethnicity) as "principle of life." Their status *as* more or less relevant to a thanatopolitics (the politics administering forms of population "death") produced the differentials in their own exposure to harm and death via this particular conduit. One has no need of Esposito's categories of "future birth" or "forestalled life" if we locate a differential thanatopolitics and precariousness in the making of women as concurrent principle of life and principle of harm to life and in the differentials of their own corresponding exposure.

In the United States the intersection of reproductive politics with assessments of women's differential value were strongly marked when the Hyde amendment denied federal funding for abortion, while leaving poor women no less free, legally, than wealthy women to access it.[25] In the ruling's declaration of the state's interest in "life," one sees the differential grievability of the reproductive lives of the poor and the wealthy. An early essay by Wendy Brown discusses Justice Stewart's commentary on this point: "by subsidizing the medical expenses of indigent women who carry their pregnancies to term while not subsidizing the comparable expenses of women who undergo abortions . . . Congress has established incentives that make childbirth a more attractive alternative than abortion for persons eligible for Medicaid. These incentives bear a direct relationship to the legitimate congressional interest in protecting potential life").[26] In fact, congressional interest in "life" bifurcated the worth of women's reproductive rights claims and lives.

In what follows, I consider further the making of effects of "fetal precariousness" as a making of maternal precariousness. I will also identify this phenomenon in the very understanding of abortion as a moral decision. One more time, this will involve a consideration of a theorist's suspended reserves. Two further questions pursued in this chapter arise from, but push the edges of Butler's discussion. One concerns the differentials of mattering in maternal precariousness. Also we can ask if some forms of ethical life amount to modes of precariousness. A Nietzschean genealogy of morals (discussed by Butler) would be just one variant allowing an affirmative answer.

I will also add to the discussion two feminist responses to Butler who have ventured an analysis of the fetus in terms of precarious life. Again I respond with an argument proposing an expanded attention to the woman in these two accounts. Before turning to these, I first review some reasons the fetus will not, for Butler, be an obvious example of precariousness.

WOMEN'S REPRODUCTIVE LIFE AS PRECARIOUS

A fetus is a living organism, but Butler's remark that it could be considered precarious life (*FW* 16) comes with a caveat. For, in this broad sense, differentially grievable life would also include animal life, and all organisms "that are living in one sense or another" (*FW* 16), and "it does not suffice to say that since life is precarious, therefore it must be preserved" (*FW* 33).

Also because an important aspect of precariousness on which Butler focuses is the capacity of power, governmentality, and epistemological framing for *dehumanization*, the fetus is a less than ideal example (as is animal life, despite the challenge by those who note her adherence to a human/animal species divide).[27] Certainly a fetus can be grievable life, and an indication of the latter's differential value (for example, as Mills has argued, by virtue of race norms or norms of health or able-bodiedness). For some it is an important example of the ambiguously human (*FW* 7). But the fetus is not established with sufficient social subjectivation to be vulnerable to a significant *unmaking* or *de*subjectivation, the annulment or deconstitution of its historical or plausible subjectivation (*PL* 91).[28] Other candidates considered by Butler possess citizenship they might lose, identity papers, political status, rights such as habeas corpus or the rights governing prisoners of war. These interned, wounded, and attacked lives differentially serve to humanize other lives whose loss will register more strongly. Examples given in *Frames of War* include those interned at Guantánamo Bay or those bombed to "humanitarian" ends in Afghanistan.[29] The two aspects of this inflection are made clear:

> The question of who will be treated humanely presupposes that we have first settled the question of who does and does not count as a human. . . . The term and the practice of "civilization" work to produce the human differentially by offering a culturally limited norm for what the human is supposed to be. It is not just that some humans are treated as humans, and others are dehumanized; it is rather that dehumanization becomes the condition for the production of the human to the extent that a "Western" civilization defines itself over and against a population understood as, by definition, illegitimate, if not dubiously human.[30]
>
> (*PL* 91)

On this view the human is always undergoing its own making, and the conditions for this making have tended to include the apprehension of otherwise default human lives as *less* than human (*FW* 93, 125). Butler is not committed to the human as an essential or ontological category. Still, there is a redoubling of differential grievability or an additional level of apprehension establishing that we are in the presence of what could count as the strongly human, so that the alternative—apprehending those lives as less than human—is describable as deconstitution of those subjects.

IN THE CLINIC I: PRECARIOUSNESS AND FETAL LIFE

While, for all these reasons, Butler's references to the possibility of thinking the fetus as precarious life have been both brief and cautious, it has seemed more promising to Catherine Mills and Fiona Jenkins. As Jenkins characterizes the debate on which Butler's work has been brought to bear: "Mills has argued that we are wrong to discount the moral relevance of emotive arguments with respect to foetal life, particularly insofar as the relation to this form of life has been changed through ultrasound imaging."[31]

When Butler's language of vulnerability is brought to bear on the technologically rendered fetus, the vulnerability of women is not far from these discussions. But both Mills and Jenkins direct attention to the fetus as the precarious life on which one might concentrate renewed feminist attention. Butler's account of how "being human requires fulfilling a usually implicit set of normative criteria that more or less effectively regulate the process of humanization" would then "highlight[t] the way in which the fetus itself is vulnerable to those criteria of humanization."[32] (This would give a means, Mills suggests, of understanding prenatal genetic diagnosis, and associations of the human with genetic perfectionism.)[33]

Yet Mills's material need not lead us only to this conclusion—we can draw on it differently. Mills could also be seen as describing how the technologically mediated and epistemically conditioned fetal imaging creates the conditions of a mother's differential humanization and individuation. Certainly, as Mills is arguing, she may be understood to bear a "decisional responsibility." This should command analytic attention, not feminist disregard. But what if the very responsibility in question, a process for which we could adapt Foucault's use of the term *responsibilization* (HS I 105), is an interpellation understandable as the woman's precariousness—one we could consider theorizing in Butler's terms?

For none of these theorists is the fetus an intrinsically valuable form of life. To claim otherwise would be, according to Butler, Mills, and Jenkins, to deny the work of framing and the necessary ambiguity with respect to "the very use of life as if we know what it means, what it requires, what it demands." In fact, though, this particular remark is made by Butler in the context of a discussion that redirects us more specifically to the precarious life of the woman. The discussion occurs in the midst of a reflection on feminism as long having engaged with questions of life and death and with difficult questions such as "whose life is counted as a life? Whose prerogative is it to live? How do we decide when life begins and ends, and how do we think life against life? Under what conditions should life come into being, and through what means?"

Butler reroutes such dilemmas to the following questions asked by feminists: "Who cares for life as it emerges? Who tends for the life of the child? . . . Who cares for the life of the mother and of what value is it, ultimately?"[34] If we were to consider the framings of reproductive life, Butler's work could facilitate reflection on how both fetus and women are made and framed so that the very question of "the one" making a possible emotional call on "the other" could even be plausible.[35]

In *Futures of Reproduction* Mills describes some of the ways in which women come to bear appropriate forms of decisional responsibility, with choices to exercise *as* subjects with technologically mediated emotional responses. Under certain circumstances, some women are, in contexts of reproduction and of reproductive choice, made "moral."[36] So consider, in addition to its technological conditions, the "many other factors" mentioned when Mills describes the conditions for the woman's emotional response: the correlative vulnerability of the body of the woman, her interdependence with the fetus, the "decisional responsibility" she bears but must also have the "freedom to exercise," the fields of law and justice in which a pregnancy takes place. Despite the interest in revisiting the fetus, these comments acknowledge the hollowing out and stimulation of the woman's subjectivity, in these respects, and the processes through which she is humanized as reproductive decision maker.

Among the options for how to analyze this subjectivation *as* a "making" moral, we could turn to Butler's *Giving an Account of Oneself* for its exploration of the contingent and normative conditions of a plausibly or legibly ethical encounter. For normative confrontations have, in the second sense of normativity,[37] prior normative conditions. As Butler has proposed: "we must ask, however, whether the 'I' who must appropriate moral norms in a living way is not itself conditioned by norms, norms that establish the viability of the subject."[38] The many framings and makings of moral subjects[39] considered by Butler range from the seeming immediacy of the Levinasian address to the forms of responsibilized moral conscience open to Nietzschean critique.[40] We are invited to recall that neither the ethical subject nor the demand from the other is ever immediate or original. Instead we are asked to interrogate this encounter's conditions of possibility and the framing Butler generally associates with precarious life.

This suggests that the analytic force of Butler's reflections on precariousness could be differently deployed as a means of considering the contingent conducts of responsibilization produced by reproductive biopolitics. Processes of subjectivation should be understood in terms of their concurrent work of differentiating desubjectivation and deconstitution. The right question would be who in these circumstances might be best understood is deconstituted (unmade, rendered illegible) by the framing conditions of reproductive choice? There are a number of ways of answering this question. Butler is among those to have considered illegibilities of sexuality and kinship stimulated by reproduction's normalization. There are also versions of maternal, or potentially maternal, life whose deconstitution one can understand in terms of precariousness. (This is not to deny the ambiguity of embryonic life, also acknowledged by Butler in *Frames of War* and elsewhere).

IN THE CLINIC II (GIVING AN ACCOUNT OF ONESELF)

Describing changes in the regulation of abortion in late twentieth-century France, Dominique Memmi has described a concurrent transformation of modes of power linking the state, the local expert, the administrator, the individual, and the fetus. She first establishes the relationship between the abolition of the death penalty in 1977 and the effective legalization of abortion in France in 1975. Connecting these phenomena, Memmi suggests that we might understand these together as a relinquishing by the state of the strong hand it had long held on *bare life,* or on *zoe*:

> What dominated biopolitics until the nineteen-seventies was the valorization of "bare" life—*zoe*, to adopt the antinomy introduced by Giorgio Agamben, albeit to the detriment of a defined existence within these material conditions (*bios*). . . . The essential vocation of medical care was to save, conserve, if not bring into being bare life. Before the nineteen-seventies and nineteen-eighties, a fairly fixed hierarchy of values was in force: no abortion, no euthanasia, no public debate about them. The State, and health professionals made life, as an ultimate value, trump all

other considerations except when it came to those who threatened these values: for example criminals, and also abortionists. In short the State-as-interdictor had largely redoubled and perpetuated religious interdictions: a clearcut priority protected by a clearcut authority. But in the seventies, other values came to compete with "bare life's" dominance. That became clear with respect to procreation, as with death.[41]

Here, Memmi is not so much referring to human life *reduced* to bare life, but to human life in what she refers to as its minimal quality of being alive. But it becomes clear that (as emphasized by Butler, Khanna, Ziarek, and others) life is never mere life.[42] This is seen in its very political value as "mere life" and in the onus on those held responsible for it.

Prior to the legalization of abortion, Memmi argues, there had been little room for arguments that euthanasia or abortion might be "more" justified in certain circumstances. The *quality or type* of life of the subject who sought suicide or of the woman who sought abortion or of the state of advancement of a fetus was not in question. The value of life was not to be differentiated by its quality, it was (as Memmi characterizes this legal and policy regime) a brute value.

Where Foucault had differentiated the death penalty associated with sovereign power to take life from the forms of biopolitical power that, administering life, had an interest in maintaining bodies in life,[43] Memmi suggests that the sovereign claim to decision making about life had been seen in the death penalty and in the illegality of euthanasia and abortion.[44] All had been forms of state control *over* life (*la vie même*). Thus the aborting woman or the euthanizing or suiciding individual bore the status of challenging the state's sovereign power over life (we could include them with other criminals whose challenge to the sovereign is characterized by Foucault: "by breaking the law, the offender has touched the very person of the prince" (*DP* 49).[45] Thus the state power to take life (as in the death penalty) or to prohibit others from taking their own life (euthanasia, laws against suicide) or to prohibit women from aborting would all be instances of state control over life. Understood as such, Memmi argues that the following change has taken place since the 1970s: "The tendency is towards a loss by the State of its dominant grasp on bare life, and over the power to put to death, or to pardon. Meanwhile others—simple individuals—recuperate a part of this power over bare life."[46] Here

Memmi suggests we identify a phenomenon she calls "biopolitical delegation" to the individual: in the case of euthanasia and abortion, responsibility for decision making has been transferred from the state to the individual. In fact, it becomes a very different kind of decision making. Now its logic is not only that of the "phantom sovereign" but also biopolitical, given an overall rubric of general well-being and its appropriate conduct. The decision making transferred to women has taken the form of a new kind of responsibilization: for physiologically and psychologically healthy choices become a new kind of biopolitical obligation. Decision making is individuated in an interface with local experts in relation to new norms for responsible conduct.

In the context of legalized and usually state-funded abortion, a woman is invited to provide a legible narrative about her choice in consultation with a second party, a health counselor or medical professional. Perhaps it is a form of testimony to the fact that she has taken an organized and reflective decision and that the decision is her own. We need not see this as a delegation of a sovereign right directly to an individual right. Nor need we see this as a redirection of the *same* kind of right. Nor need we see the life once grasped by the state in its sovereign hold over life-death decision making, as the same as the life over which the woman is understood to have acquired new powers of decision. Instead one can identify a rerouting, a replacement, one that lends itself to Foucault's interest in strange forms of survival of the biopolitical in the sovereign (and the reverse). We can see it also as the coincidence of modes whose possibility also interested Foucault, the segmentation of their techniques, their capacity for penetration.

It is *as if*, argues Memmi, so far from exercising its rights over the woman, her pregnancy, and over life, the state has withdrawn its hand to the extent of *insisting* the woman now bear this responsibility. It is *as if* something is transferred from the state to the woman. The woman must not just decide (as those with reasonable access to health care may regularly do about any number of choices and medical interventions), she must more specifically be seen to decide and in a form a second party can recognize and bear witness to.[47]

Memmi draws our attention to the recent and long period in which women in France went to sometimes dangerous lengths to obtain illegal abortions. The final abolition of this legal regime involved not only the setting aside (a precarious setting aside, we'll recall Le Doeuff's rejoinder)[48] of abortion's illegality but also a concurrent, strange distribution of a phantom sovereign will and the requirement of a performed, self-reflexive selfhood. In consequence, Memmi deems more significant than might otherwise appear the often rote *presque rien* required by the woman as a presentation to the medical counselor:

> To make oneself temporarily or permanently sterile, to have a baby artificially, to have an abortion for a various reasons, to control after the fact a sexual encounter with the morning after pill: today individuals can do many things with their own procreative body. On one condition, always the same one: to present oneself before a health professional. What will that health professional ask of you? Seemingly, almost nothing. You will be asked to take a seat, and to talk about your condition, what you are asking for, and often, the reasons. In short, what has brought you there. The authority of Church and State have retreated in favor of a regulation reduced to "almost nothing": government by means of one's words [*par parole*]. With respect to medically assisted procreation, medically assisted termination of pregnancy, and termination of pregnancy on medical grounds, even if these interviews aren't required by law, they are required by medical protocols. . . .
>
> On the whole, it is only a matter of evoking a few of the common "good reasons," to produce, consensually, the argumentation on which patients and healthgivers can agree.
>
> But all of a sudden, the administration of reproduction has been delegated to the subjects directly concerned, through these practices, and their allies in this respect—the health professionals, under the protective wing of the State: here we find a true transformation of the administration of life [*du vivant*].[49]

Women may find themselves specially attached to the expected forms of subjectivity understood as responsible choice: integration, coherent explanation of motives, thought, reflective decision, display of these before a counselor or medical expert. It is not that every woman is expected to have the same kind of reaction to pregnancy, its termination, or its continuation (they are not normalized in that sense). Rather they are normalized in the Foucauldian sense: they enter contexts in which they are differentiated somewhere on a *range* of legible behavior concerning the norms and conventions of personal decision taking and its organized self-narratives.

I have earlier argued that the interest in a framed fetus be considered in terms of complex practices of subjectivation of "decision making." As technologies, these conducts of consultation can be added to the attention long directed by a number of feminist scholars (among them Petchesky, Duden, Haraway, Barad, Berlant, Mills) to the role of sonogram or ultrasound imaging in rendering a humanized fetus. There are a number of reasons (legal, economic, political, religious, historical, traditional) that some women are describable as the relays for, and as particularly open or vulnerable or *privileged* in relation to such contingent formations of moral life. They may be seen, and made, as decision makers, making specifically "significant" choices. So they may see themselves and be expected to see themselves. In addition to imaging techniques, we will add the various forms of consultation, the role of counselors, experts, friends, and family, and a number of questions (and self-questioning) directed at or by the woman. So we will see the production of fields of knowledge (social work, sociology, psychology), the protocol of medical regimes, and self-organizing behavior related to the procedural, economic, insurance, and similar regimes associated with accessing reproductive choice. Depending on the context, there will be tacit norms for conduct in relation to medical practitioners, counseling and consultation, and interaction with the dispensers of advice. Incited reflection and interrogation will integrate with practices of secrecy, privacy, anxiety, appeal, disclosure, judgment, or tact. These may be preconditions for the emergence of the woman as moral agent in relation to decisions about life. And, for some, reproduction has come to be associated with forms (rituals, conventions) of freedom.

The conduct of such decision making has come to be understood as paradoxical in a number of ways—among these, I have suggested the coincidence of disparate modes of power and their segmented techniques. Among other resources earlier mentioned, we can turn to the "cruel optimism" described by Lauren Berlant as a form of thanatopolitics. Here the agent embodies always already failed forms of responsibility (relating to health, diet, good choices—and, we can add, reproductive choices). Good choices become a social and biopolitical expectation of oneself and toward the social body. Depending on a number of factors and available options, such organized self-management is not equally plausible for all. Moreover it reflects the expectations of the conduct of a phantasmatic sovereign subject *all* have in some way already failed. Wendy Brown has spoken to forms of responsibilization-as-failure seen in the strange intersections of biopolitical care, the redirections of the sovereign state back to the individual, combined with the making of the individual as the similarly failed sovereign.[50] The insight of these theorists is not just that contemporary biopolitics simultaneously presuppose the responsible conduct of phantom sovereign subjects. Such "responsibilizing" is also a dividing practice according to which some are produced as particularly "failed" subjects: manifesting irresponsible, unhealthy, repeating negative behavior, incoherent, less than optimal with respect to their care of themselves and others.

To explore this further, I turn to two contexts for the making of responsibility in abortion decision making, one taking place within the clinic and the other outside it. The first allows a reconsideration of technologies concurrently making ambiguous embryonic and the conduct and subjectivities of the "decision makers." These, I have suggested, include not just the more easily identifiable technologies such as the sonogram, but the conduct of consultation. Here we will find a number of ways of thinking vulnerability, for these technologies produce categories of illegibility both within the clinic and well outside its space. A reconsideration of Carol Gilligan's now classic *In a Different Voice* produces some instances of the former.[51]

IN THE INTERVIEW: GIVING AN ACCOUNT OF ONESELF II

In *In a Different Voice* Gilligan reassessed hierarchical evaluations of moral thought, according to which universalizable, impartial, objective, and abstract reasoning would be considered (as in American psychologist Lawrence Kohlberg's influential account) the more advanced form of moral reasoning. Interested in exploring the role of gender difference in moral thought and in its tacit comparative assessment, Gilligan devised studies involving a number of different groups: including a group of men and women participating in a university course on moral philosophy and a group of twenty-nine women confronted with abortion choices in the United States.[52] If there were divergences between men and women in moral reasoning and in differently valuable forms of moral thought,[53] Gilligan challenged the supposition that a relational, context-specific, and empathic approach, oriented toward the sustaining of relationships, must be deemed more rudimentary and inferior to a more principle based moral reasoning.[54]

Gilligan does not hesitate to situate abortion within the moral register, one to which women would bring what she famously described as a different voice. Beyond noting that the "dilemma of choice enters a central arena of women's lives" only when "birth control and abortion provide women with effective means for controlling their fertility" (*DV* 70), there was little room in the project to think about the contingency through which modern abortion has come to appear so intuitively as a moral issue. She gave no room to the differential and circumstantial ways in which it is framed as such, nor to the role played by differences of culture, wealth, age, religion, nation, citizenship. Nor was there room to interrogate the conduct, modes, and conditions of this emergence, nor the role of family, peers, school, religious, and other types of counselors, nor the stimulating dyadic conduct of consultation, nor the making of the "psychic" space of introspective reflection, nor the role of the architecture and spatial distribution within clinical and consultation spaces, nor the role of media, technology, or other techniques of visualization. There was no room to think about the microfactors at work, including stimulation by the subtle expectations of questions, the invitation to organize experience in terms of motives, and the tacit supposition that those interviewed had reasons, desires, and wishes, sometimes of an obscure form that might become clearer over time. One thinks of the possible mismatch between the relatively articulate eighteen year old whose "I really didn't think anything except that I didn't want it" would be greeted with *Why was that?* "There is no right decision." (*Why?*) "I didn't want it" (*DV* 73). Women who might well answer the question *How would you describe yourself to yourself?* "I don't know" (*DV* 33).

Gilligan's challenge to the hierarchy between principle-governed, universalizable abstract reasoning and empathic, relational moral thought is well-known. Yet in its representation of the relational forms of responsibility attributed to some of the women, some feminist critics, among them Joan Tronto,[55] have noted that a different kind of progressive register seemed to be reestablished. Of course, the project's aim was to observe such expressions, the language in which they were expressed, and the forms of moral thought they manifested. Gilligan noted that the language of responsibility tended to emerge as a primary concern and to undergo a number of transformations. The women were interviewed, sometimes multiply, most of them before and after an abortion. Gilligan described a number of transitions from an initial reaction that was often deemed to be "center[ed] on the self. The concern is pragmatic and the issue is survival. The woman focuses on taking care of herself because she feels that she is all alone" (*DV* 74). But, often, in a "transition that follows this position, the concepts of selfishness and responsibility first appear" (*DV* 75). Self-interest has "so far formed the based of judgment," but, suggested Gilligan, it might come to be redefined by the woman. "As the criterion for judgment shifts, the dilemma assumes a moral dimension, and the conflict between wish and necessity is cast as a disparity between 'would' and 'should'" (*DV* 77). Of one woman, Gilligan says: "the abortion decision becomes for her an opportunity for the adult exercise of responsible choice. . . . In [an] epiphany of . . . cognitive reconstruction" (*DV* 76). The woman struggles with the expectations of others, the desire not to hurt others, and the concern that her choices may be selfish or perceived as selfish. In another transitional phase, the woman may begin to "scrutinize the logic of self-sacrifice" (*DV* 82) and to find a means "to be responsible to herself as well as to others and thus to reconcile the disparity between hurt and care. The exercise of such responsibility requires a new kind of judgment, whose first demand is for honesty. To be responsible for oneself, it is first necessary to acknowledge what one is doing. The criterion for judgment thus shifts from goodness to truth" (*DV* 81–82).

For example, one woman is said to have realized that continuing her pregnancy had been a means of punishing her husband, another realized she had been doing so largely for the benefit of her parents. Gilligan also describes some women suspended in such phases, trapped in contradictions, unable to separate their own voice from that of others, unable to scrutinize their own attitudes, perhaps unable to make any decision (*DV* 82, 85). (Gilligan draws attention to the important role of counseling situations in giving a woman the opportunity for lucidity, for example, about the possibility that one's pregnancy may be overdetermined by the wish to please.)

But while room was given to the gender differences inclining some women toward the languages of responsibility and anxiety about selfishness, there was no room for thinking about the context, conduct, and technologies through which abortion and pregnancy in particular become attached to special and conventional expectations of responsible behavior and decision making attributed to a moral register. Nor was there room to think about how even the form of the interviews was participating in the process and conditions to which they bore witness. (This is a banal remark to make about interview situations, and all situations of observation, but not inappropriate here.) The project's intent may have been characterization, not stimulation of the forms of moral thinking of the women in question. But, looking back at the interviews, it is hard not to see the questions framing and contributing to the production of the appropriately introspective subject—counseling and interviewing mildly blurs in the study. (It may be recalled that some women had been referred by the clinic in hopes that the study's interviews might serve the function of further counseling.)

We see the *ways* abortion gets framed as a moral issue (dyadic discussion supposing organized selves, deep motives, and a confrontation with dilemma) in the supposition that this is an apt moment for the reflective questions posed. No doubt some of the women manifested progressive stages of moral thought, as described. Yet the temporally sequential interviews prompt the possibility of a new answer to the question: *How would you describe yourself to yourself?* A revision to *I don't know* is invited by the situation. If this is plausible, it is also because of many factors hollowing out the introspective self as reflective, transitional, progressive (or as a failure thereof)—in relation to abortion's framing as moral dilemma. These include the conduct of peers, family, doctors, teachers, fictional or cinematic depictions of abortion. Gilligan observes: "the abortion decision *comes to be seen* as a 'serious' choice affecting both self and others" (my emphasis). But the women are being prompted for "seriousness." "This is a life that I have taken, a conscious decision to terminate, and that is just very heavy, a very heavy thing" (*DV* 94) says a woman . . . before an interviewer whose questions (presented at the time she is considering an abortion) have included: *is "acting morally . . . acting according to what is best for the self or . . . a matter of self-sacrifice?"* (*DV* 84). Practices of counseling and related conventions in such contexts can work very similarly to sonograms.

Among the illegibility produced, we lose sight of the role played in psychic and moral life by incoherent wishes and desires and an absence of answers to questions about who we are and how we understand ourselves. The study renders some voices less successfully transitional, less coherently narrativizing, paralyzed, self-contradictory, if not verging on "moral nihilism." Think of the woman who has vaguely rejected the option that she might "sell" the baby "in a black market kind of thing" (*DV* 78). She is included in the pages of *In a Different Voice,* but we see the production of illegibility when Gilligan suddenly breaks the frame of *In a Different Voice,* assuming a more hermeneutic role on the woman's behalf. As if merely characterizing the interviewee's voice is suddenly intolerable, Gilligan's own voice intervenes, translating the woman's vague irresoluteness into deeper, more explicable (and coherent) motives and feelings as follows: "It is not surprising that she considers selling her child, since she feels herself to have, in effect, been sold by her parents" (*DV* 78). A production of surpluses of illegibility might then be seen in Ronald Dworkin's subsequent characterization of the women facing abortion decisions in Gilligan's study: "each was trying, above all, to take the measure of her responsibility for the intrinsic value of her *own* life . . . to see the decisions about whether to cut off a new life as part of a larger challenge to show respect for all life by living well and responsibly herself."[56] A modest variant of the same production of conditions of illegibility is seen in Gilligan's commentary that *Roe* allows a woman to legally "speak for herself" and assume the complex "responsibility for life and for death" (*DV* ix).

One of the poems about abortion discussed in Barbara Johnson's "Apostrophe, Animation, and Abortion," Gwendolyn Brooks's "The Mother," includes the eloquent line "Believe that even in my deliberateness I was not deliberate,"[57] to which Johnson adds the following commentary: "I have not chosen the conditions under which I must choose." Perhaps we can add to Johnson's reading in several ways. In an essay offering a complex elaboration of the subjectivities arising with decisions about, and experiences of, abortion, Johnson makes a case for the recognition of an emotional life that may include guilt or grief. It is not uncommon for feminist reconsiderations of abortion to characterize (other) feminist readings as having more typically failed to register or give proper account to such affect:[58] "Readers of Brooks' poem have often read it as an argument against abortion. . . . . But to see it as making a simple case for the embryo's right to life is to assume that a woman who has chosen abortion does not have the right to mourn. It is to assume that no case for abortion can take the woman's feelings of guilt and loss into consideration, that to take those feelings into account is to deny the right to choose the act that produced them."[59]

To this reading we can add that the very complexity of emotional life attributed to women's lives of reproductive choice, whether those associated with the "moral philosophers" or those of the "poets" (with the poets often being, of course, very good moral philosophers), plays its role in the normalization of some kinds of women's subjectivity in relation to reproductive choice. We are rightly invited to recognize complexity here, but complexity of emotional life in this domain also participates in a normative register: it, too, is stimulated and stimulating. It too participates in a hollowing out of psychic depth, involving the exploration of the likely presence of conflict and mixed feelings which are both widely expected (to think of one sense of normativity) and whose gradations also offer a means of differentiating and including the presence of all reactions ranging from "normal" to "abnormal" (to return to the Foucauldian sense of normativity). Without minimizing this complexity, or the difficulty of its articulation, we can recognize that nothing has come to seem more appropriate than a woman writing a complex, even a very good poem about selfhood and the ambiguity of address in some contexts of contemporary abortion.

So to return to Johnson's commentary on Brooks's "Believe that even in my deliberateness I was not deliberate": "I have not chosen the conditions under which I must choose." Some will find themselves in circumstances in which they are particularly solicited and self-prompt for "deep" forms of reflective subjectivity (musing, self-interpretive, motive oriented, the recognition of fraught and contradictory desires). But, of course, women are not just placed in these circumstances (legal, social, and historical), nor are they just passively worked on by conventions (for introspection, for emotional response, humanization, for a psychic life of complexity and contradiction in relation to certain issues, for responsibility). Women become relays just as much as they are targets or recipients of the norms of choice.

Thinking with the resources of Butler and Foucault, I have begun with two points. First, these are contexts in which normalized and normalizing forms of responsibilization are stimulated and transferred. For her part, Butler offers an argument in *Giving an Account* for a critical approach to the ethical: this would include an analysis of the normative conditions through which subjects are made *as* normative (for example, as ethical subjects). The many contexts appropriate for this kind of redoubled analysis could well include, I have argued, the modern contexts in which fetuses appear. But this is because the appearance of the "fetus" *is* the conjoined appearance of modern subjects as reproductive "decision makers." To see this as a context of precarious life is to see a process through which some (modern "decision makers") will be centered as fully human while stimulating categories of illegibility (those making other kinds of decisions or those for whom reproduction cannot be a matter of decision or indeed those who may refuse to take decisions). And, to the forms of unintelligibility mentioned so far (those who become illegible within the clinic), we must add a number of subjectivities, social and political life, priorities, and forms of commerce and choice positioned as exterior to the clinic, sometimes deprioritized by the latter's subjects.[60]

BARE LIFE

Also in conversation with Butler, Fiona Jenkins has criticized feminist approaches that excessively emphasize the "bare materiality" of the fetal body to the point that the fetal body "become[s] somehow invisible where abortion is a right."[61] A pro-abortion politics could, she claims, allow for a recognition of the ambiguity of the fetus's materiality as opposed to seeing the fetus as "nothing more than matter." Feminism can afford, she argues, to register the anomalous and ambiguous status of embryonic life and recognize that it can be a source of "affective dissonance and ethical trouble" without this amounting to the thesis of its "innate or individual human dignity."[62] With this suggestion to hand, let's return to the clinics described by Memmi. These are spaces in which the malleability of the modern fetus is inseparable from the modern conduct of decision making. In a context institutionally supportive of reproductive choice and access to abortion, Memmi depicts the multiple technologies making the fetus ontologically flexible (*making* it as makeable) in accordance with women's choices. Her account illustrates how conduct accomplishes a context of sensitive recognition of ambiguity, in a tacit upholding of the potential parent's right to this very ambiguity. It is among the signature aspects of modern reproductive choice. Again this means that the choosing agent is no more unframed than is fetal life. Similarly the biological waste or "mere biology" to which a fetus can seemingly be returned is not natural. It too is a category made by protocol producing its ambiguity of status as significant to contemporary registers of freedom and choice.

I am proposing the term *ontological tact* to characterize medical and social protocols and conduct accessed in a number of contemporary clinics.[63] Ideally, a consensual making and unmaking of the fetus takes place between women or parents and health professionals in conformity with the woman's or the parents' choices. This means that it may be as important to respect and support a fetus's lack of human, moral, or anticipatory significance as it can be important to join in the anticipatory attribution of its significance for those hoping for their pregnancies—with all the accompanying conduct, interface with technology, and affective exchanges with family and health professionals.

Similarly, the sadness of a hoped for pregnancy which results in miscarriage will be the context for a number of ambiguous overlapping modes, makings, and perceptions. The mother or parents may desire to get rid of a dead fetus as soon as possible, to avoid sight and reference, to see the fetus as mere matter with no relationship to an anticipated future, and medical protocol can support that perception. But in some cases it may be just as important to consider the embryo not as biological waste but as a regretted or deceased or forestalled humanity, perhaps mournable. In such a case, notes Memmi, the tactful medical expert might well expect to humanize the fetus, to remove it with a different ceremony, in a "slower" temporality, perhaps allowing for questions such as preferred means of disposal of the remains.[64] There may also be either slow or rapid transitions between these modes, between different "lives" of the fetus, between shared perceptions of pregnancy, of fetal life, grieved potential life, or matter. Differential conduct, legal regimes, economic conditions, medicalization, and the conduct of care play their role in the availability of "tactful protocol": the range of malleable possibilities for a fetus to appear as biological waste or as life anticipated or regretted.[65]

But this form of attentive nuance in the making of the fetus (at least in this form) is more available to women in some kinds of medical, legal, and economic circumstances. For this reason, the very possibility of such flexible protocols, the very tact in question, is part of the making of some women as human and the deconstituting of others by contrast (as when it is assumed that others belong to contexts not offering or participating in such consensual relationships and makings). Only some women can access these forms of clinically inflected ontological tact and the related malleability, etiquette, attentiveness, mindfulness, and nuanced conduct from health care and associated contexts. This is both an economic and procedural divide and also a perceptual divide. It is not to question the importance of this tact with respect to fetal ambiguity to recognize that this very possibility also plays its role in a kind of reproductive exceptionalism. It may be tacitly supposed as the right or the protocol expected of some nations, health systems, or economic classes of women or of those able to access an approach considered enlightened—and not a right or possibility attributed to others. It certainly can divide populations of women in terms of economic privilege. But while accessing this ontological tact can be an emblem of privilege, this is not to say that easier access to abortion is a consistent indicator of privilege. Freedom from imposed abortion, from differential promotion of abortion, and the freedom not to be coercively sterilized have also been among the major reproductive rights claims of many groups of women. A prior, differential biopoliticization of women as principle of life (or death) for populations will often be determining of such variations in policy, and the latter will also stimulate the former.

There are, then, broad reasons to conclude that the fetus's ambiguous status as "more" or "less" human, as grievable, disposable, waste, anticipated or desired, also distributes the precariousness of the woman. Since a woman can only have the experience on which Mills reflects (responding to 3-D uterine images as to the "call" and the "face" or interacting with a technologically and "decision oriented" fetus) by virtue of mutable legal and medical regimes, the analysis also enfolds the conditions (geographical, economic, political) which differentially place some women in clinics at all and leave others well outside them. The contingencies and normativities relevant here relate also to the conditions under which women's decisions can be taken *as* decisions. Modern responsibility takes place in a context of regimes and techniques ensuring the ontological flexibility of a fetus. Yet even this flexibility, I have suggested, amounts to a principle of division.

I have so far considered unmaking in the "clinic": the context in which some women have come to be understood as appropriately deciding agents with respect to reproductive life, while others will emerge as particularly aberrant or failed decision makers. But Jenkins's exploration of framed fetal grievability also invites us to think about fetal ambiguity, and its differential grievability, as this emerges outside the clinic. The variant discussed by Memmi (where fetal ambiguity becomes associated with advanced conducts of choice in the clinic) can be juxtaposed with a variant considered by Jenkins. It reminds of how the ambiguity of the fetus may be differently confronted outside the clinic, but in an encounter that should not be understood as less mediated or more biologically real. Again it emerges only as enmeshed in its framing conditions. It entails dangers, anxieties, complex financing, legal, medical, and criminal conducts, subjectivations and desubjectivations. Here the problem it may present of disposal and disposability demarcates some as particularly exposed to the associated regimes of punishment, affordability, the necessary networks of connections and confidences, calculations of the thresholds of time, trust, and risk. These can be seen as the framing conditions of the disposability—not just of fetuses, but in conjunction, the differential grievability and precarious life of women. Even where legal, in most countries, and for most women, access to reproductive services, technologies, and options will be determined by matters of wealth, education, religion, age, immigration status, connections, networks, and practical and/or financial mobility. Such differentials, like the revocability of their legal regimes, render potentially pregnant women precarious life: practically, subjectively, institutionally, legally, economically, and to regimes of greater or lesser concern about the harm or death to which some women are exposed by regimes with interests in reproduction.

Individualization in terms of the alternatives of responsibility and inappropriate conduct is also an effect for those whose reproductive choices must take place "outside the clinic" particularly where this involves recourse to illegal abortion. In turn, to be made a subject "outside the clinic" (in this sense) stimulates new division of legibility and illegibility. This is to add to feminist analyses of the "made fetus" discussed through the lens of Butler's work, a further exploration of the associable forms and relays of "made responsibility" (in all their concurrent inclusions and exclusions) manifesting in Cristian Mungiu's *4 Months, 3 Weeks, and 2 Days* (2007), as interpreted by Jenkins.

OUTSIDE THE CLINIC: PRECARIOUSNESS AND THE FETUS

4 Months is set in the Romania of the Ceauşescu regime, when abortion was inaccessible to most except through the illegal and dangerous measures that proved deadly to women in the thousands. Jenkins's discussion directs our attention to a scene in which a woman confronts a fetus lying on a hotel bathroom floor following her mid-term abortion. Gabriela, her friend Otilia, and the abortionist, Mr. Bebe, face the possibility of arrest and long imprisonment. Yet Gabriela jeopardizes her own and Otilia's safety by asking her friend to disregard the abortionist's detailed instructions for how to dispose of the fetus with the least risk of detection. Instead, the fetus seems to make some kind of call, prompting Gabriela's response that it ought to be buried.

These are complex stories of response, responsiveness, responsibility, and impingement in illegal medical procedures. So it matters that Gabriela is herself presenting a hapless helplessness. She is an irresponsible agent according to the limited options for appropriate decision making and covert reproductive choice under these circumstances. She is dangerously deceptive about the advanced state of the pregnancy, vague on the details she ought to have followed in setting up the abortion, vague about the money, not managing to ensure the detailed planning, not clear to her friend about the instructions, nor about the fact that she hasn't followed them. She presents a passivity to which her friend's hypercapability, in turn, seems particularly vulnerable. We find the latter compensating, organizing the money and many of the details, exposed in consequence to sex extorted by the abortionist as his condition for proceeding with the unexpectedly late-term abortion. Where Gabriela is dangerously vulnerable to the (framed) call that the fetus ought to be buried,[66] in these interconnected networks of illegality Otilia is also vulnerable. Not just her rape but her mission to dispose of the fetus, carrying it at great distance through remote urban areas late at night, are scenes reminding that the risks, exposures, and productions of subjectivity also may include a woman's concerted responsiveness under these circumstances.

So we can think differently about some of the framed modes of responsibilization of the women. We are confronted with the complex making of the conditions of their ethical life and of their differential vulnerability at the point where Jenkins is proposing an understanding of the fetus as framed and precarious: "Gabriela's response seems to suggest that to the extent that the foetus looks like a human infant it also addresses us with a human claim, the minimal claim, if not to subjectivity, then at least to having died, a condition that demands a burial rather than sheer disposal."[67]

I am suggesting an alternative in focus to the view that the mother responds to the (technologically and/or discursively framed and produced) face or ethical call of the fetus or that (according to another tradition) she is more like a hostage to the fetus.[68] Rather she might be seen as vulnerable to the stimulations of responsibilization.[69] This would also be to draw differently on the resources available in Butler's consideration of ethical formations. We would turn instead to Butler's account of the "'I' who must appropriate moral norms in a living way," and who, as such, is understood as "conditioned by norms, norms that establish the viability of the subject."[70]

This account can help keep our focus on the conditions and norms through which it might become possible for the woman (thinking of the arguments considered in this chapter) to be "called" by a fetus in a register framed as ethical. Insofar as Butler proposes (though not in a discussion of this phenomenon) a critical and paradoxical relationship to the moral register,[71] we would be invited to analyze "not the relation that a subject has to morality, but a prior relation: the force of morality in the production of the subject." In a commentary on Adorno she emphasizes, "one cannot will away this paradoxical condition for moral deliberation."[72] The phenomena described by Mills and Jenkins include the productions and relays of responsibilized subjects. The approach specific to Butler might ask us to attend to these in their genealogy, their framing conditions, the contingency of their social norms, the ways in which precariousness is both presupposed and produced in such contexts, the microdetail and the retroactive effects of such moral making. In this encounter between their resources, Butler's capacity for a critical genealogy of morals would encounter Mills's and Jenkins's stronger interest in the fetus: the result would be a reoriented means of thinking precariousness that reroutes from the arguments of all three.

An understanding of some subjects as precarious (in an establishment of the conditions for their humanization and dehumanization), specifically as they are made (in relation to certain contingent problems) as moral—and of the conditions and effects of this phenomenon—is important to feminist genealogies of the politicization and responsibilization of women in regimes of reproductive choice and also of its illegality. In other words, a critical approach to ethics available in *Giving an Account* could allow attention to the conditions of possibility of subjectification in moral choice and its concurrent function as a dividing practice.[73] It would allow analysis of the retroactive institution of some subjects confronted by reproduction made moral. This register is also a practice of division—of populations, peoples, groups, and subjects—such that some are not expected to fit modern narratives of reproductive choice.

ILLEGIBILITIES, ILLEGITIMACIES

Feminists, queer theorists, critical race theorists, and others have argued that reproductive rights may be among those rights we "cannot not want,"[74] even if they also circulate heteronormativity and progressive exceptionalism. When promoted as a general good, they can obscure race, class, and wealth differentials of access and priorities.[75] The supposition that all women's reproductive rights concern, primarily, contraception access and abortion can obscure the different priorities of some: such as the right not to be forcibly sterilized or the parenting rights of gay couples.[76]

As I have argued, the modern, individualizing images of women who make reproductive choices need to be placed in a broad context of regimes of a) women whose reproductive choices count for little; b) women whose reproduction is not legible as "choice" but as failure, of coherence, attention, responsibility, or of the will (as in depictions of "excessive" pregnancy, sometimes associated with poverty or teenage pregnancy),[77] and those who, in a register of choice, seem to make inadequate or inhuman choices; and c) the many women unable to access the reproductive rights that in some cases technically belong to them. To these we have also added the groups of d) the many who are unable to access the reproductive rights that do belong to others, so that reproductive rights in this sense also become principles of inclusion/exclusion, and e) those whose different priorities also manifest as obscurely indifferent to reproductive legibility.

This has been to argue for an intertwined analysis drawing on at least seven malleabilities. First, the malleability between the potentially reproductive woman as politicized, as biopoliticized, and as thanatopoliticized. Second, the malleability of reproduced life (for example, anticipated individual life or statistical contribution to collective life; "quickening" or "fetus"; the problem of soul, law, or choice; 2-D or 3-D imaging; distinctions between fetus or waste, underreproduction or overreproduction). Third, the malleability between the woman perceived as having a faculty of sovereign decision making, a capacity for collective biopolitical impact or as responsible for the corresponding lives and deaths. Fourth, the malleability of the law, its inverted states of exception and their chronic revocability. Fifth, I have mentioned the malleability of the techniques and segmentation of modes of power. This can intersect with the multivalence of the relevant subjects, objects, and practices. For example, vagaries in ease of access to abortion can reflect and stimulate differential human worth; it can produce the terms through which some decision makers (or those who don't, won't, or can't decide) will take on a status as less than human. Another factor reinforcing these associations is the making of reproduction as a mode of neoliberal choice, personal project, or investment in human capital. Sixth, as I suggested in chapter 4, reproduction has been associated with malleability in one's relationship to citizenship and political status. Capacity for reproduction as principle of life is a factor of concurrent inclusion in *and* exclusion from political domains as is its thanatopolitical variant (reproduction as principle of death). Seventh, I have also emphasized the malleability of the philosophical resources deployed in this project. The mobilization of a number of reserves and suspensions has been operative in this reconsideration of the biopolitics and thanatopolitics of reproduction.

FOUCAULT, POWER, AND ABORTION

One of Foucault's best-known contributions to theories of power was seen in his proposal that one will sometimes need to forgo the supposition that one group is disempowered as a means to another's empowerment. Sometimes one might more usefully ask what has been problematized (and under what conditions) such that both groups have become legible opponents in this regard, thereby sharing more common ground than may be perceived. In certain cases (and biopolitical conditions are exemplary of these) strategies of power are complex and unpredictable, involving productivities, stimulations, unexpected by-products, and complex capillary networks for which we need new forms of analysis.[78] Foucault famously claimed that power might stimulate forms of resistance, which would not therefore be in a position of exteriority with respect to power (*HS I* 95), and that such struggles would be indefinite. Such forms of resistance were least interestingly described as adversarial: "For every move by one adversary, there is an answering one by the other."[79] In interviews brief mention was made, in such terms, to resistance and counterattack by workers responding to techniques of surveillance,[80] to Oscar Wilde and Gide,[81] to the formation of the "lesbian movement."[82] He provided a similar characterization of the emergence of feminism:

> For a long time they tried to pin women to their sexuality. They were told for centuries: "You are nothing other than your sex." And this sex, doctors added, is fragile, almost always sick, and always inducing sickness.... Towards the end of the eighteenth century, this very ancient movement quickened and ended up as the pathologization of woman: the female body became the medical object par excellence.... But the feminist movements have accepted this challenge. Are we sex

by nature? Well then, let it be, but in its singularity, in its irreducible specificity. Let us draw the consequences from it and reinvent our own type of political, cultural, and economic existence. . . . Always the same movement: take off from this sexuality in which movements can be colonized, go beyond them in order to reach other affirmations.[83]

And it was amidst such reflections that Foucault took a moment to consider the politics of abortion:

As always with relations of power, one is faced with complex phenomena. . . . Mastery and awareness of one's own body can be acquired only through the effect of an investment of power in the body: gymnastics, exercises, muscle-building, nudism, glorification of the body beautiful. All of this belongs to the pathway leading to the desire of one's own body, by way of the insistent, persistent, meticulous work of power on the bodies of children or soldiers, the healthy bodies. But once power produces this effect, there inevitably emerge the responding claims and affirmations, those of one's own body against power, of health against the economic system, of pleasure against the moral norms of sexuality, marriage, decency. Suddenly, what had made power strong is used to attack it. Power, after investing itself in the body, finds itself exposed in that same body. Do you recall the panic of the institutions of the social body, the doctors and politicians, at the idea of defacto couples [*l' union libre*] or abortion? But the impression that power vacillates here is in fact mistaken; power can retreat here, shift ground, invest itself elsewhere . . . and so the battle continues.[84]

Foucault had offered an elegant argument that such resistance did not arise from a position outside what was resisted. Adversaries shared the terrain whose politics and stakes both presupposed. Yet Foucault left room for further intensifying the complexity with which such relations of power could be analyzed. For one thing, the passage seems to suppose the possibility of identifying the adversaries, if not their opposed interests. But what if we added some of the most recent battles to have emerged in the arena of reproductive rights, such as rights concerning surrogacy arrangements and the dilemmas to which they have given rise? The latter have included new variations for abortion politics, as when those paying for a surrogate pregnancy have sought abortions. The politics of surrogacy have been uncertainly parsed (as more or less exploitative) as gifting or as commercial arrangements, as more or as less regulated by the state, and as permissable or illegal. The politics of differential access will play a role: as with the politics of inclusion/exclusion seen when gay couples are sometimes denied access to surrogacy arrangements legally accessible in some states or nations by heterosexual couples. How are their reproductive rights to be understood in these and other contexts? If they include surrogacy, do they also include surrogate abortion? The politics of surrogacy will be complicated by economic differentials, given that some nations makes less expensive surrogacy options available to citizens from wealthier nations. The differential value of pregnancies will be seen in the lesser value of the pregnancy accompanied by medical problems. It may begin to seem unsatisfactory to see the adversaries of abortion politics as bearing calculably opposed interests. Foucauldian resources will, however, allow us to intensify our understanding of such complexity. So let's turn, not to the cases that have been reported with a largely unanimous abhorrence,[85] but to variants where the question of who has become whose adversary is harder to determine—as is an appropriate language of reproductive rights.

Recent instances of the conditional circumstances through which gay marriage rights have been granted have seen the denial of equal adoption rights or access to assisted reproduction technologies legally available to heterosexual couples. Thus there has been considerable confusion between gay marriage and debate about the fate of the "children."[86] But (returning for a moment to that language) to see gay reproductive rights as counterattacks and countereffects will not do justice to the complexity of power to which Foucault himself refers—particularly in developing his reflections on biopolitics. Let's consider a complicated case of the politics of reproductive technologies,[87] depicted in Zippi Brand Frank's 2009 documentary *Google Baby*.

Two gay men living in Israel seek a surrogate to bear a child for them. An entrepreneur, who explains that most "would like to have a Caucasian donor," facilitates a form of international commerce now commonly accessed in countries where commercial surrogate arrangements are legal: such as the United States, India, the Ukraine, and Thailand. The couple's sperm is transported to North America to fertilize the eggs of a commercially contracted white American donor. The resulting zygotes are transported to India, where cheaper commercial surrogacy is available. The arrangement is only viable because an Israeli passport for the resulting baby will (in a departure from the policies of a number of other nations) be issued by the Israeli government. Yet this reflects neither the vigor of their national pro-natalism nor a progressive political affirmation of the diversities of kinship nor of gay rights. For surrogacy contracts, although legal in Israel, have been regulated by the state and restricted to heterosexual couples. Willingness to issue such passports divides countries such as Israel and Australia from others such as Germany and France (where surrogacy is illegal *and* passports are also not issued for children born overseas to foreign surrogates).[88]

Adding to the complications, the Israeli couple will gain financially from choosing over a U.S. surrogate for the pregnancy a surrogate based in India. This is most easily understood as the latter's economic subordination. But the payment, amounting to a "lot of money" for the Indian surrogate mother, will buy a simple house,[89] whereas the going fee in the United States (for a U.S.-based surrogate in the context of most North American real estate forms and economies) would not.

Then one would want to factor the conditions set by the surrogacy clinic for the surrogate's participation: both physiological (she must already have had an unproblematic pregnancy) and psychological. Again we will find the requirement of performance before a witness of psychic motives and norms for a responsible decision, also understandable as contributing to the carving out of new forms of psychic space. The clinic's director explains: "the women need to have a *strong desire* to improve and upgrade their lives." How should we understand the interest in this question and in a surrogate's subjectivity being configured in this particular way? Why must their desire be "strong," why must it concern a desire for improvement and life "upgrade"? What kinds of psychic lives and motivations would present as *less* appropriate to or legible as an optimal surrogacy?

Moreover, the interests at work in the requirement to desire an "improved" and "upgraded" life are complicated. In one case, a common answer—the desire to buy a house—is provided by the husband by the side of the woman who is being interviewed as a possible surrogate. Later we are confronted with a husband's declaration, about his wife's work as a surrogate, that "women are good for very little." But some women are financing the purchase of houses by this means. This will also impact their economic relationships with their husbands and families in unpredictable ways. Another uncertainty concerns their health and their risks: the American egg donor talks about her fears of cancer from the hormone stimulation. The Indian surrogate, reminded that she could die in childbirth, is informed that, if so, neither the couple nor the clinic will bear responsibility.

In a special deal, offered by the clinic, embryos will be implanted in two surrogates to maximize the chances of successful pregnancy. One of the prospective fathers makes a nervous joke (or is it a plan?), as he realizes the risk, that one or both pregnancies might lead to twins. We hear one father on the phone as the couple considers the offer: "OK you will have four children. So we'll do a selective abortion. (*Laughter.*) That was good..."

"We would do a reduction," reassures the entrepreneur, seriously.

And so they could and may (*can we calculate*?). But they may also find—as embryo transforms into anticipated life or back to possible disposability—that this is not (or else it is)—so lightly done.

The surrogates are among the cheapest, globally: is their status mere disposable life? For whose ends? Is the husband really making the decision to "send his wife to work," is she entirely subordinate, or might he also be nostalgically performing the rhetoric and gesture of a sovereign patriarchal power, given that this is being reconfigured by a number of forces in play? And, true, the Israeli couple and entrepreneur are, comparatively, economically privileged, and they stand to save and make money from this arrangement. Yet the entrepreneur seems hesitant to mention the couple's homosexuality when told the clinic will "only accept genuine cases for surrogacy":

"What do you mean genuine?"
"Genuine cases mean that medically it should be genuinely indicated."
"OK."

User's guides to international commercial surrogacy in India have distinguished between clinics understood to be gay friendly and those that are not. As of January 2013, restrictions in India on visas to gay couples—and single individuals—seeking these surrogacy arrangements were introduced.

The reference to genuine medical cases comes from the clinic's director, and she is a complicated figure: careful in warning the surrogates of their death risks (yet differently careful in warning the clinic bears no financial liability). Naming herself a feminist, telling a husband that she would like the purchased house to be in his wife's name alone. And to another she will say—but, who knows, perhaps she is referring to the gay male parents (*can we calculate*)?—"one woman helping another woman. She cannot have a child [for] which she longs, which you are going to give, and you cannot have a house. You cannot educate your son beyond school. For that, they are going to pay." And, in relation to his hopes for such a son, the surrogate's husband will say, later (*can we calculate?*): "How will I make his future and pay his fees? I will have to send her to be a surrogate again. I will do whatever it takes to make him an army officer. And if not I will send him into the police force."

Just how definitively can the subordination of the woman to the man, to the interests of her husband's or her own reproductive futurism, the commercial interests of the clinic, or to the interests of her son be calculated here? Is this exploitation of her reproductive body and, more generally, the subordination of third world Indian surrogates to first world reproductive futurisms pursued at bargain prices? How to understand the relations between nations, between state and individual rights, the differentials of biopolitical citizenship, the variably progressive aspects of reproductive rights, controls, and technologies, the state's role as bearing both sovereign and biopolitical interest in the question, and a number of further politics and modes of power, in the geopolitical distinctions between countries that will recognize these arrangements from those that will not? How definitively are some subjects rendered illegitimate, or illegible, in these interpenetrating regimes, powers, and politics of reproductive rights?

The ontological tact accessed by this couple in relation to the possibility that they could "do a reduction" is premised on the denial of that same ontological tact to the Indian surrogate who is cautioned accordingly: "you don't have a right over the baby . . . you have to give the baby to them." For the parents depicted by Memmi and for the male couple in

Google Baby, reproductive freedom is importantly connected not only to the ability to access abortion and surrogacy but also to the associated ontological tact I have discussed: the consensual making of embryonic life as valued potential life, or as biological waste, and its consensual making as a flexibility between these possible perceptions and outcomes. In this case, couples access the ontological tact associated with their reproductive freedom through a tacit occlusion of the surrogate mother's subjectivity. (We are not presented with a reflection on the possible claims of the surrogate with respect to this abortion.) The commercial arrangement is premised on the supposition that the surrogate does not access fetal reversibility on equivalent terms. It is assumed that, having borne her own child with personal interest, she could bear another couple's embryo impersonally. It is also supposed she will have no right to participate in the latter's malleability of status (as it oscillates between business proposition, bargain, fetishized future child, or "reduction"), unlike the couple for whom this very malleability has just become a fundamental reproductive freedom. Amrita Pande has discussed the contradictory demands negotiated by surrogates in this respect, given that they are expected to be, simultaneously, disciplined contract workers and nurturing mothers but selfless mothers.[90]

Yet this is not to presuppose that the most importantly foreclosed freedom is the surrogate's decision making with respect to that developing fetus, nor equal access to consensual tact with respect to its ambiguous ontological status. We can say that the tact accessed by the couple is premised on a denial of an equivalent tact to the surrogate in these particular circumstances: but we cannot say that the exclusion of the latter is the best way of understanding the cost of the former's reproductive freedoms. Nor should we assume it is not.

Thus a critical analysis of these complex interrelations must try to factor what cannot always be factored: expense, occlusion, illegibility, penetration. This would be the concerted attempt to acknowledge the component of incalculability in delegitimations, sacrifices, the making of disposable life, its expense, the complexity of concurrent forms of power, techniques, penetrations, segmentations, and malleabilities. This has also been to unfold (with Mills and Jenkins) the resources offered by Butler's work—not necessarily anticipated by the latter—such that biopoliticized reproduction might become thinkable as precarious life.

At this point it might also become thinkable in terms of a critical ethics. This I am defining as the ethics that will always require genealogy, all the while that this genealogy is willing to negotiate with the question "can we calculate?"

REPRODUCTIVE BIOPOLITICS AS HYPERGENEALOGY

Judith Butler's engagement with Foucault has been as singular as that of each of the theorists considered in this project. Each has articulated missing links in Foucault, oversights, blind spots, and unasked questions. To the extent that they have done so in the mode of critique, I have suggested that this mode has demarcated limit points: For Derrida, I suggested this limit point arose with Foucault's biopolitics. For both Agamben and Esposito, I suggest the limit would be a consideration of biopoliticized reproduction become thanatopolitics. For Foucault, it concerned the making of biopoliticized reproduction as a "power of death" manifesting in the very making of women's agency as threatening and as capable of impacting peoples in an excess to projects of governability (where the thanatopolitical parallel in his work was the atomic bomb or virus or any biopolitical measure reconfiguring both as power of death *and* as risk of governmental paradox).

The many respects in which Butler has critically explored Foucault's work have not, specifically, thematized his biopolitics. But Butler has queried the status of both life and death in Foucault's work.[91] Foucault's inattention to the phenomena of desubjectivation, a phenomena she considers in both individual and population terms. Butler's engagements with Foucault have also included her interrogation of critique: the term has been one of their most important points of theoretical encounter.[92] It arises also in *Giving an Account of Oneself*.[93] Responding to the term *critique*, Foucault eventually articulated his own variant of a genealogy of ethics. Engaging with this, Butler offers the prospect of a critical ethics.[94] Although her resources speak to the availability of the ethical encounter to genealogical critique, she has not foregrounded the way in which certain types of subjects emerge as particularly accessing moral status, normatively humanizing ethical decision-making conduct as itself a problematic mechanism of desubjectivation, a stimulation of illegibilities, and a principle of population division.

In exploring this alternative possibility, I have directed it into the consideration of abortion politics foregrounded neither by Foucault nor Butler. The biopoliticization of abortion and modern responsibilization in relation to embryonic life could be seen as limit points in the analyses of both. My view is not that Foucault or Butler "ought" to have given these phenomena more extensive consideration. To the contrary, we gain insight into the parameters of Butler's *Frames of War* project by understanding why the modern fetus can emerge only briefly in its prefatory remarks. Moreover, Butler comments that biopolitical analysis might be "for other scholars to do."[95] And, despite the elements discussed in chapter 3, we cannot turn back to Foucault for an adequate treatment of reproductive biopolitics. By contrast, I have suggested that the mutual engagement between the suspended reserves of Foucault, Butler, Mills, and Jenkins is productive in this regard.

Through this distinctive form of mutual encounter (not between arguments or texts but between suspended reserves) we can foreground the genealogical conditions of calls, responsibilities, and ethical encounters, their agencies, subjectivities, and objects, their framing conditions, their privileges and deprivileging with Butler's resources suggesting the importance of asking which subjects and problems are generated as illegible to, or excluded by, such ethical encounters. I have asked this question in relation to responsible decision making in modern reproduction, the dilemmas sometimes manifesting as reproductive ethics, and the responsibilization of women as "life and death" decision makers or "quality of life" decision makers, as fundamentally responsive, consequential, or moral agents.

This has also been to agree with those who have queried the formulation of abortion rights as the platform for personal responsibility, for responsibility for and to others, and as a means of being enfolded into life. The critique that abortion delivers antisociality, or even death (whether of futures, peoples, potential, growth), is not best rebutted with the claim that women's reproductive choice is instead a claim to quality of life, to only the most wanted children and the most deliberative parents, to responsibility, care for the self, or an aesthetics of existence. This is to support the argument presented in chapter 2: such claims operate too easily as a dividing principle. Too much and too many fall outside this claim to inclusive sociality, too many categories of antilife and of illegibility and nonconformity are stimulated in relation to these modes of reproduction as responsible life choice. That some claims to ethical life and the normative protocols of decision making play an overvigorous role in stimulating registers of illegibility and antilife is not an argument made by Butler. Yet, I have argued, this phenomenon—as becomes clearer as one broadens the consideration of those inevitably excluded from its parameters—has its place among the phenomena she has termed *precarious life,* as does the argument that forms of moral responsibility arise in conditions to be understood politically and biopolitically.

In chapter 2 we saw Puar's discussion of homonationalism make mention of the corresponding phenomenon of gender exceptionalism.[96] An even more specific "reproductive rights exceptionalism" is seen if reproductive rights claims reinforce conventional associations of class and cultural difference and norms for responsible conduct. Those taken to counter the interests of reproductive rights certainly have included those grouped by virtue of nation, community, or culture, in addition to religion or politics, as the putative deniers of rights. The language of reproductive choice also produces categories of those whose reproduction is assumed to be coerced, unenlightened, those for whom choice is assumed to be unavailable or irrelevant or whose agency might not be legible as choice. Those representing an impediment to the imaginary of reproductive choice are also seen in figures of reproductive irresponsibility, disorganized motives, incoherent behavior, the imposition on others of social burden, late, vague, or "poor" choice. To mention the latter might seem a challenging invitation: the defense of poor choice and irresponsibility has rarely suited a feminist imaginary. Yet the very implausibility indicates the contingency of modern reproductive choice. Consider, I suggested, that the right to poor, uninformed, reckless, and irresponsible decision making in voting often goes unquestioned, as it is in many other respects, even where negative impact on others might be supposed a concern. And consider the immediate associability of certain groups with irresponsible reproductive choice or poor parenting, incapacity of choice or a reproduction assumed not to count as "choice." These tacit assumptions about the groups or types making good or poor reproductive decisions, combined with suppositions that some forms of reproduction are less than human when considered from the perspective of responsibilized decision making, manifests the biopolitical hierarchies and principles of division with which reproductive choice is intertwined.

Lauren Berlant has suggested that biopower is at work when specific populations, groups, or subgroups of bodies come to be seen less competent at maintaining health or other conditions of social belonging. Their agency is deemed destructive or they "represent embodied liabilities to social prosperity of one sort of another."[97] The analyses of Berlant and Brown have been particularly insightful in identifying the biopolitical making of failed responsibility as a principle of population management and division. In this final chapter I have considered variants of this phenomenon in relation to reproductive choice, rights, freedoms, a making of both responsibility and illegible irresponsibility and a making of some groups and subjectivities as excluded from such freedoms. These are phantom responsibilities and failed responsibilities stimulated by the clinical consultations emerging in Gilligan's study but also by the spaces of illegal abortion evoked by the Romanian hotel rooms of *4 Months*. To describe the conditions under which groups of subjects are *made* as those excluded from rights, freedoms, responsibilities, or as those whose irresponsibility makes them a liability, is, Berlant has suggested, to describe one of the fundamental operations of biopower.[98]

This is also to conclude in agreement with the formulation that reproductive rights are what we cannot not want.[99] It means they can be pursued while at the same time articulating, as strenuously as possible, questions such as the following: At whose expense? Where are the generated figures of impediment and antifuture? What is the contingency of the relevant "life," "lives," and "deaths," of concern and of the providential state? Of neoliberalism? Of the personal and collective project and the care of the self? Of the making of risk and security? And it is also to do so while affirming the need to multiply such questions to the point of affirming their incalculability. Pushed to its limit, an analysis of the paradox of rights will also undermine a stable understanding of the paradoxes at work, their positive and negative impact.[100]

Considering the multiple conducts and counterconducts of *Google Baby* as an example, what coinciding regimes and registers we will *not* find: postcolonial, sovereign, nostalgic, and phantasmatic; state, states of risk, and risk aversion; biopolitical, thanatopolitical, divisions of the biological continuum; differentials in worth of life, neoliberalism; a number of projects of care of the self, both consistent and conflicting. These can't settle into a stability: of meaning, of mode of power, of subordination, of exploitation, of progress, of rights, of self-development, of self-making, of optimization, of harm, of choice, of rights, of freedom, of the latter's occlusions and illegibilities. We might better understand these as coinciding, sometimes in the mutually reinforcing conjunctions of an apparatus, sometimes in relations of dissonance or mutual resistance.

I have concluded by suggesting that the multiplication of modes of power, their techniques, segments, subjects, objects, expenses, penetrations, became so complicated as to make unstable the answers to questions such as "who pays?" At whose expense is this subject's rights claims pursued? What counts as power, what as resistance, what as conduct, what as counterconduct? This is both a point arising from Foucault's work, while also constituting the point of resistance to some of Foucault's formulations of "resistance"—if, for example, the identification of "counterconducts" would require a stabilization of a mode of power, or a formation, rendered less plausible by the complexity of segments and penetrations to which his own analyses also speak.

This is a project building on the commitment to a genealogy of ethics: in this case a genealogy of the reproductive decision makers, responsibilized as "moral philosophers," who have emerged with the biopolitical, as have its objects, its lives and deaths, its legibilities and illegibilities. Speaking to the project of critique, Butler has included its capacity to undertake genealogical, and political, interrogation of the ethical subject (its framing conditions, its imbrication in power and making, its status as formation) while reminding that this need not amount to invalidation of the ethical register. The stories we would need to tell about the retroactively self-forming and deconstituting activity of a moral agent, its norms, conducts, spaces, ends, how the latter are pursued, by whom, under what conditions, in conjunction with whom and what, as opposed to what, at whose expense, are complex. For we are not just "moral agents," we are moral agents in particular spaces, with particular conduct, about particular problems and in relation to appeals that come to seem self-evident. There is no "ethics" proper, Foucault will argue: there are contingent ethics in relation to concurrently coalescing objects for concurrently forming agents or microagencies or collective agents. This is the analysis we need of the ethical life, moral philosophy, and responsibilization of reproduction. This kind of genealogy of ethics will ask: About what? In relation to what aims? How? By whom? In relation to what? Constituting what parts of ourselves? Through what kinds of acts and conducts? In what kinds of relationships, through what kinds of transformations? Presupposing what?[101] Undone by what? Dividing whom? Deconstituting whom?

This is to explore the possibility that rights claims, and normative reflection, could be pursued while pursuing, and tolerating, critique of their framing conditions, their political, biopolitical, necropolitical, and thanatopolitical conditions, their interrelation with modes of power and their exposure to genealogical critique. So we would be brought, not just to genealogy but to critical genealogy, and to critical ethics: for which one formulation is the genealogy of ethics that would not invalidate ethics. In the discussion of these chapters I suggested another formulation: the ethics that will always require genealogy, but a genealogy that negotiates with the question "can we calculate?"

NOTES

INTRODUCTION

1. "No-one talks about that last part. Even though the book is a short one . . . I suspect people never got as far as this last chapter. All the same, it's the fundamental part of the book." Michel Foucault, "The Confession of the Flesh," in Michel Foucault, *Power/Knowledge: Selected Interviews and Other Writings, 1972–1977*, ed. Colin Gordon (New York: Pantheon, 1980), 194–229, 222 (translation modified). Presumably such readers preferred the chapter's concluding remarks in which different futures for sex are imagined.

2. In his recent dialogue with Lauren Berlant, Lee Edelman reasserts (not specifically as a comment about the different interpretations of *The History of Sexuality*) sex's importance given that contemporary critical thought is, he claims, "all too eager to put the subject of sex behind it. Critical discourse now centers instead on questions of rights (civil, natural, and human) of sovereign power and states of exception, of the definition and limits of the human, and of the distribution and control of populations through the categories of citizen and noncitizen." Lauren Berlant and Lee Edelman, *Sex, or The Unbearable* (Durham: Duke University Press, 2013), 63.

3. While not using this term, new work in this long-neglected area within Foucault scholarship includes Claire Blencowe, *Biopolitical Experience: Foucault, Power, and Positive Critique* (London: Palgrave Macmillan, 2013); Chloe Taylor, "Foucault and Familial Power," *Hypatia* 27, no. 1 (2012): 201–18; Jemima Repo, *The Biopolitics of Gender* (Oxford: Oxford University Press, 2015); Michelle Murphy, *Seizing the Means of Reproduction: Entanglements of Feminism, Health, and Technoscience* (Durham: Duke University Press, 2012); and see also contributions by Katherine Logan, "Foucault, the Modern Mother, and Maternal Power: Notes Towards a Genealogy of the Mother," 63–81, and Vikki Bell, "Foucault's Familial Scenes: Kangaroos, Crystals, and Continence and Oracles," 39–62, among important essays in Robbie Duschinsky and Leon Antonio

Rocha, eds., *Foucault, the Family, and Biopolitics* (New York: Palgrave Macmillan, 2012).

4. An expression proposed by Jasbir Puar in *Terrorist Assemblages: Homonationalism in Queer Times* (Durham: Duke University Press, 2007), 10, 32, 34, 35–36.

5. A collage of these "concerns for women" expressed in contemporary North American antiabortion campaigns is assembled by the brilliant John Oliver at https://www.youtube.com/watch?v=DRauXXz6toY (accessed March 2, 2016).

6. See Ladelle McWhorter, *Racism and Sexual Oppression in Anglo-America: A Genealogy* (Bloomington: Indiana University Press, 2009), Elsa Dorlin, *La Matrice de la race: généalogie sexuelle et coloniale de la nation française* (Paris: Découverte, 2006); Gisela Bock, *Zwangssterilisation im Nationalsozialismus. Studien zur Rassenpolitik und Frauenpolitik* (Opladen: Westdeutscher Verlag, 1986); Dorothy Roberts, *Killing the Black Body: Race, Reproduction, and the Meaning of Liberty* (New York: Vintage, 1998); and see Esposito's mention of Bock in Roberto Esposito, *Bios: Biopolitics and Philosophy*, trans. Timothy Campbell (Minneapolis: University of Minnesota Press, 2008), 217n91.

7. Achille Mbembe, "Necropolitics," *Public Culture* 15, no. 1 (2003): 11–40.

8. "Every genocidal system is said to follow the same script: a process that starts from a situation of 'de-individualization,' and 'moral disengagement,' culminating in all-out 'dehumanization.' . . . As the experts on genocide agree, this is how one goes about creating 'bare life.'" Simona Forti, *New Demons: Rethinking Power and Evil Today*, trans. Zakiya Hanafi (Stanford: Stanford University Press, 2014), 142–43.

9. Although there is (see note 3, this chapter) a new literature on the role in Foucault's work of family, parenting, and reproduction, their associations with distributions of death is not a dominant theme.

10. With the exception of brief passages in essays by Achille Mbembe such as "At the Edge of the World: Boundaries, Territoriality and Sovereignty in Africa," *Public Culture* 12, no. 1 (2000): 259–84 and "On Politics as a Form of Expenditure," in J. L. Comaroff and J. Comaroff, eds., *Law and Disorder in the Postcolony* (Chicago: Chicago University Press, 2006), 299–336, the role of sex, gender, reproduction, sexuality, and sexual violence has largely been occluded from his discussions of necropolitics. For criticism on this point, see Melissa W. Wright, "Necropolitics, Narcopolitics, and Femicide: Gendered Violence on the Mexico-U.S. Border," *Signs: Journal of Women in Culture and Society* 36, no. 3 (2011): 707–31, 710; and see Cihan Ahmetbeyzade, "Gendering Necropolitics: The Juridical-Political Sociality of Honor Killings in Turkey," *Journal of Human Rights* 7, no. 3 (2008): 187–206.

11. José Esteban Muñoz, *Cruising Utopia: The Then and There of Queer Futurity* (New York: New York University Press, 2009), 15.

12. These can be, he proposes, "nonetheless reworked in the service of a different politics and understanding of the world" (ibid., 16).

13. See Catherine Mills, *The Philosophy of Agamben* (Stocksfield: Acumen, 2008); and Ranjana Khanna, "Disposability," *differences* 20, 1 (2009): 181–98. Thanks to both for discussion of ideas here and elsewhere in this book; to Estelle Ferrarese and Francesca Raimondi, whose exchange about Agamben and feminism at the Bare Life Workshop

(Centre Marc Bloch, Berlin, November 12–13, 2015) stimulated some of the comments here; and to Elizabeth Wilson, Laura Bieger, and Francesca Raimondi for their very helpful comments on this introduction.

1. SUSPENSIONS OF SEX

Chapter epigraphs come from Jacques Derrida, "'To Do Justice to Freud': The History of Madness in the Age of Psychoanalysis," in his *Resistances of Psychoanalysis*, trans. Peggy Kamuf, Pascale-Anne Brault, and Michael Naas (Stanford: Stanford University Press, 1988), 70–118, 118; Michel Foucault, "Polemics, Politics, and Problematization: An Interview with Michel Foucault," in *The Foucault Reader*, ed. Paul Rabinow (New York: Vintage, 1984), 389.

1. Agamben's *Homo Sacer* was framed by its proposal to flesh out a Foucauldian "blind spot" and what was "logically implicit" in Foucault's work. See Giorgio Agamben, *Homo Sacer: Sovereign Power and Bare Life,* trans. Daniel Heller-Roazen (Stanford: Stanford University Press, 1998), 6; and, for his sharp discussion of Agamben's stance toward Foucault, see Jacques Derrida, *The Beast and the Sovereign*, vol. 1, ed. Michel Lisse, Marie-Louise Mallet, and Ginette Michaud, trans. Geoffrey Bennington (Chicago: University of Chicago Press, 2009), 1:330. For an entirely different language of correction, see Wendy Brown, *Regulating Aversion: Tolerance in the Age of Identity and Empire* (Princeton: Princeton University Press, 2008), 95.
2. Roberto Esposito, *Bios: Biopolitics and Philosophy*, trans. Timothy Campbell (Minneapolis: University of Minnesota Press), 44–50, hereafter *Bios*.
3. Didier Fassin, "Another Politics of Life Is Possible," *Theory, Culture, and Society* 26, no. 5 (2009): 44–60, 48–49.
4. Ibid., 53–54.
5. Wendy Brown, *Undoing the Demos: Neoliberalism's Stealth Revolution* (Brooklyn: Zone, 2015), 72–73.
6. Achille Mbembe, "Necropolitics," *Public Culture* 15, no. 1 (2003): 11–40.
7. For the immune paradigm, see Esposito's *Bios* and, for reflections on insecurity, disorder, and the emergence of a vocabulary of thanatopolitics and necropolitics supplementing or reconfiguring Foucauldian biopolitics, see the inclusions in Patricia Ticineto Clough and Craig Willse, eds., *Beyond Biopolitics: Essays on the Governance of Life and Death* (Durham: Duke University Press, 2011); and François Debrix and Alexander D. Barder, *Beyond Biopolitics: Theory, Violence, and Horror in World Politics* (New York: Routledge, 2012).
8. Derrida, *The Beast and the Sovereign*, 1:330.
9. Instead, given the role played by Freud in Foucault's thresholds, Derrida redirects Foucault back to the resources of Freud for thinking the radical ambiguity of the aims of power and pleasure and to the late Freud's life and death drives.
10. Michel Foucault, *The Birth of Biopolitics: Lectures at the Collège de France, 1978–1979*, ed. Michel Senellart, trans. Graham Burchell (New York: Palgrave Macmillan, 2008), 3.

11. A term used by Foucault (signing as "Maurice Florence") in "Foucault," in *Essential Works of Foucault, 1954–1984* (in three volumes): vol. 2: *Aesthetics, Method, and Epistemology*, ed. James D. Faubion (Harmondsworth: Penguin, 1998), 459–463, 459. See also his discussion of civil society, madness, and sexuality as "transactional realities" (*réalités de transaction*): "those transactional and transitional figures that we call civil society, madness and so on, which, although they have not always existed are nonetheless real, are born precisely from the interplay of relations of power and everything which constantly eludes them, at the interface, so to speak, of governors and governed" (Foucault, *The Birth of Biopolitics*, 297).
12. Foucault, "Foucault," 459.
13. Foucault's *The Birth of the Clinic: An Archaeology of Medical Perception*, trans. Alan. M. Sheridan (London: Tavistock, 1973) is the work in which Foucault most strenuously repudiates the image of objects of knowledge awaiting their correct observation by a perceiving subject, in which the fantasy of fidelity to the object would equate with an ideal of the absence of imagination, superstition, myth, interpretive presuppositions, interpretive grids, or similarly historical conditions for our modes of perception. This continued to be the demarcating, repudiated alternative in *The Order of Things*: "I am not . . . concerned to describe the progress of knowledge towards an objectivity in which today's science could finally recognize itself" (Foucault, *The Order of Things*, xxii [translation modified]). The term *archaeology* is developed among Foucault's alternatives for the methodology of history. Foucault distinguishes the former from the latter's assertion of the independence of objects of knowledge. If one assumes that independence, a history of the evolution of medicine, psychiatry, linguistics, economics, or biology might claim (as Foucault does not) to describe the "growing perfection" of their understandings. If one's object of study is instead the transactional unity of subject and object, the pretention to account for a growing perfection in understanding becomes less viable. Foucault proposed as an alternative the analysis of the "conditions of possibility" for the formation, not of the object, but of these unities, understood in terms of contextualized "styles" and modes of knowledge, and *ways* of seeing, taking place in "spaces" of knowledge which would then become one's object of study: "Such an enterprise is not so much a history, in the traditional meaning of that word, as an 'archaeology'" (ibid., xxii).
14. See, for example, the discussion in *The Order of Things* of exchange, capital, and forms of production as emerging in the space of knowledge (ibid., 252).
15. In other words, he adds, it is a matter of determining its mode of subjectivation. Foucault, "Foucault," 459.
16. This is developed well in Claire Blencowe's *Biopolitical Experience: Foucault, Power and Positive Critique* (New York: Palgrave Macmillan, 2013), 3. Blencowe focuses on continuities in Foucault's accounts of transorganic and historically produced life, from *The Birth of the Clinic* through *Care of the Self*, giving a basis for a similar approach to his discussions of death.
17. See Foucault, *The Birth of the Clinic*, 91.
18. Judith Butler, *Frames of War: When Is Life Grievable?* (London: Verso, 2009), 1, 34.

19. Ibid., 7.
20. As elaborated by Bichat, see Foucault, *The Birth of the Clinic*, 91, 134, and, more broadly, 88–106 and 124–48.
21. See Michel Foucault, *Abnormal: Lectures at the Collège de France, 1974–1975*, ed. Valerio Marchetti and Antonella Salomoni, trans. Graham Burchell (New York: Picador, 2003), and Michel Foucault, *The History of Sexuality*, vol. 1: *An Introduction*, trans. Robert Hurley (New York: Vintage, 1980), 54, 125, hereafter *AB* and *HS I*.
22. Michel Foucault, *Security, Territory, Population: Lectures at the Collège de France, 1977–78*, ed. Michel Sennelart, trans. Graham Burchell (London: Picador, 2007), 81, hereafter *STP*.
23.
> There is not the legal age, the disciplinary age, and then the age of security. Mechanisms of security do not replace disciplinary mechanisms, which would have replaced juridico-legal mechanisms. In reality you have a series of complex edifices in which, of course, the techniques change and are perfected, or anyway become more complicated, but in which what above all changes is the dominant characteristic, or more exactly, the system of correlation between juridico-legal mechanisms, disciplinary mechanisms, and mechanisms of security.
>
> (*STP* 8)

24. In the last lecture of *Society Must Be Defended* Foucault discusses the Nazi state, of which he says,

> No State could have more disciplinary power than the Nazi regime. Nor was there any other State in which the biological was so tightly, so insistently, regulated. . . . No society could be more disciplinary or more concerned with providing insurance. . . . Controlling the random element inherent in biological processes was one of the regime's immediate objectives. But this society in which insurance and security were universal, this universally disciplinary and regulatory society, was also a society which unleashed murderous power, or in other words, the old sovereign right to take life.

Michel Foucault, *Society Must Be Defended: Lectures at the Collège de France, 1975–76*, ed. Mauro Bertani and Alessandro Fontana, trans. David Macey (London: Picador, 2003), 259, hereafter *SMBD* (translation modified).

25. Lemke offers a good summary of discipline in these terms: "To preclude a possible misunderstanding: According to Foucault discipline is a technology of power that works in very different social formations and historical epochs. He concentrated in his texts on the analysis of processes of discipline from the seventeenth to the nineteenth century, but also stressed their importance for fascist . . . socialist . . . and liberal-democratic regimes in the twentieth century." Thomas Lemke, "Comment on Nancy Fraser: Re-reading Foucault in the Shadow of Globalization," *Constellations* 10, no. 2 (2003): 172–79n2. In addition to remarks made in *Discipline and Punish* and elsewhere about

techniques of surveillance predating disciplinary societies, a number of similar examples are provided in STP. Among the points given emphasis to this end: premodern spectacular punishments were intended to have a deterrent effect on others. Instances of "cell" techniques for the distribution, observation, and self-regulation of bodies could be found in premodern religious contexts and also in the treatment of debtors (STP 8–9). Premodern legal codes embody techniques not only of punishment but also of security, of risk aversion (STP 6–7).

26. Lemke, "Comment on Nancy Fraser, 172n12.
27. This disassembling approach could be seen as consistent with one of several different strategies with which Foucault is interpreted by Jasbir Puar in *Terrorist Assemblages: Homonationalism in Queer Times* (Durham: Duke University Press, 2007). Most obviously, see Gilles Deleuze's *Foucault*, trans. Seán Hand (Minneapolis: University of Minnesota Press, 1988) and his "What Is a Dispositif?" in Timothy Armstrong, ed., *Michel Foucault Philosopher* (London: Harvester Wheatsheaf, 1992), 159–68.
28. The suggestion is made that one could understand either the techniques, or the correlations between them, as mutating.
29. Fassin, "Another Politics," 52.
30. Even so, here the formulation is framed with the concessive, "but if it is true that . . . "
31. His best-known characterization refers to its "ancient and absolute form" (HS I 136), the defining power to take life, "derived, no doubt," from the ancient Roman *patria potestas* (HS I 135).
32. HS I 89 (my emphasis).
33. For example, Foucault may "contrast" sovereign power and biopolitics, but, argues Lemke, what is really being described is "the integration," "rearticulation," and the "transformation of sovereign power into biopower." Thomas Lemke, *Biopolitics: An Advanced Introduction* (New York: New York University Press, 2011), 34, 35, 40–41. Lauren Berlant takes it that, on Foucault's account, "biopower . . . does not substitute for but reshapes sovereignty." Lauren Berlant, "Slow Death: Sovereignty, Obesity, Lateral Agency," *Critical Inquiry* 33 (2007): 754–80, 756. Agamben characterizes Foucault's view that "sovereign power is progressively transformed into what Foucault calls 'biopower'." Giorgio Agamben, *Remnants of Auschwitz: The Witness and the Archive*, trans. Daniel Heller-Roazen (Brooklyn: Zone, 1999), 82.
34. Michel Foucault, *The Punitive Society: Lectures at the Collège de France, 1972–1973*, ed. Bernard E. Harcourt, trans. Graham Burchell (Basingstoke: Palgrave Macmillan, 2015), 5; "décomposer en ses éléments": Michel Foucault, *La Société punitive: Cours au Collège de France 1972–3*, ed. François Ewald, Alessandro Fontana, and Bernard E. Harcourt (Paris: Gallimard, 2013), 7.
35. Foucault resisted offering "histories of institutions" (including the family) and an overly successive account of the waxing and waning of formations of power in part by describing the segmentation of different modes of power and the techniques typically associated with them. For example, he emphasized that those techniques typically associated with disciplinary power had already formed within religious communities in

medieval contexts, but operated differently in societies generally dominated more by sovereign forms of power. Isolated segments of disciplinary techniques might be present, as in monastic contexts, but the difference is that they are not interlinked with the "political power-individual body" syntheses important to the nineteenth century, for which disciplinary techniques were "central." Michel Foucault, *Psychiatric Power: Lectures at the Collège de France, 1973–74*, ed. Jacques Lagrange, trans. Graham Burchell (New York: Palgrave Macmillan, 2006), 41, hereafter *PP*.

36. *The Punitive Society* begins this discussion with the example of punishment by fining or appropriation of assets. It might involve the suspension of a person's status within a community or their expulsion from it and so belong to tactics of exclusion. But financial penalties can also be paid in a compensatory capacity by participants in a political space. As such they can be strategies of inclusion. Fines, or other forms of financial appropriation could serve as markers of subordination to sovereign authority, of being governed, ruled, or perhaps unjustly dominated—but not of being illegible—within a political space.

37. Foucault, *Société punitive*, 12; *The Punitive Society*, 11.

38. One could differentiate a seemingly similar technique (such as an execution) as, in fact, quite a different technique, according to the mode of power, tactic, aim, or governmentality with which it is integrated.

39. Derrida, *The Beast and the Sovereign*, 1:332. In *HS I* Foucault had proposed that capital punishment could be seen as biopower's "limit . . . scandal and . . . contradiction" (*HS I* 138).

40. He does refer to such a decline, and Derrida, in his *Death Penalty*, also refers to a general acceleration of abolitionism since the Second World War. Derrida stresses, however, that the opposite trend has been seen in the United States. See Jacques Derrida, *The Death Penalty*, trans. Peggy Kamuf (Chicago: Chicago University Press, 2013), 1:91.

41. Puar, *Terrorist Assemblages*, 32.

42. It is both "an eminently corporeal mode of behavior . . . a matter for individualizing disciplinary controls that take the form of permanent surveillance . . . but it is also" as he argues, "in broad biological processes that concern . . . the multiple unity of the population," (thus, simultaneously, the disciplinary and the biopolitical). But here the image used is that of an *intersection* of differentiable axes in, for example, the formations of sexuality and the work of norms (*SMBD* 251–52).

43. See, among his many discussions of the term, Derrida's reading of Freudian life in *Beyond the Pleasure Principle*, "'To Do Justice to Freud,'" 118; and *The Beast and Sovereign*, vol. 2, trans. Geoffrey Bennington (Chicago: University of Chicago Press, 2011), 2:130–32. See also Frédéric Worms, "Pouvoir, création, deuil, survie: La vie, d'un moment philosophique à un autre," in *Le moment philosophique des années 60 en france*," ed. P. Maniglier (Paris: PUF, 2011).

44. Occupying just a few pages in *The History of Madness*, it led to considerable debate in the context of Descartes scholarship in France and to Derrida's famous critique, published as "Cogito and the History of Madness" in *Writing and Difference*, trans. Alan Bass (Chicago: University of Chicago Press, 1978), 36–76. Judith Revel discusses this in

her forthcoming book, *Une Controverse philosophique: Foucault, Derrida, et l'"affaire Descartes."*

45. For example, Descartes may (as Foucault first argued in *The History of Madness*) institute the Cogito as a simple exclusion of madness. But, on Foucault's own account also, Descartes retains a Cogito perpetually threatened by the risk of unreason, given the lurking possibility both of dreaming and of a deceptive evil genius. Freud is presented by Foucault as a hinge figure, representing a number of different tendencies. He is said to carry over, and be tributary to, the lineage of Pinel and Tuke and their thaumaturgical forms of expert authority, associated by Foucault with the classical age. But, insofar as Freud also commits to listening to the voice of unreason rather than relegating it to the pathological, he can also be aligned with the different affiliation of Hölderlin, Nerval, Nietzsche, Van Gogh, Roussel, and Artaud; see Foucault, "'To Do Justice to Freud,'" 86; and see Michel Foucault, *The History of Madness*, ed. Jean Khalfa, trans. Jonathan Murphy (London: Routledge, 2006), 157.
46. Foucault, *The Order of Things*, 318–23.
47. Derrida, "To Do Justice to Freud," 93.
48. As when Foucault describes Diderot as "prefiguring" the unreason of Nietzsche, see ibid., 89.
49. Derrida also goes on to connect this principle of disturbance with the possibility of the Foucauldian event.
50. Colin Koopman, *Genealogy as Critique: Foucault and the Problems of Modernity* (Bloomington: Indiana University Press: 2013), 51.
51. As Trumbull claims, the debate concerns not whether Foucault has the capacity to think everything named in his work as power as disrupting and undoing itself. Rather, the question is whether Foucault must nonetheless commit to a sufficiently coherent sense of power's (or an epoch's) ("gathered") identity to make viable the genealogy which may then recount its profound ambiguity, transformation, de-segmentation, or plasticity. In referring to the ambiguity of pleasure and power, life and death drives, Derrida thinks to identify a more radical challenge to power's identity than is accomplished when Foucault presupposes some kind of "gathering principle." See Robert Trumbull, "Power and the 'Drive for Mastery': Derrida's Freud and the Debate with Foucault," in *Foucault/Derrida Fifty Years Later: The Futures of Genealogy, Deconstruction, and Politics*, ed. Olivia Custer, Penelope Deutscher, and Samir Haddad (New York: Columbia University Press, 2016), 151–65, 160.
52. Derrida, "To Do Justice to Freud," 115.
53. Ibid., 117.
54. And see the elaboration of this theme, *SMBD* 252.
55. See Lynne Huffer, "Looking Back at *History of Madness*," in *Fifty Years Later*, 21–37, 29.
56. Lynne Huffer, *Mad for Foucault: Rethinking the Foundations of Queer Theory* (New York: Columbia University Press, 2009).
57. "Reply to Derrida ('Michel Foucault Derrida e no kaino'. *Paideia* (Tokyo) February 1972)," in *The History of Madness*, 575–90, 575–76.

58. Ibid., 223.
59. Ibid., 606, 609.
60. Jacques Derrida, *Of Grammatology*, corrected ed., trans. Gayatri Chakravorty Spivak (Baltimore: Johns Hopkins University Press, 1997), 153, 158.
61. See Foucault's "What Is an Author?" in *Essential Works of Foucault, 1954–1984*, vol. 2: *Aesthetics, Method and Epistemology*, ed. James D. Faubion, 3 vols. (Harmondsworth: Penguin, 1998), 2:205–21, and see his "Discourse on Language," in Michel Foucault, *The Archaeology of Knowledge*, trans. A. M. Sheridan Smith (New York: Vintage, 2010).
62. See Foucault's "Reply to Derrida" (1972), the revised version published in the same year as "My Body, This Paper, This Fire," both in *The History of Madness*. For related comments on the status of text and of commentary (preoccupations and functions to which he had reduced Derrida in his reply), see Foucault's "What Is an Author?" and "Discourse on Language."
63. Jacques Derrida, "Violence and Metaphysics: An Essay on the Thought of Emmanuel Levinas," in *Writing and Difference*, trans. Alan Bass (Chicago: University of Chicago Press, 1987), 79–102.
64. Derrida, *Of Grammatology*, 153, 158.
65. See the more circumspect, brief comments by Foucault in 1984 about the difference between his method and deconstruction, "Polemics, Politics, and Problematization: An Interview with Michel Foucault," in *The Foucault Reader*, ed. Paul Rabinow (New York: Vintage, 1984), 381–90, 389.
66. Revel suggests we see a dueling quality in the innovative, brilliant methodologies the two were concurrently developing (Revel, *Une Controverse philosophique*).
67. For her sympathetic reading of the text of sex and the sex of text in Derrida's work, see Sarah Kofman, *Lectures de Derrida* (Paris: Galilée, 1984), 144. This is counterbalanced by Luce Irigaray's less sympathetic response to Derrida in "Le V(i)ol de la lettre," in *Parler n'est jamais neutre* (Paris: Minuit, 1985), 149–68. A rich reading of this exchange is to be found in "Derrida, Irigaray, and Feminism," in Tina Chanter, *Ethics of Eros: Irigaray's Rewriting of the Philosophers* (New York: Routledge, 1985). Questions raised in this chapter about the profitable suspended resources of Foucault and Derrida could come into interesting conversation with Chanter's speculations, perhaps similar in spirit, about the relationship between Irigaray and Derrida.
68. *AB* 313–14. On this see Mary Beth Mader, "Foucault's Metabody," *Journal of Bioethical Inquiry* 7 (2010): 187–203.
69. Again I refer to Huffer's analysis of *The History of Madness* in *Mad for Foucault*, and see a number of comments on sexuality, including Foucault's articulation of the possibility of an archaeology of sexuality in Michel Foucault, *Archaeology of Knowledge and a Discourse on Language* (New York: Pantheon, 1972), 193. In 1971 Foucault flagged the promise of archaeological and genealogical approaches to sexuality; see his "Discourse on Language," 233.
70. Further discussed in the next chapter.

71. Jacques Derrida, *Glas*, trans. John P. Leavey and Richard Rand (Lincoln: University of Nebraska Press 1990); Geoffrey Bennington and Jacques Derrida, *Jacques Derrida* (Chicago: University of Chicago Press, 1993).
72. For this term, see Jacques Derrida, *Aporias*, trans. Thomas Dutoit (Stanford: Stanford University Press, 1993), 8.
73. Derrida, *The Beast and the Sovereign*, 1:333.
74. Derrida, "To Do Justice to Freud," 89.
75. Jacques Derrida, *The Politics of Friendship*, trans. George Collins (London: Verso, 1997), 266–67, citing Victor Hugo, "Introduction," in *Paris Guide par les principaux écrivains et artistes de la France* (Paris: Libraire Internationale, 1867), 1–44, 43, and see 104–6, 110, 114, 118–24.
76. Ibid., 265, citing Hugo, "Introduction," 2–3, 4.
77. Derrida, *The Death Penalty*, 188.
78. Ibid. Derrida depicts Hugo's association of progress with the metaphor of the seed as follows: "progress is germinating, it is irreversible, and that this organism is going to develop . . . it is a kind of teleological geneticism, organicism, in this vision of the irreversible progress of the abolition of the death penalty. Which is a progress of life. It is the right to life, and it is normal to describe the progress of the right to life as an organic, genetic process" (ibid.).
79. Derrida, *The Politics of Friendship*, 265, citing Hugo, "Introduction," 5 ("l'ovaire profond du progrès fécondé").
80. On women's reproductive bodies as complex spatialities and temporalities, insofar as their own lives and vitality is understood to enfold those of real or prospective children and national, collection, and population futures, see Nathan Stormer, "Prenatal Space," *Signs: Journal of Women in Culture and Society* 26, no. 1 (2000): 109–44, 115–19; and see Michelle Murphy, *Seizing the Means of Reproduction: Entanglements of Feminism, Health, and Technoscience* (Durham: Duke University Press, 2012).
81. But for new work in this respect, see the contributions to Robbie Duschinsky and Leon Antonio Rocha, eds., *Foucault, the Family, and Politics* (New York: Palgrave Macmillan, 2012); Blencowe, *Biopolitical Experience*; and, most recently, Jemima Repo, *The Biopolitics of Gender* (Oxford: Oxford University Press, 2015).
82. Discussed further in chapter 4.
83. Thus it is not quite the case that there is no Foucauldian thanatopolitics. When Foucault used the term in "The Political Technology of Individuals," he referred to a phenomenon that emerges at the end of the eighteenth century: formations of the police (in the sense of *Polizeiwissenschaft* as developed, for example, by von Justi, his reference at this point) and similarly of a state whose object was "to foster the citizen's life and the state's strength." Von Justi compares this new positive task to the more negatively defined tasks of upholding laws, fighting internal enemies (with the law) as one fights external enemies with military force. This more positive role aimed to impact the conduct of the governed. But, as Foucault comments, this was not just a new type of role but also a new kind of governed object, the "population": "or, in other words,

the state has essentially to take care of men as a population. It wields its power over living beings as living beings, and its politics, therefore, has to be a biopolitics. Since the population is nothing more than what the state takes care of for its own sake, of course, the state is entitled to slaughter it, if necessary. So the reverse of biopolitics is thanatopolitics." Michel Foucault, "The Political Technology of Individuals," in *Power: Essential Works of Michel Foucault, 1954–1984*, ed. James D. Faubion (New York: New Press, 2000), 403–17, 415–16.

84. Of course, analogy receives considerable attention in one of the epistemic contexts for considering relations between macrocosm and microcosm in a cosmos understood in terms of similitude, discussed in Foucault, *The Order of Things*.

85. See the inclusions in Clough and Willse, *Beyond Biopolitics* and Debrix and Barder, *Beyond Biopolitics*.

86. See note 43, this chapter.

2. REPRODUCTIVE FUTURISM, LEE EDELMAN, AND REPRODUCTIVE RIGHTS

1. Lee Edelman, *No Future: Queer Theory and the Death Drive* (Durham: Duke University Press, 2004), 14, hereafter *NF*.
2. *NF* 157n18.
3. For example, compare this with Wendy Brown's interest in "political coalitions among groups that otherwise would not instantly fit together" or Deborah Gould's discussion of members of ACT UP who have engaged in actions defending abortion clinics and their clients against Operation Rescue. See Wendy Brown, with Christina Colegate, John Dalton, Timothy Rayner, and Cate Thill, "Learning to Love Again: An Interview with Wendy Brown," *Contretemps* 6 (2006): 25–42, 38; and Deborah Gould, "Becoming Coalitional: The Strange and Miraculous Alliance Between Queer to the Left and the Jesus People," paper delivered at Northwestern University, October 17, 2013.
4. The formulation in an early piece by Wendy Brown represents the sentiment commonly expressed in a reproductive rights context, "abortion is not a positive good but an unhappy necessity." Wendy Brown, "Reproductive Freedom and the Right to Privacy: A Paradox for Feminists," *Families, Politics, and Public Policy: A Feminist Dialogue on Women and the State*, ed. I. Diamond (New York: Longman, 1983): 311–88, 323. Or in the words of *After Tiller's* Susan Robinson, "Nobody *wants* an abortion." See *After Tiller*, directed Martha Shane and Lana Wilson (2014).
5. *No Future* has been seen as the "contemporary queer theorists' negation of feminist influences," a view characterized by Cassia Paigen Roth, http://www.academia.edu/4470955/_Queering_Feminism_Center_for_the_Study_of_Women_UCLA_Newsletter_October_2009_ (accessed February 15, 2015). But the emergence of queer theory has combined with nuanced arguments for taking provisional breaks from the foci of feminist genealogies and politics. For important reflections on this question, see Janet Halley, *Split Decisions: How and Why to Take a Break from Feminism* (Princeton: Princeton University

Press, 2006); and the contributions to Elizabeth Weed and Naomi Schor, eds., *Feminism Meets Queer Theory* (Bloomington: Indiana University Press, 1997).

6. He mentions the remark of a former mayor of Lourdes, for whom homosexuals were the "'gravediggers of society'—those who care nothing [for] the future" (*NF* 74), in addition to this citation from Gary Bauer, a member of the "Family Research Council" (*NF* 39). As Edelman notes, this phrase is "itself a commonplace in anti-abortion polemics" (*NF* 40). The homophobic comments mentioned here referred to forms of sex deemed to reject the aims of reproduction. Among the many works on the broader associations of homosexuality and death, including those that took shape in the context of the AIDS epidemic, see Deborah Gould, *Moving Politics: Emotion and ACT UP's Fight Against AIDS Chicago* (Chicago: University of Chicago Press, 2009); Leo Bersani, *Is the Rectum a Grave? and Other Essays* (Chicago: University of Chicago Press, 2009); and Judith Butler, "Sexual Inversions" in *Foucault and the Critique of Institutions*, ed. John Caputo and Mark Yount (University Park: Pennsylvania State University Press, 1993), 81–98.

7. In the United States a widely cited contribution to this debate was a 2013 declaration of support for legally recognized gay marriage by the American Academy of Pediatrics. Their review of some eighty studies, books, and articles, conducted over thirty years, concluded that same-sex parenting was not more harmful to children than heterosexual parenting, while legalizing same-sex marriage would benefit children by eliminating the precarious legal status of their same-sex parents. See also Judith Butler's discussion of debates abut gay marriage in France, insofar as these also prompted and engaged with "expert" views on the impact on children of gay parenting, in "Is Kinship Always Already Heterosexual," *differences* 13, no. 1 (2002): 14–44.

8. See http://www.washingtonpost.com/news/wonk/wp/2013/03/27/sorry-justice-scalia-theres-no-evidence-that-gay-parents-arent-great-parents/ (Accessed 01/23/2017).

9. The Defense of Marriage Act, 1996, was a law blocking federal recognition of gay marriage, struck down by the U.S. Supreme Court in 2013.

10. As per the findings of the research summary on gay parenting adopted by the American Psychological Association, at http://www.apa.org/about/policy/parenting.aspx. (Accessed 11/19/2016).

11. "The National Longitudinal Lesbian Family Study" of 154 mothers in same-sex relationships whose children were conceived through artificial insemination is cited by Benjamin Siegel, one of the authors of the American Academy of Pediatrics report. As the *Washington Post* reports his assessment: "the children did fine—better, even, than children in a similar study involving more diverse families." https://www.washingtonpost.com/national/health-science/social-science-struggles-with-the-effects-of-same-sex-parenting-on-children/2013/03/26/a6fa50ca-9655-11e2-8b4e-0b56f26f28de_story.html?utm_term=.be8b1af2b51d. Accessed 12/15/2016.

12. So one might expect a positive response from Edelman to Derrida's formulation of the *à-venir*. While the latter is, by definition, unpredictable and unanticipatable, Edelman nonetheless identifies what he takes to be Derrida's residual reproductive futurism, see Lee Edelman, "Against Survival: Queerness in a Time That's Out of Joint," *Shakespeare Quarterly* 62, no. 2 (2011): 148–69. I have elsewhere argued that this underestimates

Derrida's affirmation of the monstrous potential of the "future" in Penelope Deutscher, "The Membrane and the Diaphragm: Derrida and Esposito on Immunity, Community, and Birth, *Angelaki* 18, no. 3 (2013): 49–68 (special issue on Roberto Esposito). A similar dialogue takes place with Judith Butler, for whom we assume responsibility for a collective future whose direction and contours we cannot know in advance: "the future, especially the future with and for others, requires a certain openness and unknowingness." Judith Butler, "The Question of Social Transformation," in *Undoing Gender* (New York: Routledge, 2004), 204–31, 226. Edelman's response to Butler's reading of Antigone is discussed later in this chapter. Where Butler reads Antigone as a figure standing for the possibility of illegible kinship, and unpredictable transformation of kinship structures, Edelman again argues that these remain conservatively projected futures, at least insofar as they suppose that the unpredictable transformation of social forms are to be understood positively.

13. The specter of the "obstacle to futurity" is projected onto figures of *sinthom*osexuality, in particular, he notes, the gay man. But since the preservation of the (never present) past and present would be, in any case, impossible, we therefore lack self-presence in our very constitution, we are our own "obstacle" to any aim at preservation. Edelman suggests we are *all*, in this sense, the *sinthom*osexual: "Futurism makes *sinthom*osexuals, not humans, of us all" (*NF* 153).

14. From an address first delivered at an MLA "Lesbian and Literature" panel, at the Modern Language Association in December 1977, written in a period when Lorde confronted imminent death from cancer. Her formulation spoke to the vulnerability of African American women's visible blackness in America, only to then redirect it at "most of you here today, black or not": "Most of all, I think, we fear the very visibility without which we also cannot truly live.... Even within the women's movement, we have had to fight and still do, for that very visibility which also renders us most vulnerable, our blackness. For to survive in the mouth of this dragon we call america, we have had to learn this first and most vital lesson—that we were never meant to survive. Not as human beings. And neither were most of you here today, black or not." It might be said that Lorde's declaration presupposes the identity of the one who confronts her mortality. Republished in Audre Lorde, *The Cancer Journals: Special Edition* (San Francisco: Aunt Lute, 1997), 20.

15. Connecting with a long trajectory of associations between the queer and the antisocial—see in particular Robert Caserio, "The Antisocial Thesis in Queer Theory," *PMLA* 121, no. 3 (2006): 819–21; and Leo Bersani, *Homos* (Cambridge: Harvard University Press, 1996).

16. Whose hand is "limp and heavy, deathly cold, ... a lifeless thing." Daphne du Maurier, *Rebecca* (New York: Doubleday, 1993), 66. Halberstam has offered a critique of Bersani and Edelman's "excessively small archive" of negativity, an archive she considers confined to the "anti-social queer aesthetes and camp icons." Judith Halberstam, "The Politics of Negativity," *PMLA* 121, no. 3 (2006): 823–25, 824; and see Caserio, "The Antisocial Thesis in Queer Theory," 820. So we should not forget Edelman's (Hitchcockian) birds, nor the directions opened up by figures such as Mrs. Danvers, Katherine, and Ellen, however briefly.

17. For this reason, Halberstam proposes the figures of Valerie Solanis and Jamaica Kincaid as "antisocial theorists who articulate the politics of an explicitly political negativity" (Halberstam, "The Politics of Negativity," 824); they do not (at least in this respect) correspond to female figures of the *sinthom*osexuality mentioned by Edelman.
18. Judith Butler, *Antigone's Claim* (New York: Columbia University Press, 2002), 72.
19. Ibid., 6. Also troubling the view that Antigone represents the claims of kinship, versus those of the state, is Butler's suggestion that by defiantly asserting her agency, sovereignty, and "manly" authority her language approximates that of Creon, thereby "embodying the norms of the power she opposes" (10). There is no simple opposition here between the claims of kinship and sovereignty; instead their reliance on each other deforms the ideal norms for both (6).
20. Though consider Bonnie Honig's discussion of Edelman's comments on Antigone. Honig does not side with the birds (she is mounting a case for an agonistic humanism and attributing to Antigone a politicized form of mourning and a politics of counter-sovereignty). Yet she has fun reading with Edelman so as to amplify his own resources. After pushing Edelman to up the ante in considering the burst balloon of *Strangers on a Train*, Honig then remarks on Edelman's neglect of Antigone's birds: "in an extended reading of Hitchcock's *The Birds*, Edelman invokes the birds as a marker of *in*humanity's expansiveness but, even though he does discuss Sophocles' *Antigone* as well, he neglects the complex role played by birds in Sophocles' play.... Carol Jacobs notes that when the sentry compares the mourning Antigone to a mother bird at an empty nest, the comparison [also] gestures [to] ... a more devouring relation, since birds are at that very moment feasting on Polynices' body." Bonnie Honig, *Antigone, Interrupted* (Cambridge: Cambridge University Press, 2013), 52.
21. Butler, *Antigone's Claim*, 23–24.
22. Lines 900–920 (cited ibid., 9).
23. Edelman notes that some of the *sinthom*osexuals he discusses are enmeshed in narratives of conversion: as when Scrooge finds the meaning of Christmas and Katherine appears, at least, to have become docile. Thus *sinthom*osexuality would then be contained or rerouted at the point where Scrooge finds the meaning of Christmas and Katherine comes to approximate an obedient spousal femininity.
24. And see his own description: "*No Future*, by contrast, approaches negativity as society's constitutive antagonism, which sustains itself only on the promise of resolution in futurity's time to come, much as capitalism is able to sustain itself only by finding and exploiting new markets." Lee Edelman, "Antagonism, Negativity, and the Subject of Queer Theory," *PMLA* 121, no. 3 (2006): 821–23, 822.
25. *NF* 13, citing a review by Walter Wangerin, whose formulation is "if there is a baby, there is a future, there is redemption."
26. Consider nineteenth-century women's rights claims formulated in England, the United States, and some European countries in opposition to the legal tradition of coverture, according to which a wife had no independent legal status, no right to her own earnings, no right of divorce, and no legal rights over her children. More recently, consider

2. REPRODUCTIVE FUTURISM   205

also the emergence of political movements promoting "father's rights" (understood in opposition to those of mothers).

27. Ann Stoler discusses this issue in the context of research on illegal immigration and child trafficking. Here, she writes, a child might be figured as "at risk" in the context of trafficking or when accompanying adults on dangerous immigration journeys. But the figure of the child can also redouble into that which *poses* a risk. The question of the child as at risk/or as posing a risk is permeated with age divisions: "The Homeland Security Act of 2002 transferred the care of unaccompanied alien children who were apprehended for immigration violations to the Office of Refuge Resettlement. Children are perceived as both at risk and as risks themselves. In that delicate balance, 'the politics of compassion' as [Greta] Uehling notes, stops at adolescence: children elicit it, teenagers decidedly do not." Ann Stoler, " Beyond Sex. Bodily Exposures of the Colonial and Postcolonial Present," in *Genre et Postcolonialismes. Dialogues transcontinentaux*, ed. Ann-Emmanuel Berger and Elena Varikas (Paris: Archives Contemporaines 2011), 185–214, 207.

28. In her reading of Lasse Hallstrom's *Once Around* (1991), Lauren Berlant describes the wife whose "body bears the burden of keeping these gendered, racial, class, ethnic, and national identities stable and intelligible. . . . [She is] an identity machine for others, producing children in the name of the future, in service to a national culture whose explicit ideology of national personhood she is also helping to generate." See Lauren Berlant, "America, Fat, the Fetus," in *The Queen of America Goes to Washington City: Essays on Sex and Citizenship* (Durham: Duke University Press, 1997), 85. A model deeming the woman passively appropriated to the genealogical, national, sentimental reproductive futurisms of others would be wrong here. She may actively participate in the "fetal motherhood" (see note 30 below) at play when pregnancy is attached to pursuits of meaning, identity, teleology, coherence (personal, familial, genealogical, cultural, national).

29. A classic essay (discussing the iconic image of an "eighteen week fetus" which appeared on the cover of *Life* magazine in 1965) is Rosalind Pollack Petchesky, "Fetal Images: The Power of Visual Culture in the Politics of Reproduction," *Feminist Studies* 13, no. 2 (1987): 263–92.

30. See ibid. Developing the argument, Berlant describes a historically recent transformation in ways in which some women could access a form of (albeit ambiguous) recognition through the route of "the promise of maternal value [which] has defined a source of power and social worth." However problematic and ambivalent those long-standing sources of personal, public, and nationalist-inflected status, she describes a newer phenomenon, to which she gives the term *fetal motherhood:* the "fetus" has replaced this space of value and the pregnant woman becomes "more minor and less politically represented than the fetus, which is in turn made more *national*" (Berlant, "America, Fat, the Fetus," *The Queen of America Goes to Washington City: Essays on Sex and Citizenship* (Durham: Duke University Press, 1997), 84–85).

31. Ronald Dworkin, *Life's Dominion: An Argument About Abortion, Euthanasia, and Individual Freedom* (New York: Vintage 1994), 60.

32. A remark from one of the doctors practicing third-term abortions in *After Tiller* speaks to the normative conduct problematically associated with responsibility in this context:

Why is that fair, what if you're just not a good story teller? Why would it be okay for me to say, "no you've got to tell me a better story than that"? Because what I believe is that women are able to struggle with complex ethical issues and arrive at the right decisions for themselves and their families. . . . So if somebody comes in and says, "I want an abortion," whether or not she is articulate about it, let alone whether she has a great story to tell, isn't the point, the point is that she has made this decision.

33. Whereas a number of histories of women's rights claims describe the philosophical alternatives between formulations emphasizing women's equality or those emphasizing women's difference. Joan Scott, *Only Paradoxes to Offer: French Feminists and the Rights of Man* (Cambridge: Harvard University Press, 1996) describes a number of instances of historical French feminism in which, more paradoxically, claims to equality were formulated by means of a concurrent emphasis of sexual difference.

34. Among the figures discussed by Scott, one could consider Olympe de Gouges's interest in the founding of state-funded, dedicated public hospitals for women in order to improve their survival rates in childbirth and her association of maternity, public duty, and political rights claims. As Scott argues, de Gouges linked women's equal agency in reproduction (and in other respects) to their claims to a public voice (Scott, *Only Paradoxes to Offer*, 43); and see Olympe de Gouges, "Projet d'un théatre et d'une maternité" (1789), in Olympe de Gouges, *Oeuvres*, ed. Benoîte Groult (Paris: Mercure de France, 1986), 78–82. See also Scott's discussion of Jeanne Deroin's association of women's political claims with their maternal role (Scott, *Only Paradoxes to Offer*, 70–73); and, for a detailed account of the unfolding of similar arguments, see Karen Offen, *European Feminisms, 1700–1950: A Political History* (Stanford: Stanford University Press, 1999).

35. See Claire Démar, *Ma loi d'avenir, suivi d'un Appel d'une femme au people sur l'affranchisement de la femme* (Paris: Bureau de la Tribune des Femmes, 1834); and, for her discussion of this particular formulation (and as discussed also by Benjamin in his *Arcades Project*), see Christine Blättler, "Claire Démar: Heroine der Moderne und Opfer des Saint-Simonismus," *Märtyrer-Porträts: Von Opfertod, Blutzeugen und heiligen Kriegern*, ed. Sigrid Weigel (Munich: Wilhelm Fink, 2007), 191–95.

36. Démar, *Ma loi d'avenir*, 54. Démar also reminds her readers of Abraham's near infanticide, of Brutus and Jephthah slitting their children's throats (ibid., 52).

37. Ibid.

38. Ibid., 58. They might be all the more prone to egoism if preoccupied with earning their income, but Démar affirms they *should* be so preoccupied.

39. "Et comment le pourrait-elle, si toujours elle est condamnée à absorber une partie plus ou moins longue de sa vie dans les soins qui réclame l'éducation d'un ou plusieurs enfants? Ou la fonction sera negligée, mal remplie, ou l'enfant mal élevé, privé des soins que réclament sa faiblesse, sa longue croissance" (ibid., 58).

40. Ibid., 59.

41. Ibid., 25.

42. Mary Wollstonecraft, "A Vindication of the Rights of Woman," in *A Vindication of the Rights of Men and a Vindication of the Rights of Woman and Hints*, ed. Sylvana Tomaselli (Cambridge: Cambridge University Press, 1995), 65–295, 240.
43. See Condorcet:

    It is said that no woman has ever made an important scientific discovery, or shown signs of genius in the arts or in literature, and so on, but we would hardly attempt to limit citizenship rights only to men of genius. . . . Why, then, should we exclude women, rather than those men who are inferior to a great many women? . . .

    It has been said that . . . women have no real idea of justice and follow their feelings rather than their conscience. There is more truth in this observation, but it still proves nothing since this difference is caused, not by nature, but by education and society. . . . If we accepted such arguments against women, we would also have to deny citizenship rights to anyone who was obliged to work constantly and could therefore neither become enlightened nor exercise his reason.

    Jean-Antoine-Nicolas de Caritat, Marquis de Condorcet, "On the Emancipation of Women. On Giving Women the Right of Citizenship" (1790), in *Political Writings*, ed. Steven Lukes and Nadia Urbinati (Cambridge: Cambridge University Press, 2012), 156–63, 157, 158–59.

44. Consider Anna Wheeler, who collaborated with William Thompson in writing *Appeal of One Half of the Human Race, Women Against the Pretensions of the Other Half*: "The love of rational liberty forms no part of the nature of this willingly degraded sex, and their very propensity for slavery. . . . Women's personal courage is never exerted but to fight for a master and their mental courage is chiefly exhibited in the indurance [sic] of oppression exactly where it is unworthily exercised . . . a woman will fight, with all the zeal of desperation which belongs to a more generous cause to perpetuate the oppression of all mankind, but rarely has she yet been found sacrificing herself for the hallowed cause of human emancipation. Women may burn in thousands ever year, no woman murmurs! Women are not so ignorant, but they are passive, and indifferent to the suffering of their species. Whether from superstition or its stupefying effects on the characters of women, their hearts seem incapable of loving anything but man as he is tyrannical, cruel, selfish, oppressive. There is something very depressive in contemplating this true, but dark side of the human picture.

    Anna Wheeler, "A Letter From Anna Wheeler, November 18, 1832," in Marie Mulvey Roberts and Tamae Mizuta, eds., *The Rebels: Irish Feminists* (London: Routledge/Thoemmes, 1995), 1–6, 3–4.

45. The characteristic so often attributed, see also Olympe de Gouges's "The Declaration of the Rights of Woman": "Women have done more harm than good. Constraint and dissimulation have been their lot. What force had robbed them of, ruse returned to them. . . . Poison and the sword were both subject to them; they commanded in crime as in fortune." In *Women in Revolutionary France, 1789–1795*, trans. with notes and commentary

by Darline Gay Levy, Harriet Branson Applewhite, and Mary Durham Johnson (Urbana: University of Illinois Press, 1980), 85–96, 93., See also Claire Démar: "vous ne pouvez nier la puissance de la femme . . . elle a des armes qui sont propres à sa faiblesse: elle *minaude, agace, ruse, ment, et ment effrontément*, car le mensonge est l'arme familière de l'esclave, arme d'autant plus envenimée qu'on la trempe dans la haine et qu'on l'aiguise dans l'ombre" ("Appel d'une femme au people sur l'affranchisement de la femme," 67).

46. Wollstonecraft, "A Vindication of the Rights of Women," 269.
47. Similarly when she speaks to the programs of education women should be offered, she argues for the basics of medical care and health. This too would save many lives including those of the children in women's care: "In public schools women, to guard against the errors of ignorance, should be taught the elements of anatomy and medicine, not only to enable them to take proper care of their own health, but to make them rational nurses of their infants, parents, and husbands; for the bills of mortality are swelled by the blunders of self-willed old women, who give nostrums of their own, without knowing anything of the human frame" (Wollstonecraft, "A Vindication of the Rights of Woman," 274). Wollstonecraft's partner William Godwin emphasized her concern that women's poor education and poor sense was exposing children and contributing to the mortality rate: "from the mismanagement to which children are exposed, many of the diseases of childhood are rendered fatal, and more persons die in that, than in any other period of human life. Mary had projected a work upon this subject, which she had carefully considered, and well understood. . . . Mr Anthony Carlisle, surgeon of Soho-Square . . . had promised to revise her production." William Godwin, "Memoirs of the Author of the Rights of Women," in Mary Wollstonecraft, *A Short Residence in Sweden, Norway and Denmark and Memoirs of the Author of the Rights of Women* (Harmondsworth: Penguin, 1987), 205–74, 207.
48. Wollstonecraft, "A Vindication of the Rights of Woman," 240.
49. By contrast, Dworkin's *Life's Dominion* contrasts certain European legal regimes whose legalization of abortion remains connected to a legal recognition of the value of human life, whereas the American variant renders abortion rights a matter of privacy. Abortion should, Dworkin argues, be recognized as a matter of deep responsibility.
50. Edelman, "Antagonism, Negativity, and the Subject of Queer Theory," 821.
51. Ibid., 822.
52. This constitutes the terrain of the debate with Halberstam, given her aim of producing a more political version of queer negativity.
53. Judith Halberstam, *The Queer Art of Failure* (Durham: Duke University Press, 2011), 106.
54. Ibid., 106 (my emphasis).
55. Love cites *NF* 27.
56. Heather Love, *Feeling Backward: Loss and the Politics of Queer History* (Durham: Duke University Press 2009), 22 (my emphasis).
57. Tim Dean, "The Antisocial Homosexual," *PMLA* 121, no. 3 (The Antisocial Thesis in Queer Theory) (2006): 826–28, 827. Dean cites *NF* 16.
58. In an unrepresentative passage Edelman uses a language which does not assume importance in *No Future*: "queerness attains its ethical value precisely insofar as it accedes

to [the place of the social order's death drive], accepting its figural status as resistance to the viability of the social while insisting on the inextricability of such resistance from every social structure" (*NF* 3).

59. Brown, "Learning to Love Again," 37.
60. Herman Cain, "Face the Nation," October 30, 2011, interview with Bob Schieffer, CBS. Cain leveled the accusation (based partly on a reference to the early twentieth-century eugenic sympathies of Margaret Sanger and partly on a disputed claim that Planned Parenthood centers are disproportionately located in black neighborhoods) at organizations facilitating abortion, rather than at those in the African American community who seek abortions.
61. As Alveda King has expressed this view, "Every baby scheduled for abortion is like a slave in the womb of his or her mother. The mother decides his or her fate and does so at will." Alveda King, *How Can the Dream Survive If We Murder the Children? Abortion Is not a Civil Right* (Bloomington: Authorhouse, 2008), 2. And see the countering commentary of Loretta Ross of Sister Song Women of Color Reproductive Justice Collective:

> Our opponents began a misogynistic attack to shame-and-blame black women who choose abortion, alleging that we endanger the future of our children. After all, many people in our community already believe that black *men* are an endangered species because of white supremacy. Our opponents used a social responsibility frame to claim that black women have a racial obligation to have more babies—especially black *male* babies—despite our individual circumstances.... Either we were dupes of abortion providers, or we were evil women intent on having abortions—especially of black male children—for selfish reasons. In their first narrative, we were victims without agency unable to make our own decisions, pawns of racist, profit-driven abortion providers. In their second narrative, we were the uncaring enemies of our own children, and architects of black genocide.

http://www.rhrealitycheck.org/blog/2011/02/24/fighting-black-antiabortion-campaign-trusting-black-women (accessed November 5, 2011). Also at http://www.ontheissues magazine.com/2011winter/2011_winter_Ross.php/ Thanks to Lisa Guenther for her suggestions at the 2011 SPEP meeting concerning this debate and the concurrent figuring of women as potential race protectors or race destroyers. For another variant, see the notorious 2006 "I don't snuff my own seed" radio advertisements voiced by Cain and funded by the organization America's PAC (here men are figured as the reproductive agents attributed with the "racial" responsibility not to "snuff the seed").

62. As in the language of billboards which went up in New York, Atlanta, and Oakland under the slogan "Betrayed." These depict Jesse Jackson and the Congressional Black Caucus as supporters of abortion and so as threatening the black community, reproduced at AbortionInTheHood.com. (Accessed 11/05/2016.) See also http://www.bet.com/news/health/2011/08/16/new-anti-abortion-billboard-points-fingers-at-black-leaders.html (accessed 12/10/2016). More recent examples of billboard campaigns, and related arguments, can be found at: www.the-restoration-project.org ; www.theradiance foundation.org ; and www.toomanyaborted.com.

63. Wendy Brown, "Suffering Rights as Paradoxes," *Constellations* 7, no. 2 (2000): 230–41.
64. Love's *Feeling Backward* and Halberstam's *The Queer Art of Failure* both critically engage with Edelman in works in which Foucault also plays an important role (though the latter is not brought directly into dialogue with the former). In expanding an archive of queer negative affect, Love includes Foucault's archival interest in the "infamous," the marginal, those of "no importance." Both Halberstam and Love work to reconcile their interest in Foucault's repudiation of the repressive hypothesis, with their own interest in an expanded queer archive attentive to figures of (in Love's case) shame, melancholia, pathos, depression, grief, regret, and despair and (in Halberstam's case) a group of affects Love thinks have been more easily associated with possibilities of action: "rage, rudeness, anger, spite, impatience, intensity, mania, sincerity, earnestness, overinvestment, and brutal honesty. . . . Dyke anger, anticolonial despair, racial rage, counterhegemonic violence, punk pugilism" (Halberstam, "The Politics of Negativity," 824). One of the interesting effects of the readings is that, while he is not directly positioned by either in such terms, Edelman's negativity effectively becomes either an alternative to or an alternative way of thinking about a queer archive of *affect*. Love responds to Edelman that she is more interested in looking back at instances of "ruined or failed sociality" (Love, *Feeling Backward*, 22). She attributes to Edelman, in distinction to her own, a project of suspending the future. For her part, she proposes other possibilities for imagining the future: for example, *through* a "backwards" kind of future. On this version, one might engage in an alternative politics of envisaging futures, absent the projections of optimism, redemption or reproductive imperatives. As such her interest in "*experiences*" of failure is contrasted with his interest in the *role* of negativity (ibid., 23). A starker version of the engagement with Edelman in contemporary debates about affect is seen in Halberstam's response to *No Future*. She contrasts a range of "affective responses" that she attributes more to a gay male archive with those she associates with a number of alternatives including Valerie Solanis, Patti Smith, and Jamaica Kincaid ("The Politics of Negativity," 824).
65. See, however, Edelman and Berlant's *Sex, or The Unbearable*, for the former's brief suggestion that reproductive futurism (or, more specifically, as mentioned here—the conventions of teleological narrative, the future, or future anterior orientation given to the value of life, many forms of sexual—or reproductive or tacitly reproductive—optimism) "compels a regulatory discipline," that is also understandable, "with apologies to Michel Foucault . . . as Panoptimism." Lauren Berlant and Lee Edelman, *Sex, or The Unbearable* (Durham: Duke University Press, 2013), 3.
66. Ibid.
67. I am thinking here of Christoph Holzey and Luca Di Blasi's interest and promotion of this kind of theory "tension," or *Spannung*, as presented in their cowritten epilogue to Forst and Brown's dialogue on tolerance and toleration. See Christoph Holzey and Luca Di Blasi, "Epilogue: Tensions in Tolerance," in Wendy Brown and Rainer Forst, *The Power of Tolerance: A Debate*, ed. Christoph Holzey and Luca Di Blasi (New York: Columbia University Press, 2014), 71–103.
68. Jasbir Puar, *Terrorist Assemblages: Homonationalism in Queer Times* (Durham: Duke University Press, 2007), 211.

69. Ibid.
70. Ibid.
71. Ibid.
72. And see his comment: the "figural Child alone embodies the citizen as an ideal, entitled to claim full rights to its future share in the nation's good, though always at the cost of limiting the rights 'real' citizens are allowed" (*NF* 11). Thus there is a biopolitical component, albeit not developed in these terms, by Edelman. A Foucauldian analysis might take particular interest in Edelman's account of the shared and mutually consolidating tactics of the reproductive futurists and of those understood as obstacles to the former's aims.

3. FOUCAULT'S CHILDREN

Chapter epigraph is from *HS I* 105 (translation modified).

1. For discussions of this issue, see Ellen K. Feder, *Family Bonds: Genealogies of Race and Gender* (Oxford: Oxford University Press, 2007); and Jon Simons's "Foucault's Mother" (1996), in Susan Hekman, ed., *Feminist Interpretations of Michel Foucault* (University Park: Pennsylvania State University Press, 1996), 179–209. These consider the role in Foucault's work of family formations, and mothers, while making the point that this theme deserved more attention from him. See also Ladelle McWhorter, *Racism and Sexual Oppression in Anglo-America: A Genealogy* (Bloomington: Indiana University Press, 2009), particularly the discussion at 171ff.; and the collection edited by Robbie Duschinsky and Leon Antonio Rocha, *Foucault, the Family, and Politics* (New York: Palgrave Macmillan, 2012). The latter presents different approaches to the status of biopoliticized reproduction in Foucault's work, arguing, as does McWhorter, that the theme is more strongly present in Foucault's work than has been appreciated. The closer attention has been stimulated by the posthumous publication of a number of Foucault's lectures, and in particular Collège de France lectures such as *Psychiatric Power* and *Abnormal* in which there is more material on the theme. Feminist scholarship was long dominated by other debates. These included the extent to which Foucault ought to have brought the perspective of sexual difference more significantly to his analyses; the extent to which he ought to have offered analyses of power, knowledge, technologies, and disciplines relating to gender; and the extent to which his work could be productively deployed to the ends of such analyses. Some prominent feminist responses to Foucault include Judith Butler, "Sexual Inversions," in *Foucault and the Critique of Institutions*, ed. John Caputo and Mark Yount (University Park: Pennsylvania State University Press, 1993), 81–98; Judith Butler, *Gender Trouble: Feminism and the Subversion of Identity* (New York: Routledge, 1990); Teresa de Lauretis, *Technologies of Gender: Essays on Theory, Film, and Fiction* (Bloomington: Indiana University Press, 1987); Irene Diamond, and Lee Quinby, eds., *Feminism and Foucault: Reflections on Resistance* (Boston: Northeastern University Press, 1988); Lois McKnay, *Foucault and Feminism: Power, Gender, and the Self* (Cambridge: Polity, 1992).

2. At the conclusion of this chapter, I turn to the differences between Mbembe, Esposito, and Agamben's usage of these terms, further discussed in chapter 4. They are often used indistinguishably, as particularly evident in contributions to the anthology edited by Patricia T. Clough, and Craig Willse, *Beyond Biopolitics: Essays on the Governance of Life and Death* (Durham: Duke University Press, 2011). Michelle Murphy's use of the term would also be representative: "biopolitics thus also always involved necropolitics—distributions of death effects and precariousness—at the same time as it could foster life." She makes a remark distinctive in the literature, insofar as she indicates the procreative variant of necropolitics, specifically: "It was through this multiscaled, *differential governing* of the diversity within the mass, for the greater good of that mass, that individuals in the twentieth century were so often enjoined to participate in the governing of their own potentialities and reproduction." Michelle Murphy, *Seizing the Means of Reproduction: Entanglements of Feminism, Health, and Technoscience* (Durham: Duke University Press, 2012), 13. For critical remarks about minimal consideration by Mbembe of the relation between necropolitics and gender, sex, sexual violence, and reproduction, see Melissa W. Wright, "Necropolitics, Narcopolitics, and Femicide: Gendered Violence on the Mexico-U.S. Border," *Signs: Journal of Women in Culture and Society* 36, no. 3 (2011): 707–31, 710; and see Cihan Ahmetbeyzade, "Gendering Necropolitics: The Juridical-Political Sociality of Honor Killings in Turkey," *Journal of Human Rights* 7, no. 3 (2008): 187–206.

3. For particularly relevant discussions of this phenomenon, see Murphy, *Seizing the Means of Reproduction*; Elsa Dorlin, *La Matrice de la race: Généalogie sexuelle et coloniale de la nation française* (Paris: Découverte, 2006); Alys Weinbaum, *Wayward Reproductions: Genealogies of Race and Nation in Transatlantic Modern Thought* (Durham: Duke University Press, 2004); Gisela Bock, *Zwangssterilisation im Nationalsozialismus. Studien zur Rassenpolitik und Frauenpolitik* (Opladen: Westdeutscher, 1986); McWhorter, *Racism and Sexual Oppression in Anglo-America*.

4. While one can speculate about the possibilities for dialogue between these figures as they appear in *HS I* and in *No Future*, the many ways in which one would differentiate them would include the psychoanalytic inflection given by Edelman to the formation of the *sintho*mosexual.

5. The "nervous woman" is said to be the "negative image" of the Mother and the "most visible form of [the] hystericization" of women's bodies (*HS I* 104).

6. Emile Zola, *Fécondité* (Paris: Le Trésors de la littérature, 2007), discussed in an earlier version of chapter 4 published as "Sacred Fecundity: Agamben, Sexual Difference, and Reproductive Life," *Telos* 161 (2012): 51–78.

7. See the discussion of the campaign, or "crusade," against children's masturbation in these terms, in *Abnormal*, in which the latter term is used a number of times.

8. He shows that, like the surveillance of masturbation, the practice of reproductive control or selectivity associated with the "Malthusian couple" is also, and frequently, understood as a claim to a controlled and optimal future: possible inflections of repression and constraint blur with a language of incentive, and collective and individual interest, and flourishing, and so with a different kind of freedom associated with vitality, prolifera-

3. FOUCAULT'S CHILDREN   213

tion, optimization. See for example, Anne Cova, *Féminismes et néo-malthusianismes sous la IIIe republique: La liberté de la maternité* (Paris: L'Harmattan, 2011).
9. Jasbir Puar, *Terrorist Assemblages: Homonationalism in Queer Times* (Durham: Duke University Press, 2007), 206.
10. Ibid., 24.
11. Despite the diversity of theorists working with concepts of intersectionality, Sara Ahmed's pithy definition, as Holland observes, characterizes the field well: "given that relationships of power intersect, how we inhabit a given category depends on how we inhabit others." Sara Ahmed, *Queer Phenomenology: Orientations, Objects, Others* (Durham: Duke University Press, 2006), 136, citing Sharon Holland, *The Erotic Life of Racism* (Durham: Duke University Press, 2012).
12. Jasbir Puar, *Terrorist Assemblages*, 212.
13. For this reason, the work prefers a Deleuzean modeling of assemblages to a Foucauldian modeling of disciplinary bodies.
14. Puar, *Terrorist Assemblages*, 206.
15. Rey Chow, *The Protestant Ethnic and the Spirit of Capitalism* (New York: Columbia University Press, 2002), 7. See also McWhorter's *Racism and Sexual Oppression in Anglo-America*, 212ff., for her extensive account of the intersections of racial difference and sexual difference pursued through a reading of Foucault, a project that integrates the concern with governmentalities of reproduction as race defense. McWhorter gives particular, and very helpful, attention to the conceptual overlaps of perversions of race and perversions of sex.
16. Chow, *The Protestant Ethnic*, 2; Ann Stoler, *Foucault's History of Sexuality and the Colonial Order of Things* (Durham: Duke University Press, 1995). Among the readings to have reconsidered *HS I* in light of Foucault's Collège de France lectures of 1975–76 (now published as *Society Must Be Defended*), Stoler's pathbreaking project was the first book-length study arguing for a greater attention to the status of race in the work, and establishing the link between the formations of sex and the role of colonial sexuality. While not foregrounding the imbrication of queer sexualities, she does consider the associations between a history of sexuality and colonialist worries about race perversion. Forms of sex in colonial and race-hierarchical contexts can present concurrently as sexual *and* race perversion. Thus Puar distinguishes Stoler's work for the consideration it does give to the "'evil' of homosexuality as a *racializing* discourse" (Puar, *Terrorist Assemblages*, 239n93, my emphasis), making similarly positive reference to McWhorter's project.
17. Chow, *The Protestant Ethnic*, 6. (Citing HS1 141)
18. Ibid., 3.
19. Ibid.
20. See Stoler, who emphasizes this aspect of *HS I* and in the associated Collège de France lectures. Showing that these aspects are insufficiently developed in the former, she argues that one cannot disconnect *HS I*'s account of the formations of sex from those of colonialism, yet the latter disrupt some aspects of *HS I*'s narrative.
21. Puar, *Terrorist Assemblages*, 34–36.

22. This separation manifests in approaches as various as Robert Bernasconi, "The Politics of Race Mixing: The Place of Biopower Within the History of Racisms," *Bioethical Inquiry* 7:205–16; Thomas Lemke, *Biopolitics: An Advanced Introduction* (New York: New York University Press, 2011); and Claire Blencowe, *Biopolitical Experience: Foucault, Power, and Positive Critique* (London: Palgrave Macmillan, 2013). By contrast, McWhorter, in *Racism and Sexual Oppression in Anglo-America*, integrates the making of sex, racism, sexual perversion, and governmental reproduction, if not through attention to the same figures or problematic foregrounded by Puar. Dorlin's *La Matrice de la race* is another project interestingly assessed from the perspective proposed by Puar. *La Matrice*, a work intermittently referring to Foucault, considers connections between colonialist expansion, the government of reproduction, sexuality, and specters of overlapping racial and sexual perversion. At the same time, it is more in proximity with McWhorter's project (which gives attention to the emergence of the latter phenomena in the eugenics movement in America and elsewhere) in not foregrounding the overlaps of race hierarchy, sex, and defensive biopolitized reproduction *with* the concurrent making, more specifically, of the queer other. The overlaps of race and sexuality and biopolitics have, by contrast, become a point of reference in the field of black queer studies. For example, in a recent work critical of the status of race in Foucault's work, Alex Weheliye integrates considerations of biopolitics, race, and sexual perversion in a discussion of Hortense Spiller's reading of sexual difference and slavery and the racialized pornotroping of violence and sexual violence in the tradition of slave ownership and its representation, which is discussed also by Sharon Holland, *The Erotic Life of Racism* (Durham: Duke University Press, 2012); Alex Weheliye, *Habeas Viscus: Racializing Assemblages, Biopolitics, and Black Feminist Theories of the Human* (Durham: Duke University Press, 2014); and see Hortense Spillers, *Black, White, and in Color: Essays on American Literature and Culture* (Chicago: University of Chicago Press, 2003). See also the discussion of Spillers with Foucault in Feder, *Family Bonds*.
23. Discussed also in Puar, *Terrorist Assemblages*, 128.
24. Ibid., xii.
25. For example, the phantasmatic terrorist of *Homonationalism*, who is generally associated with homophobia, may also be taken to be antifeminist, violently opposed to reproductive rights, and has been associated with proneness to sexual violence. Thus there is a feminist correlate to the Puar's argument concerning homonationalism (Puar suggests the term *gender exceptionalism*) as when the putative antifeminism of other peoples, religions, cultures similarly becomes the pretext for war and invasion, organized by a narrative of the delivery of Western rights. See Puar, *Terrorist Assemblages*, 5, 22, 59; and Inderpal Grewal, *Transnational America: Feminisms, Diasporas, Neoliberalisms* (Durham: Duke University Press, 2005).
26. Weheliye's *Habeas Viscus* proposes that we need not turn to figures such as Foucault and Agamben to accomplish such theoretical work. While offering critical readings of the latter, he also proposes alternatives: a turn, for example, to Spillers (also more closely read with Foucault by Feder in *Family Bonds*). But, insofar as Foucault's texts remain a point of reference in these debates (including the work of Weheliye, Puar,

and Spillers), they can also be engaged maximally from the perspective of the questions they occlude.
27. See the discussion of this in chapter one. For an often referenced, very helpful historical overview emphasizing contingency of concepts of reproduction, see Ludmilla Jordanova, "Interrogating the Concept of Reproduction in the Eighteenth Century," in *Conceiving the New World Order: The Global Politics of Reproduction*, ed. Faye Ginsburg and Rayna Rapp (Berkeley: University of California Press, 1995), 369–86.
28. Giorgio Agamben, *Homo Sacer: Sovereign Power and Bare Life*, trans. Daniel Heller-Roazen (Stanford: Stanford University Press, 1998); Nikolas Rose, *The Politics of Life Itself: Biomedecine, Power, Subjectivity in the Twenty-First Century* (Princeton: Princeton University Press, 2007); Roberto Esposito, *Bios: Biopolitics and Philosophy*, trans. Timothy Campbell (Minneapolis: University of Minnesota Press, 2008); Robert Bernasconi, "The Politics of Race Mixing: The Place of Biopower Within the History of Racisms," *Bioethical Inquiry* 7 (2010): 205–16; Donna V. Jones, *The Racial Discourses of Life Philosophy: Négritude, Vitalism, and Modernity* (New York: Columbia University Press, 2010); Weheliye, *Habeas Viscus*; David Halperin, *Saint Foucault: Towards a Gay Hagiography* (Oxford: Oxford University Press, 1995); Didier Eribon, *Insult and the Making of the Gay Self* (Durham: Duke University Press 2004); Eve Kosofsky Sedgwick, *Epistemology of the Closet* (Berkeley: University of California Press, 1990); Janet Halley, *Split Decisions: How and Why to Take a Break from Feminism* (Princeton: Princeton University Press, 2006).
29. "Given these conditions, you can understand how and why a technical knowledge such as medicine, or rather the combination of medicine and hygiene, is in the nineteenth century . . . of considerable importance because of the link it establishes between scientific knowledge of both biological and organic processes (or in other words, the population and the body" (*SMBD* 252).
30. So, for Vikki Bell, it will make sense that sex is "one of the most important of the biopolitical apparatuses" [the point from which much contemporary biopolitical theory has surely distanced itself] and also "more than an example of power." Because sex is the link between the two poles of bio-power, and between the 'body' and population, it "became a crucial target of a power organized around the management of life." Vikki Bell, *Interrogating Incest: Feminism, Foucault, and the Law* (London: Routledge, 1993), 36, citing *HS I*.
31. See Blencowe, *Biopolitical Experience*; Murphy, *Seizing the Means of Reproduction*; Duschinsky and Rocha, *Foucault, the Family, and Politics*.
32. For his analysis of the problematic role in scientific research (and its public funding) of strategies of exclusion *and* of inclusion of the gender and race identities associated with the individuating disciplines, see Steve Epstein, *Inclusion: The Politics of Difference* (Chicago: University of Chicago Press, 2007).
33. Fassin has explored the emergence of the biopolitically based rights claimant, and so the emergence of what he terms *biolegitimacy*: as when health-based claims can trump politically based claims to asylum, and, in this specific context, "biological life" will take on a claim as the "highest value." Didier Fassin, "Quand le corps fait loi: La raison

humanitaire dans les procédures de régularisation des étrangèrs," *Sciences sociales et santé* 19, no. 4 (2001): 5–34.

34. See, for example, Astrid Deuber-Mankowsky, "Nothing Is Political, Everything Can Be Politicized: On the Concept of the Political in Michel Foucault and Carl Schmitt," *Telos* 142 (2008): 135–61; and Maria Muhle, "A Genealogy of Biopolitics: The Notion of Life in Canguilhem and Foucault," in Vanessa Lemm and Miguel Vatter, eds., *The Government of Life: Foucault: Biopolitics, and Neoliberalism* (New York: Fordham University Press, 2014), 77–97.
35. Blencowe's *Biopolitical Experience* includes an analysis of the status of life and death in Foucault's work that connects his treatment of biopolitics with his considerations of contingent forms of life and death more broadly throughout his work, particularly in projects such as *The Birth of the Clinic* and *The Order of Things*.
36. Teresa de Lauretis identifies *HS I* to be elaborating the technology of sex as a conflation of sexuality with reproduction; see her "Habit Changes: Response," in *differences* 6, nos. 2 and 3 (1994): 296–313, 299 (in a special issue, "Feminism Meets Queer Theory").
37. The Reichian hypothesis would be that the repression of sexuality functions to stimulate a (re)productive, procreative sexuality, friendly to the interests of capitalism; see Bell, *Interrogating Incest*, 19; and, for Foucault's broad response to psychoanalysis in which his response to Reich played its role, see Mauro Basaure, "Foucault and the 'Anti-Oedipus Movement': Psychoanalysis as Disciplinary Power," *History of Psychiatry* 20, no. 3 (2009): 340–59.
38. To be sure, Foucault stresses, here and elsewhere (particularly in *Security, Territory, Population*) that the regulation of population includes concerns with health, diet, habitation, immigration, urban space, order, economic stability, employment, etc. But at its heart, he claims, is sex—sex thinkable in terms of rates of fertility and sterility and birthrate.
39. And at this point, it is possible for those interested in Foucault's account of biopolitics *as* race division to highlight (critically or in an account understood as expanding his project), in response to *SMBD* and to some extent *HS I*, the new threshold role he would need to attribute more concertedly (consistent with his own account of the technologies of biopolitics, the concerns of the society that must be defended, and the emergence of theories of degeneracy) to the emergence of biopoliticized procreation with respect to the defensive, race-divided futurities of peoples, races, nations, and colonies he describes. See, for example, Murphy, *Seizing the Means of Reproduction*, 13, 24; McWhorter, *Racism and Sexual Oppression in Anglo-America*; Feder, *Family Bonds*.
40. See, for example, Malthus's reference to Susmilch's tables, included in his *Gottliche Ordnung*, which provides comparative rates of deaths, marriages, and births for Prussia and Lithuania from 1692 to 1757.
41. Michel Foucault, *The Order of Things: An Archaeology of the Human Sciences* (New York: Vintage, 1979), 187.
42. Claude-Jacques Herbert, *Essai sur la police générale des grains* (London, 1753), cited in *HS I* 25.

43. Adam Smith, *The Wealth of Nations* (New York: Random House, 1994), 92, and see Foucault, *The Order of Things*, 258.
44. Lars Behrisch, "'Politische Zahlen.' Statistik und die Rationalisierung der Herrschaft im spaten Ancien Regime," *Zeitschrift für historische Forschung* 31, no. 4 (2004): 51–57, 56.
45. On the turn of the century (neo-)Malthusian movement and its proximity with turn-of-the-century feminist movements in a number of countries, see Cova, *Féminismes et néo-malthusianismes;* Kevin Repp, "'More Corporeal, More Concrete': Liberal Humanism, Eugenics, and German Progressives at the Last Fin de Siecle," *Journal of Modern History* 72, no. 3 (2000): 683–730; Lucy Bland, *Banishing the Beast: Sexuality and the Early Feminists* (New York: New Press, 1995); and Murphy, *Seizing the Means of Reproduction.*
46. This is not to suggest that the moral and political movements known as Malthusian or neo-Malthusian followed the moral principles of Malthus—with a view to population impact such movements turned specifically to a use of contraception Malthus considered abhorrent, and sometimes to a eugenically oriented approach to choice of reproductive partner.
47. Thomas R. Malthus, *Essay on the Principle of Population* (Cambridge: Cambridge University Press, 1992), 313.
48. Francis Galton would repeat, with the notorious alternative focus on procreative selectivity and "quality," the vision of the moral obligation of a procreative agent toward something conceived as population future.
49. Malthus, *Essay on the Principle of Population*, 213–14.
50. Simons, in "Foucault's Mother," reviews such formations of maternity in the context of his account of the family, also suggesting the possibility of variants involving performative subversion, resistance, or counterconduct on the part of women. In a generous characterization of *HS I*, Véronique Mottier allows that Foucault makes some brief recognition in *HS I* of the specific role of mothers in biopolitical *dispositifs*, "Foucault suggested that biopower invests women in particular ways, highlighting the ways in which medical discourses and interventions pathologize women by reducing them to their reproductive functions." But she identifies in Foucault's discussion of hysterical mothers (*HS I* 153) a depiction of "the workings on power on women's bodies primarily in individualizing terms, . . . producing the 'hystericization' of individual women". Even allowing for *HS I*'s reference to this phenomenon, she agrees that Foucault "failed to acknowledge (and consequently . . . under-theorized) the ways in which women's reproductive bodies become particular targets of population policies such as eugenic policy-making, despite his own use of eugenics as an illustration of biopolitics in modern times at the end of *History of Sexuality, Volume one*." Véronique Mottier "Gender, Reproductive Politics and the Liberal State: Beyond Foucault," in *Foucault, the Family and Politics*, ed. Duschinsky and Rocha, 142–57, 149. Mottier goes on to outline directions in which the more specific analysis she proposes might have taken him. Michelle Murphy similarly concludes, based on a reading of *The History of Sexuality* that Foucault largely occluded this particular question. It is true that his discussions of eugenic concerns rarely foreground sexual difference, as Mottier has suggested they should. Yet these theorists are also bringing to light that the Foucauldian material is in the vicinity

of an analysis of biopoliticized reproduction, and maternities, in its attention to families, parents, couples, children, birthrate, population. See Mottier, "Gender, Reproductive Politics and the Liberal State," 149; and Murphy's *Seizing the Means of Reproduction*.

51. See Jordanova, "Interrogating the Concept of Reproduction in the Eighteenth Century."
52. That differentiation would lead Foucault to both antifeminist accounts, attributing to women specific duties in this respect, and pro-feminist variants that also accorded women a more specific responsibilization than was borne by the "couple." See, for example, R. S. Steinmetz, "Feminismus und Rasse," *Jahrbuch für Sozialwissenschaft* 7, no. 12 (1904): 751–68.
53. See Cova, *Féminismes et néo-malthusianismes*.
54. Katherine Logan, "Foucault, the Modern Mother, and Maternal Power," in Duschinsky and Rocha, *Foucault, the Family and Politics*, 63–81, 64.
55. Jacques Donzelot, *The Policing of Families*, trans. Robert Hurley (New York: Random House, 1979), 20. As Foucault describes this, the family becomes, from a political, medical, expert and philanthropic perspective, a problem of health optimization (*AB* 179) and child raising becomes a biopolitical problem of optimizing collective health. As he argues, descent is then no longer (or not only) organized around the conjugal axis, but rather around the parent-child axis, now oriented around optimization of the health of the child, and concurrently considered a collective governmental problem. Like breast-feeding (whose collective- and future-oriented forms of responsibilization he also mentions), the conduct of child raising is reconfigured as a matter not only of parental responsibility toward the individual life, health, and longevity of the child but also toward the population. The conduct of reproduction itself (this might include the conduct of selection of partner, of timing, or rate of procreation) might become a matter of biopolicized "responsibility" toward a collective future. But one must turn to other commentators (Donzelot providing an early instance) for a sexual differentiation of mother and father in this context.
56. Foucault comments: "at this point the central object of the maneuver or crusade is revealed: the constitution of a new family body" (*AB* 248). Foucault is discussing P.-M. Rozier's *Des habitudes secrétes ou des maladies produites par l'onanisme chez les femmes* (Paris 1825), 81–82. The editors of *Abnormal* identify this as the edition used by Foucault, where the same work was also published under the title *Lettres médicales et morales* in 1806, and, importantly, under the title, *Des habitudes secrétes ou de l'onanisme chez les femmes. Lettres médicales, anecdotiques et morales à une jeune malade et à une mère, dédiées aux mères de famille et aux maitresses de pensions* (Paris, 1825).
57. See, for example, Michel Foucault, "The Politics of Health in the Eighteenth Century," in *Power/Knowledge: Selected Interviews and Other Writings, 1972–1977*, ed. Colin Gordon (New York: Pantheon, 1980), 166–82.
58. There are a number of similar references to unindividuated "parents" and "couples" in *HS I*.
59. McWhorter, in *Racism and Sexual Oppression in Anglo-America*, reviews a number of the texts considered by Foucault not only with respect to their differentiation of male and female "abnormals" but also, for a degree of a differentiation between the roles of

the mother and father. For example, she gives her attention to debates about whether mothers, specifically, could be expected to control successfully for masturbatory activity in their children.
60. See Logan, "Foucault, the Modern Mother, and Maternal Power," 64.
61. The reference to maternal power may be mildly misleading: she would be individuated with respect to the deployment of sexuality; she would be a vector of disciplinary power. For one discussion of the relation between the maternal and power that could be elaborated in Foucault's discussion of the family, see Danielle Rancière (n85, this chapter) for another that stresses the family as a space of vectors of multiple modes of power, see Chloë Taylor, "Foucault and Familial Power," *Hypatia* 27, no. 1 (2012): 201–8.
62. Insofar as Foucault discusses new parental obligations such as ensuring the child's health, controlling for masturbation, deterring corrupting outside influences, controlling for the manifestations of dangerous instincts, instilling obedience, and monitoring for the manifestations of various forms of behavioral or congenital abnormality, the child is individualized in terms of the gradations of normal to abnormal in these respects, while (we can add) the mother is simultaneously individualized in terms of meeting private and public responsibilities with respect to the child's upbringing.
63. See Donzelot, *The Policing of Families*, 18.
64. An exemplary version of this trend in interpretation is Mauro Basaure, "Foucault and the 'Anti-Oedipus Movement': Psychoanalysis as Disciplinary Power," *History of Psychiatry* 20, no. 3 (2009): 340–59.
65. In addition to essays examining Foucault's discussions of family spaces, Duschinsky and Rocha's *Foucault, the Family and Politics* includes a short translated section of *Le désordre des familles*.
66. See also the discussion in these terms of the *lettres de cachets* in Gilles Deleuze, *Foucault*, trans. Seán Hand (Minneapolis: University of Minnesota Press, 1988), 28.
67. Arlette Farge and Michel Foucault, *Le désordre des familles: lettres de cachet des Archives de la Bastille au XVIIIe siècle, présenté par Arlette Fage et Michel Foucault* (Paris: Julliard/Gallimard, 1982), 46 (my translation).
68. This point is helpfully stressed in Taylor's "Foucault and Familial Power," as is the multiplicity of different forms of power Foucault sees intersecting in family spaces.
69. In particular, he makes an important distinction in *HS I* between working-class and bourgeois families. Primarily discussing the metropolitan French context, he identifies the emergence of concern about the possible presence of children's sexuality, arguing that the discourse and culture of scrutiny for masturbation may have importantly emerged in the bourgeois family some half-century before it did in working-class families. Moreover, the concern about childhood sexuality in the latter took the form more of a polemics about the possibility of incest arising from excessive physical proximity between adults and children, and between children, in working-class family environments that, in other respects also, had come to be considered unhealthy as a matter of public health and philanthropic concern (the latter is further discussed in Donzelot's *The Policing of Families*.)
70. Where an exception is to be found in Taylor's "Foucault and Familial Power."

71. See *HS I* 106, 147, 149; and on this see Taylor, "Foucault and Familial Power," 206–8.
72. In this case, the term [*pénétré*] used to describe the penetration of sovereign forms of power by the mechanisms of biopower (*HS I* 89).
73. *HS I* 89. It is not uncommon for commentators to stress the uncannily coherent operations of the disparate-become-compatible, and an excellent example of this approach is to be found in Mauro Basaure, "Foucault and the 'Anti-Oedipus movement'". The compatible effects of disparate elements is also one of the interpretations given to contingency in Foucault's work, about which, for a superb account, see Colin Koopman, *Genealogy as Critique: Foucault and the Problems of Modernity* (Bloomington: Indiana University Press: 2013). Alternative interpretations, for which Deleuze surely provides the best-known example, can be positioned at the opposite pole to Basaure's version in stressing that the heterogeneity in apparatuses (heterogeneity of, in, and between techniques, modes, and apparatuses—the multiple participating multiplicities, so to speak) allows for a stronger degree of the complex, dehiscent, incompatible, surprising, and random. Deleuze does not, of course, minimize the extraordinary coalescence of a *dispositif* described by Foucault, but he provides an important alternative to the more "clockwork," stable, and integrated variation provided by Basaure. In Deleuze's version, there is more necessary divergence within what has taken shape as an apparatus, and this is also connected strongly with the possibility of fractures and new directions. Unsurprisingly, Deleuze also rejects the linear interpretation of Foucauldian modes of power. See Gilles Deleuze, *Foucault*, trans. Seán Hand (Minneapolis: University of Minnesota Press, 1988); and Gilles Deleuze, "What Is a Dispositif?," in Timothy Armstrong, ed., *Michel Foucault Philosopher* (London: Harvester Wheatsheaf, 1992), 159–68.
74. In *The History of Sexuality*, referring to a number of variants of the family in anatomo-political, demographic, alliance, and biopolitical contexts, Foucault also discusses the concurrently individualized and collective variants of the forms of threatened "death" in question, also proposing multiple times in *HS I* the term *transposition*. An example of his use of the term is seen where he speaks to the conversion of what had been an aristocratic interest in bloodlines and genealogy (integrated with the alliance mode) into a bourgeois concern (*HS I* 124): the diseases and defects lurking in one's biological inheritance, a "transposition" connected to a concern with "the indefinite extension of strength, vigor, health, and life" (now integrated with the biopower mode).
75. Again marking a degree of class differentiation on such points, he adds that this "became routine [*canonique*] in the course of the century when working-class housing construction was undertaken."
76. As described in the accounts of family presented in *AB* and *STP*, though some further disaggregation of Foucault's "parents" into the respective responsibilization of father and mother is called for.
77. Foucault makes this point in *Abnormal*, while Taylor stresses the conflicting (but also true) point: families can also lose jurisdiction over those in their care where their children are deemed insufficiently "disciplined"; see Taylor, "Foucault and Familial Power," 205.

78. Eighteenth-century physiocrats such as François Quesnay discussed habits and trends within the population that eluded the governmental efforts of the sovereign, yet could be treated indirectly, by working on "milieu" (STP 71).
79. Jean-Baptiste Moheau, *Recherches et considérations sur la population de la France* (Paris: Moutard, 1778).
80. See Andrea Rusnock, "Quantifying Infant Mortality in England and France, 1750–1800," in *Body Counts: Medical Quantification in Historical and Sociological Perspectives*, ed. Gerard Jorland, Annick Opinel, and George Weisz (Montreal: McGill-Queen's University Press, 2005), 65–88, 80, and see Andrea Rusnock, *Vital Accounts: Quantifying Health and Population in Eighteenth-Century England and France* (Cambridge: Cambridge University Press, 2002).
81. His earliest reference to "bio-politique" is to be found in 1974: Michel Foucault, "La naissance de la médicine sociale," in *Dits et écrits: 1954–1988*, in four volumes, vol. 3: *1976–1979*, ed. Daniel Defert and François Ewald, with L. Lagrange (Paris: Gallimard, 1994), 207–28, 210. Perhaps his last published reference to the term is seen in his "course summary" of research presented in the 1978–1979 Collège de France lecture series, published in the Annuaire du Collège de France and in Michel Foucault, *The Birth of Biopolitics*, trans. Graham Burchell (Basingstoke: Palgrave Macmillan, 2008), 317. The theme was to have been biopolitics, here described as "the attempt, starting from the eighteenth century, to rationalize the problems posed to governmental practice by phenomena characteristic of a set of "living" beings forming a population: health, hygiene, birthrate, life expectancy, race. . . . We know the increasing importance of these problems since the nineteenth century, and the political and economic issues they have raised up to the present." Similarly, in this epoch of reception of Foucault's work, Donzelot characterizes "what [Foucault] calls the biopolitical dimension" as "the proliferation of political technologies that invested the body, health, modes of subsistence and lodging—the entire space of existence in European countries from the eighteenth century onward. All the techniques that found their unifying pole in what, at the outset, was called *policing*: not understood in the limiting, repressive sense we give the term today, but according to a much broader meaning that encompassed all the methods for developing the quality of the population and the strength of the nation" (Donzelot, *The Policing of Families*, 6–7).
82. By contrast, an important aspect of Mbembe's introduction of the term *necropolitics* is, precisely, that its modality is analogous to the biopolitical: it is an administered and diffused proliferation of murderousness, bloodshed, and chaos which is not based on a repressive model but is instead (as is the characteristic definition of Foucauldian biopolitics) stimulating, capillary, and infectious.
83. Donzelot, *The Policing of Families*, 6.
84. Ibid., 66.
85. At the time of publication of Donzelot's *The Policing of Families*, Genevieve Fraisse and Danielle Rancière queried what seemed to be an oversimplified account, if not a critique, from Donzelot of the alliance of interests of moralizing philanthrophists and feminists (Donzelot, *Policing of Families*, 36). Donzelot describes forms of power that

became possible when wives and mothers took on a revalorized status as manager and "guardienne" of the household, of children, of the husband's morality, and of household work. Thus they took on a new importance in the apparati of discipline, surveillance, and moral control, becoming a kind of "double agent" of state and capitalism. In consequence, according to Rancière's commentary on his claims, some feminisms aligned their demands, perhaps unwittingly, with the attribution to women of politically exploitable "natural virtues." To describe such alliances need not amount to a critique of feminism. As Rancière points out, it might form part of a complex genealogy of different formations of feminism. But Fraisse identifies a critical tenor in Donzelot's account of feminist defenses of maternity and its social importance. Is he insinuating that feminism became (in this respect) the historical dupe of reactionary forces? Rancière adds that the account disregards the complex responsibilities and capacities of women in households (responsibility for provision of food for children, capacity also to confine some dissolute spouses), a complexity pinpointed, by contrast, in Farge and Foucault's collaborative *Le désordre des familles*; and see Farge's *L'histoire ébruitée*. Donzelot, according to this argument, would disregard the complexity of philanthropic projects, of the role played by mothers, and of formations of maternal and paternal authority. Rancière invites us to speculate about the type of genealogy of maternal and family formations that would really be needed here, in contrast to Donzelot's efforts in this respect. See Danielle Rancière, "Le Philanthrope et sa famille," *Les révoltes logiques* 8–9 (1978): 99–115, 104–5; Arlette Farge, "L'histoire ébruitée: Des femmes dans la société pré-révolutionnaire parisienne," in *L'histoire sans qualité* (collective volume, with contributions by Christiane Dufrancatel, Christine Fauré, Geneviève Fraisse, Michelle Perrot, Élisabeth Salvaresi, Pascale Werner) (Paris: L'espace critique, 1979), 15–39; and Genevieve Fraisse, *La raison des femmes* (Paris: Plon, 1992), 127.

86. I refer back to the earlier discussion of Puar's argument that attribution of sexual intolerance and death mongering to the (frequently Islamic) "terrorist" foreigner becomes the pretext for violence against this same stereotypical figure (ranging from invasion, illegal incarcerations, to differential legal regimes, including the conduct of immigration policies).

87. See Stoler, *Race and the Education of Desire*; Bernasconi, "The Politics of Race Mixing"; Dorlin, *La matrice de la race;* McWhorter, *Racism and Sexual Oppression in Anglo-America;* Weinbaum, *Wayward Reproductions*.

88. Stoler, *Race and the Education of Desire*, 170.

89. She notes that nineteenth-century degeneracy theory developed as a national and a class-specific project that converged with wider purity campaigns for improved natality and selective sterilization (Stoler, *Race and the Education of Desire*, 31).

90. Dorlin, *La matrice de la race*.

91. For discussion of eugenic decision making in which the role of the woman is specially foregrounded, see Angelique Richardson, *Love and Eugenics in the Late Nineteenth Century: Rational Reproduction and the New Woman* (Oxford: Oxford University Press, 2003). This is a study of turn-of-the-century British literature (some by feminist authors) in which concerns about degeneracy figure the woman as primarily exposed to risk. Her

duty (and that of her parents) is, first hermeneutic, in that she must seek (and be cautioned to do so) for signs of dissipated habit and tainted biological inheritance in a prospective husband, a physiological truth (and truth of conduct) he is unlikely to disclose. A bad choice will transmit diseases such as syphilis, and expose her and her children to the harmful physical proximity of his dissipation, and expose her to the transmission of a harmful heredity. The resulting family is depicted as a deadly environment of sapped physiology.

92. Threshold of transmission: she must be all the more careful (and hermeneutic) in her selection of a partner. She is reconfigured as overlapping obligation to herself, her children, to the health of the population, the nation, and the vitality and futurity of all these bodies. One can consult a vast literature on the antifeminist and pro-feminist versions of this understanding of responsibility. Antifeminist variants argued for the denial of careers to women, since this would exclude talented women from reproductive stock, or for coercive intervention (through medical or similar advice, policy, laws, or force) into the reproductive decision. Pro-feminist versions could associate women's rights claims (political and civic rights and reproductive rights) with women's (reproductive) importance to population. In all cases, including those where women were seen as thresholds of harmful impact, they were also associated with capacities for choice—dangerously or positively. Thus debate takes shape as to the conditions (ranging from the restrictive to the liberal) under which the best choices would be made and best population impact would be seen. These are race-divisive or race-hierarchical politics, avowedly or not, insofar as "quality" choices in reproduction will have a flagrant or implicit racial bias. Secondary studies include Ann Taylor Allen, "Feminism and Eugenics in Germany and Britain, 1900–1940: A Comparative Perspective," *German Studies Review* 23, no. 3 (2000): 477–505; Cova, *Féminismes et néo-malthusianismes*; Richardson, *Love and Eugenics in the Late Nineteenth Century*; Weinbaum, *Wayward Reproductions*; Dorothy Roberts, *Killing the Black Body: Race, Reproduction, and the Meaning of Liberty* (New York: Vintage, 1988); Dennis Hodgson and Susan Cotts Watkins, "Feminists and Neo-Malthusians: Past and Present Alliances," *Population and Development Review* 23, no. 3 (1997): 469–523.

93. Murphy, *Seizing the Means of Reproduction*, 11.

94. See, for example, Murphy's cautions, in the context of her analysis of legal and similar regulation of reproduction. Arguing that one should be wary of defaulting to a primarily repressive model in reproductive rights theory, she offers as an alternative a formulation of feminist and other counterconducts in this context (ibid., 183n3).

95. Among various formulations of such arguments (with different conclusions) see Wendy Brown, "Reproductive Freedom and the Right to Privacy: A Paradox for Feminists," in Irene Diamond, ed., *Families, Politics, and Public Policy: A Feminist Dialogue on Women and the State* (New York: Longman, 1983): 311–88; Mary Poovey, "The Abortion Question and the Death of Man," *Feminists Theorize the Political*, ed. Judith Butler and Joan Scott (New York: Routledge, 1992), 239–56; and Ruth A. Miller, *The Limits of Bodily Integrity: Abortion, Adultery, and Rape Legislation in Comparative Perspective* (Aldershott: Ashgate, 2007), further discussed in the following chapter.

224 3. FOUCAULT'S CHILDREN

96. For Foucault's fleeting use of the term see my chapter one, n83, p20. For post-Foucauldian biopolitical theory see, for example, see François Debrix and Alexander Barder, *Beyond Biopolitics: Theory, Violence, and Horror in World Politics* (New York: Routledge, 2012); and Patricia Clough and Craig Willse, eds., *Beyond Biopolitics: Essays on the Governance of Life and Death* (Durham: Duke University Press, 2011).
97. See, in particular, Achille Mbembe, "Necropolitics," *Public Culture* 15, no. 1 (2003): 11–40. Mbembe argues, in the wake of Foucault, that we ought to identify, as a contemporary mode of biopolitics, sovereign rights over mortality in a form differing from the forms of sovereign right over life described by Foucault. Mbembe discusses administration through disseminated disorder, insecurity, panic, unease, precarity, and the administered promotion of a seemingly disorganized chaos.
98. Roberto Esposito, *Terms of the Political: Community, Immunity, Biopolitics*, trans. Rhiannon Noel Welch (New York: Fordham University Press, 2012), 72–73.
99. Ibid., 74.

4. IMMUNITY, BARE LIFE, AND THE THANATOPOLITICS OF REPRODUCTION

The chapter epigraph comes from Ruth A. Miller, *The Limits of Bodily Integrity: Abortion, Adultery, and Rape Legislation in Comparative Perspective* (Aldershot: Ashgate, 2007), 173.

1. Roberto Esposito, *Bios: Biopolitics and Philosophy*, trans. Timothy Campbell (Minneapolis: University of Minnesota Press, 2008), 45, hereafter *Bios*.
2. As such, we saw that it is mostly presented as distinguishable from an ancient, sovereign right to kill, of which it is not the return and with which it should not be confused. Thus Foucault refers to the "old power of death that symbolized sovereign power" coming to be meticulously overlaid (*recouverte soigneusement*) with an "administration of bodies and calculated management of life" (*HS I* 139–40).
3. That's to say, executions, attacks, massacres, wars, genocides are given an biopolitical inflection if and where they are considered to optimize the life of some, thereby effecting the "break into the domain of life" associated by Foucault with biopolitical aims, between "what must live and what must die" (*SMBD* 254).
4. Translation modified. This seems not to undermine the *HS I* discussion, partly because it also makes reference to this kind of "penetration"; see *HS I* 89.
5. In fact, Foucault is referring to a biopolitical deployment of sovereign power. The reference occurs in the midst of a broader discussion of this possibility, and the paradox he goes on to mention in this particular passage is a deployment of sovereign power by "this power to guarantee life."
6. The closest account might be seen in Foucault's identification of security's aims and strategies. For example, *Security, Territory, Population* describes the mercantile aim of averting scarcity in advance by a thorough control of prices, a strategy that could only produce the opposite effect to that intended (*STP* 32–33; *SMBD* 246, 249). *Society Must*

Be Defended describes the "regulatory technology of life . . . which tries to control the series of random events that can occur in a living mass, a technology which tries to predict [their] . . . probability (by modifying it, if necessary) or at least to compensate for their effects. This is a technology which aims to establish a sort of homeostasis, not by training individuals, but by achieving an overall equilibrium that protects the security of the whole from internal dangers" (*SMBD* 249). Perhaps the more comprehensive the strategy of risk aversion, the more this provokes destructive or self-negating outcomes. That might be a way of understanding technologies of security whose aim is to defend against internal and external dangers: that they are bound to become autoimmune? But such broader conclusions are not Foucault's interest, and do not form part of his discussion. In the passage mentioned here, Foucault draws, temporarily, a different conclusion. He describes a withdrawal by biopower from forms of death deemed to be outside its control in favor of a possible management of mortality. Here, at least, it is not described as inevitably self-destructive so much, I think, as tending to generate new permutations and possibilities of government (*SMBD* 249).

7. See this point, discussed as principle one ("life and death as transactional unities") in chapter 1.
8. *Bios* 3–7.
9. Esposito refers to ethnic rape aiming at "positive eugenics," occurring during genocide and as "the most extreme immunitary practice, which is to say, affirming the superiority of one's own blood to the point of imposing it on those with whom one does not share it," but also as "destined to be turned against itself, producing exactly what it wanted to avoid" given the "multiethnic outcome of the most violent racial immunization" (*Bios* 7). See note 58 for debate about the use of the terms *ethnic* and *genocidal rape*.
10. For example, described in *HS I* as operating, in conjunction with the growth in importance of biopower, "more and more as a norm" rather than as the juridical arm of sovereign authority (*HS I* 144), and again in *Security, Territory, Population* as a tactic. Here he distinguishes the traditional function of the law as accomplishing obedience of subjects to the sovereign through their obedience to the law, in contrast to the emergence of governmental aims such as ensuring population increase or its sufficient subsistence. Instead of being "impos[ed] . . . on men," the law will then become just one of a series of tactics (which could include alterations in taxation, for example), arranging and disposing so as to achieve instrumental ends (*STP* 99).
11. This to the difference of Agamben, as discussed later in this chapter.
12. Neither the explanatory structure of immunity through which Esposito interprets the thanatopoliticization of biopolitics, nor his aim to loosen the latter's grip and that of (what he has identified as) new sovereign powers by opening life through a reconfiguration of the terms *flesh, norm,* and *birth,* in what he calls a "constructive deconstruction," belong to Foucault (see *Bios* 12).
13. The closest Foucault might be said to come to describing any such necessity is in his account of how "racism justifies [*assure*] the death-function in the economy of biopower," "we are dealing with a mechanism that allows biopower to work. So racism is bound up with the workings of a State that is obliged to use race, the elimination of

races and the purification of the race, to exercise its sovereign power. The juxtaposition of—or the way biopower functions through—the old sovereign power of right over death implies the workings, the introduction and activation, of racism. . . . So you can understand how and why, given these conditions, the most murderous States are also, of necessity, the most racist" *SMBD* 258). Also *HS I* characterizes a "tendency" toward biopower's death function (*HS I* 136–37) and deems it an increasing tendency. But Esposito will develop, as Foucault does not, an account of the inevitability of these developments and of the philosophical imperatives to which they give rise: the development, for example, of alternative understandings of community, individuality, life, flesh, and defense.

14. Maria Muhle distinguishes Foucault from Agamben, on parallel grounds, in "A Genealogy of Biopolitics: The Notion of Life in Canguilhem and Foucault," in Vanessa Lemm and Miguel Vatter, eds., *The Government of Life: Foucault, Biopolitics, and Neoliberalism* (New York: Fordham University Press, 2014), 77–97.

15. See Anne O'Byrne's "Communitas and the Problem of Women," *Angelaki* 18, no. 3 (2013): 125–38, for her discussion of Esposito on the "suppression of birth" (special issue on Roberto Esposito); and see Catherine Mills, *Futures of Reproduction: Bioethics and Biopolitics* (Dordrecht: Springer, 2011), 113.

16. Gisela Bock, *Zwangssterilisation im Nazionalsozialismus: Studien zur Rassenpolitik und Frauenpolitik* (Opladen: Westdeutscher, 1986).

17. These including the trumping of sovereign power and political process by neoliberalism and the thwarting of political process by big money, as elaborated in Wendy Brown, *Undoing the Demos: Neoliberalism's Stealth Democracy* (Brooklyn: Zone, 2015).

18. Briefly mentioned in Wendy Brown's account of eroded, nostalgic, and phantasmatic forms of contemporary state sovereignty, exerting themselves all the more in outward manifestations ranging from laws and policies restricting immigration, the erecting of border walls, engagement in war, all the while, as she argues, that political authority and capacity to ensure democratic process is eroded by a number of forces including the extreme of influence of global capitalism. These are the factors and expressions on which she concentrates. In one comment, in which she discusses her thesis that "as it is weakened and rivaled by other forces, what remains of nation-state sovereignty becomes openly and aggressively . . . theological," she mentions George W. Bush, invoking "God to legitimate his use of veto powers or proposed constitutional amendments to protect 'unborn life' (from abortion) and the 'sanctity of marriage' (from homosexuals) inside the United States and to withdraw funds from organizations promoting condom use or abortifacients in other nations." Wendy Brown, *Walled States, Waning Sovereignty* (Brooklyn: Zone, 2010), 62–63. This can be interpreted in conjunction with a discussion in *Regulating Aversion* of the "corrective [Brown] would add to Foucault's account." Brown recognizes Foucault's well-known challenge to the assumption that the state is the major agent of governmentality. But she argues that we need more attention to the legitimacy (and capacities) of state governance, a preoccupation that may accompany its erosion and, in some domains, irrelevance. She argues that Foucault neglects such crises of legitimacy (whose forms may therefore take shape as nostalgic, phantasmatic, compensatory exertions of sovereign power): "even as [Foucauldian]

governmentality captures both the unboundedness of the state and the insufficiency of the state as a signifier of how modern societies are governed, it fails to convey the extent to which the state remains a unique and hence vulnerable object of political accountability . . . state legitimacy needs determine at least some portion of political life." Wendy Brown, *Regulating Aversion: Tolerance in the Age of Identity and Empire* (Princeton: Princeton University Press, 2008), 83. Brown can be added to other post-Foucauldian theorists discussed in this chapter who identify lacunae in the Foucauldian account and revise the Foucauldian critique of sovereign models of power. But there is also potential for reading together Brown's account of phantasmatic and nostalgic expressions of state sovereignty with Foucault's "it is as if," given that the latter suggests the production of new objects and new governmentalities at the very point of their incapacity.

19. Or, in Butler's reformulation, it could be seen as the power that emerges retrospectively with the suspension of the law, so that *there will seem to have been* a power to suspend the law. For this reformulation see Judith Butler, *Precarious Life: The Powers of Mourning and Violence* (London: Verso, 2004), 61–62, hereafter *PL*.

20. Certainly Foucault describes the ways in which modes of power make their objects and subjects, but Judith Butler claims we don't find in his work an equivalent attention to its power to *unmake* (*PL* 98).

21. See, for example, *SMBD* 240. Notwithstanding Agamben's critical response on this point, in fact Foucault had, as Muhle nicely puts it, "coherent reasons" for omitting to give a definition of life. See Muhle, "A Genealogy of Biopolitics," 78; and see Giorgio Agamben, "Absolute Immanence," in *Potentialities: Collected Essays in Philosophy*, trans. Daniel Heller-Roazen (Stanford: Stanford University Press 1999), 220–43. Connecting the accounts of life (in all its exposure) proposed by Agamben and Foucault, Paul Patton suggests that the life described by Foucault as commanded by sovereign power (and the lives therefore suspended between life and death since ultimately living at the sovereign's pleasure) correspond most closely to the phenomenon described by Agamben as bare life (and, as such, should be differentiated from the life Foucault considers to be biopolitically governed), see Paul Patton, "Agamben and Foucault on Biopower and Politics," in Matthew Calarco and Steven DeCaroli, eds., *Giorgio Agamben: Sovereignty and Life* (Stanford: Stanford University Press, 2007), 203–18, 213.

22. Thus, to claim, as Agamben does, that Foucault neglected a discussion of the camp (*HS* 76) is not to claim that Foucault omitted all reference to Nazi governmentality, but that he omitted a discussion of the specific forms of power (recoined by Agamben as the sovereign making of the biopolitical) in which qualified life is reduced to bare life.

23. Giorgio Agamben, *Remnants of Auschwitz: The Witness and the Archive*, trans. Daniel Heller-Roazen (New York: Zone, 2012), 83.

24. As Agamben notes, in *Society Must Be Defended*, Foucault addresses paradoxes (see *SMBD* 240, 253) both with respect to the life governed (and death taken) by sovereign power and with respect to the following formula (as Agamben articulates its paradoxical status for Foucault): "How is it possible that a power whose aim is essentially to make live instead exerts an unconditional power of death" (*Remnants of Auschwitz*, 84).

However, it could also be said that Foucault identifies the paradox at the point where the capacities (including the deadly capacities) of biopolitical governance instead become incapacities. I have argued that, on his account, the sheer fact of biopolitical powers of death do not, alone, amount to governmental incapacity. Agamben argues that his redefinition of the biopolitical as a sovereign reduction to bare life obviates (just as Esposito argues of the accelerating immune paradigm of biopolitics) the paradox seemingly confronted by Foucault. Discussing Foucault's genealogy of racism, and the caesura it introduces into the biological continuum as divisions between Aryan and non-Aryan and between people and population (ibid., 84), Agamben indicates that such distinctions and their caesura are consistent with exactly the distinction Foucault failed to give (eventually, the distinction between zoe and bios). Since his claim is also that these distinctions allow one to identify a point at which these caesurae transcend race and become pure biopolitical substance (ibid., 85), here we can refer to Alex Weheliye's criticism of Agamben's analytic efforts to think a biopolitical substratum as transcending race (and sexual difference). In the Nazi context discussed by Agamben, the making of human lives as lives not worthy of being lived, coincided, as Agamben notes, with the aim to protect hereditary health, giving rise to laws regulating procreative unions, sterilization, and abortion that preceded and continued during the Final Solution. It could be argued that, insofar as he identifies the reduction to bare life in a genocide that includes the aim of protecting hereditary health, his own account tacitly recognizes the inclusion of a biopoliticized reproduction embodying a biopoliticized sexual difference (ibid., 84); and see Alex Weheliye, *Habeas Viscus: Racializing Assemblages, Biopolitics, and Black Feminist Theories of the Human* (Durham: Duke University Press, 2014), 4–5, 34.

25. In this context one could also return to Derrida's discussions of the death penalty in the United States. Between 1972 and 1976 it was suspended following a Supreme Court ruling that it procedurally violated the Eighth Amendment. Since it was not deemed unconstitutional per se, it could therefore, from 1976, be progressively reinstated by states who introduced new legal procedures through which capital punishment did not incur the terms of the suspension. The reinstatements claim their exception to the (still recognized) terms of the suspension, which in turn had claimed a suspension of the (still recognized) legality of capital punishment. See Jacques Derrida, *The Death Penalty*, vol. 1, trans. Peggy Kamuf (Chicago: University of Chicago Press, 2014). Derrida discusses, several times in the seminar, the common combination of support for the death penalty and opposition to abortion, but only in passing remarks.

26. See the dicsussion of *Roe* in Mary Poovey, "The Abortion Question and the Death of Man," in Judith Butler and Joan Scott, eds., *Feminists Theorize the Political* (New York: Routledge, 1992), 239–56, 244.

27. Ruling cited at www.law.cornell.edu/supremecourt/texts/410/113 (accessed 12/10/2016).

28. "Fetal heartbeat bills" have been introduced in at least nine states, have been passed in Houses of Representatives or Senates in at least four states, then postponed or suspended in committees or legally struck down.

29. As reported in the *New York Times*: "Similar measures to ban abortions when fetal heartbeats are detected are under consideration in several other states, including Kansas

and Ohio." John Eligon and Erik Eckholm, "New Laws Ban Most Abortions in North Dakota," *New York Times*, March 26, 2013, http://www.nytimes.com/2013/03/27/us/north-dakota-governor-signs-strict-abortion-limits.html (accessed 12/10/2016).

30. A subsequent landmark case held before the Supreme Court, *Planned Parenthood of Southeastern Pennsylvania v. Casey* (1992), ruled that states could lawfully introduce measures whose effect was to reduce practical availability of abortion so long as they did not impose an "undue" burden on women's right to choose an abortion, leaving a wide margin of interpretation on what might be considered undue. Having said that, in 2016, two state statutes were passed in Alabama concerning the regulation of abortion. The first forbade the granting or reissuing of licenses to abortion clinics within 2000ft of a public K-8 school. The second was to prevent the "dilation and evacuation" method of abortion—the most common in the second trimester—unless the physician first stops the fetal heartbeat. In October 2016 the first was overturned and the second was suspended by Judge Myron H. Thompson in the District Courts on the grounds that it placed an undue burden (in accordance with the "undue burden test") on women accessing their constitutional rights (https://www.scribd.com/document/329234060/West-Alabama-Women-s-Center-v-Miller accessed 12/19/2016).

    And yet overturning these laws does not necessarily preclude them from producing deleterious effects. In its "roundup" of state abortion restrictions published in January 2016, the Guttmacher Institute noted that there had been nearly as many restrictions regarding abortion introduced in the previous five years as in the fifteen years before that (https://www.guttmacher.org/article/2016/01/2015-year-end-state-policy-roundup accessed 12/19/2016). Even where these were later struck down by various courts of appeal (in many cases, long before they reached the Supreme Court), it seems that it is this *climate* that is increasing the burden for women to access abortion. For in this same five-year period the number of abortion clinics have significantly diminished, particularly in states that already had a very small number.

31. See comments by Tammy Kromenaker, director of the Red River Women's Clinic in Fargo, on why new regulations restricting admitting privileges would oblige the shutdown of the only abortion clinic in North Dakota: they imposed a radius within which there were only two hospitals, one of which accorded admitting privileges only to doctors who admitted at least ten patients annually. This excluded Red River doctors who fly in from other states to perform the abortions. She interpreted the fetal heartbeat law as follows: "In the past it's been, 'We're going to try and make it more difficult, more hoops, more obstacles for women to have to jump through or jump over. But this is specifically: 'Let's ban abortion. Let's do it. Let's challenge Roe v. Wade. Let's end abortion in North Dakota.'" Eligon and Eckholm, "New Laws Ban Most Abortions in North Dakota."

32. Ranjana Khanna has developed the term *disposability* as a means of expanding and nuancing Agamben's bare life, correcting the conceptual annihilation of difference she identifies in his failure to factor in the specificity of the political exclusion of slaves, women relegated to households, or the exposure of women to sexual violence, and also as a means of developing a better framework for a new feminist internationalism. See "Disposability," *differences* 20, no. 1 (2009): 181–98.

33. Unlike the American right to privacy, the right to abortion is negotiated in Germany in the context of the 1949 *Grundgesetz* whose first two articles constitutionally establish human life to be a fundamental value. This is considered to apply to unborn life, but also to the free development of one's "personality" without undue harm to others. Thus the legality of abortion must be established within these framing constitutional conditions as the weighing up of different "life" interests.
34. In Britain, abortion was a crime from 1803 onward, still illegal under the 1861 Offenses Against the Person Act. Through the twentieth century, increasingly broad exceptions were granted by the Infant Life (Preservation Act) of 1929, allowing term-limited abortions to protect the woman's life only; the Bourne Ruling of 1938, extending the exception to include psychological grounds; and the Abortion Act of 1968, which consolidated the legality if there was a threat to the physical or mental health of mother or existing childcare and if certified by two doctors. Australian law was first governed by the British 1861 Act. Despite its widespread availability (under grounds of an assortment of exceptions including economic, social, and medical grounds and usually with time limits), abortion has not been fully legalized in any state except the Australian Capital Territory that passed the Abolition of Offence of Abortion Act in 2002.
35. Michèle Le Doeuff, *Hipparchia's Choice: An Essay Concerning Women, Philosophy, etc.*, trans. Trista Selous (Oxford: Blackwell, 1991), 247. She considers this phenomenon a failure to enshrine women's control of their own fertility in the constitution as a fundamental right. Though there have been changes to French abortion law since the publication of *Hipparchia's Choice,* the conditional nature of its legality has persisted. For example, under the Penal Code of 1992, abortion becomes a woman's right during (but only during) the first twelve weeks, and abortions are still prohibited if conducted in such a way as to violate public health guidelines.
36. Giorgio Agamben, *State of Exception*, trans. Kevin Attell (Chicago: University of Chicago Press, 2005), 2, 7.
37. Ibid., 87.
38. Giorgio Agamben, *Means Without End: Notes on Politics*, trans. Vincenzo Binetti and Cesare Casarino (Minneapolis: University of Minnesota Press, 2000), 6–7.
39. Catherine Mills notes that Agamben associates women with the potential of infancy in "For a Philosophy of Infancy," trans. Elias Polizoes, *Public* 21 (2001), at http://www.yorku.ca/public/public/backissu/v21c.html, and that he depicts women as offering a prospect of (hetero)sexual fulfillment associated with the in-human and unsavable life in Giorgio Agamben, *The Open: Man and Animal*, trans. Kevin Attell (Stanford: Stanford University Press, 2004). He refers to female faces in pornography evoking the pleasure of everyday life in Giorgio Agamben, *Idea of Prose*, trans. Michael Sullivan and Sam Whitsitt (Albany: State University of New York Press, 1995). For this discussion, see Catherine Mills, *The Philosophy of Agamben* (Stocksfield: Acumen, 2008), 114–15.
40. Catherine Mills acknowledges that a feminist stress on the phenomenology of embodiment will not be appropriate to Agamben's work (ibid., 115).
41. Astrid Deuber-Mankowsky, "Homo Sacer, das bloße Leben und das Lager," *Die Philosophin* 25 (2002): 95–115, 103. English translation by Catharine Diehl available at https://adm.blogs.ruhr-uni-bochum.de/publikationen.

42. Weheliye, *Habeas Viscus*, 4–5, 34.
43. See for example, Rosi Braidotti, "The Politics of Life as Bios/Zoe," in A. Smelik and N. Lykke, eds., *Bits of Life: Feminism at the Interactions of Media, Bioscience, and Technology* (Seattle: University of Washington Press, 2008), 172–92; Melinda Cooper, "The Silent Scream: Agamben and the Politics of the Unborn," in Rosi Braidotti, Claire Colebrook and Patrick Hanafin, eds., *Deleuze and Law: Forensic Futures* (Edinburgh: University of Edinburgh Press, 2010), 142–62; Deuber-Mankowsky, "Homo Sacer"; Catherine Mills, "Biopolitics, Liberal Eugenics, and Nihilism," in Calarco and DeCaroli, *Giorgio Agamben: Sovereignty and Life*, 180–202; Mills, *The Philosophy of Agamben*; Ewa Ziarek, "Bare Life on Strike: Notes on the Biopolitics of Race and Gender," *South Atlantic Quarterly* 107 (2008): 89–106.
44. For views that European colonialism, slave trading, and the slave plantation are exemplary of Agamben's camp (not withstanding their criticisms of Agamben's disinterest in racism and colonialism, see Weheliye's *Habeas Viscus*; and Paul Gilroy, *Postcolonial Melancholia* (New York: Columbia University Press, 2006), 48–50. For Weheliye's criticism that, in universalizing—or ontologizing—the camp, and the modern zone of indetermination in which we all are rendered the virtual homo sacer, Agamben is unable to explain why certain groups of humans are more exposed to a personification or actualization of the homo sacer; see Weheliye, *Habeas Viscus*, 35.
45. When Melinda Cooper describes Agamben as "identif[ying] a biological substratum isolated from all political form or identity but nevertheless subject to the full force of law of the modern state," she asks if embryonic life might qualify as the kind of biological substratum in which he might be interested. She is right to draw attention to Agamben's omission of this possibility from his discussion. For it could seem, as she puts it, that "Agamben consistently and inexplicably eludes the one figure of contemporary political life that would seem to illustrate most fully his philosophical conception of bare life. This is the figure of the 'unborn'–a purely potential life which, according to some, has become dangerously exposed to the sovereign violence of women, the state and science." One reason for not including embryonic life could be found in the fact that Agamben's analysis has been directed instead at the loss, removal, or forced exclusion of political form or identity from forms of life. This means, at least, that the fetus is not like the slave, the immigrant who loses statehood, the camp internee, the state of coma. Cooper's argument is that the possible conceptual proximity of embryonic life and bare life allows for a closer inspection of a tacit relationship in his work with Christian, Thomist theology (giving another angle for a feminist and critical point of access into the elaboration, see Cooper, "The Silent Scream," 142).
46. Ziarek, "Bare Life on Strike," 89.
47. For Ziarek, this is an omission, but it remains unclear how easily it could be rectified within the terms of the homo sacer project. She presents a meticulous and innovative response to Agamben and some preliminary notes on how one would need to *supplement* the project. But she also offers the most acute account available of why, within Agamben's terms, these omissions are "no accident."
48. Ann Laura Stoler, "Beyond Sex: Bodily Exposures of the Colonial and Postcolonial Present," in Anne-Emmanuelle Berger and Eleni Varikas, eds., *Genre et postcolonialismes:*

Dialogues transcontinentaux, 185–214 (Paris: Archives Contemporaines, 2011). See her comment, "Key to the sexual politics of colonial rule was never just enacted sexual violation but the distribution of social and political vulnerabilities that nourished the potential for them" (ibid., 186).

49. Stoler, "Beyond Sex," 207–8.
50. In giving a different definition to biopolitics, and arguing not only for its longer lineage but for the status of the bare life produced by sovereign power interpreted as the ontological (*HS* 182) or transcendental (see Muhle, "Genealogy of Biopolitics," 83) condition of the political, he omits much of what is critical to Foucault's account— the stress on politico-technological means and measures for thinking of populations in massive and statistical terms, for example. On this see Mills, "Biopolitics, Liberal Eugenics, and Nihilism" and Patton, "Agamben and Foucault on Biopower and Politics."
51. Mills, *The Philosophy of Giorgio Agamben*, 114–15.
52. Johanna Oksala, "Violence and the Biopolitics of Modernity," *Foucault Studies* 10 (2010): 23–43, 29.
53. Mills, *The Philosophy of Giorgio Agamben*, 141n12.
54. See the related interrogation of the problematic status of slavery for Agamben in Ziarek, "Bare Life on Strike," 93–94.
55. As Khanna comments, "Agamben's term *severance* . . . would not obtain for those who never could participate in political life anyway, though they resided within the city limits," see Khanna, "Disposability", 190.
56. Considering Agamben's account from the perspective of slavery, Ziarek expresses the problem this way, "The notion of slavery as a substitute for death complicates Agamben's central thesis that sovereign decision/bare life constitutes the foundational political paradigm in the West. First, although the extreme delegitimation and the nullity of enslaved life make it another instantiation of bare life, the very fact that such life undergoes substitutions of one form of destruction for another undermines from the start the centrality of *just one* paradigm of politics" (Ziarek, "Bare Life on Strike," 96).
57. In Patterson's account of slavery as social death, and its associated liminal and paradoxical status (discussed in conjunction with Agamben in Ziarek's "Bare Life on Strike"), Patterson includes the exposure of women slaves to rape. Orlando Patterson, *Slavery and Social Death: A Comparative Study* (Cambridge: Harvard University Press, 1985), 206, 193. For her criticism of the tacit subordination of women in such accounts of this social death as rupturing traditional kinship, and her emphasis of sexual difference, the sexing of enslavement, and of women under slavery as exposed to rape and a reproduction from which they were alienated, see Spillers, " Mama's Baby, Papa's Maybe."
58. The term is used to describe the politically inflected aim to inflict pregnancy through rape with a racial or ethnic dimension intended to damage kinship relations and political communities, often as an organized political orr military tactic. Engle offers a wary account of the term as used in both feminist and legal representations. While not disputing the long-term group detention of Bosnian women for the purposes of rape, leading to prosecution and convictions by the International Criminal Tribunal for the former Yugoslavia, Engle has argued that the aim of systematic enforced pregnancy,

and particularly the view that their aim was genocidal, may have been overemphasized in their reporting. See Karen Engle, "Feminism and its (Dis)Contents: Criminalizing Wartime Rape in Bosnia and Herzegovina," *American Journal of International Law* 99, no. 4 (2005): 778–816, 816.

59. The distinction was explicitly made in the first constitution of 1791, in which the category included women and domestic servants. So-called universal citizenship, instituted in the 1792 version, covered only men over twenty-one; thus the status of women as the passive citizen persisted (until 1945). See James F. McMillan, *France and Women, 1789–1914* (New York: Routledge, 2000), 16.
60. Also discussed by McMillan, ibid.
61. Emmanuel-Joseph Sieyès's "Préliminaires de la constitution," in *Ecrits politiques* (Paris: Editions des Archives, 1985); and see remarks by Jean-Denis Lanjuinais cited in W. H. Sewell, "Le citoyen/La Citoyenne: Activity, Passivity and the Revolutionary Concept of Citizenship," in Colin Lucas, ed., *The French Revolution and the Creation of Modern Political Culture*, vol. 2: *Political Culture of the French Revolution* (Oxford: Pergamon, 1988), 105–25, 105.
62. See McMillan, *France and Women*; Joan Wallach Scott, *Only Paradoxes to Offer: French Feminists and the Rights of Man* (Cambridge: Harvard University Press, 1996); Candice E. Proctor, *Women, Equality, and the French Revolution* (New York: Greenwood, 1990).
63. McMillan's *France and Women* discusses remarks in this vein by André Amar and Pierre Gaspard Chaumette, such as Chaumette's declaration: "Since when is it permitted to give up one's sex? Since when is it decent to see women abandoning the pious cares of their households, the cribs of their children, to come to public places, to harangue in the galleries, at the bar of the senate? Is it to men that nature confided domestic cares? No, she has said to man: 'Be a man: hunting, farming, political concerns, toils of every kind, that is your appanage.' She has said to woman: 'Be a woman. The tender cares owing to infancy, the details of the household, the sweet anxieties of maternity, these are your labours"; McMillan, *France and Women*, 30–31, citing Chaumette's speech reproduced in Darlene Gay Levy, Harriet Branson Applewhite, and Mary Durham Johnson, eds., *Women in Revolutionary France* (Champaign: University of Illinois Press, 1980), 219–20. McMillan discusses further examples from Mirabeau and Prudhomme for whom women's maternal role was similarly the grounds for the denial of citizenship.
64. For its peculiar paradigm, one could suggest a more specific variant of the coma state than that discussed by Agamben (see his discussion of Karen Quinlan, *HS* 163–64, 186): extreme cases in which women have been maintained in coma states to allow the further development of an unborn fetus.
65. See Rayna Rapp, *Testing Women, Testing the Fetus: The Social Impact of Amniocentesis in America* (New York: Routledge, 1999), 127, 131, 307.
66. A phenomenon analyzed at length, with respect to the contemporary public policy context in Finland, by Mervi Patosalmi, "The Politics and Policies of Reproductive Agency," PhD diss., University of Helsinki, 2011. My thanks to Mervi Patosalmi for stimulating conversations about her research on this phenomenon in Finland.

67. Ziarek, "Bare Life on Strike," 93.
68. See Khanna, "Disposability," for the discussion of Agamben's omission of sexual difference.
69. Jill Lepore, "Birthright: What's Next for Planned Parenthood?," *New Yorker*, November 14, 2011, 44–55, 48.
70. Miller's argument is more specifically indebted to Agamben in its interest in paradigmatic spaces of the biopolitical and so in conceptualizing the womb in such terms. As an analogue of Agamben's use of the term, she is interested in a paradigm of which we also find a general distribution of its characteristics. When Miller proposes replacing the camp as the biopolitical paradigm of the modern, with an account of the womb as the paradigm space, she is thinking specifically of that variant of sovereignty described by Agamben. Adding to the argument that we have all been reduced to a virtual homo sacer, she adds that we are a virtual version of the biopoliticized womb. The argument connects with a downside of increasing emphasis on the importance of consent. In regard to sexual violence, she identifies a correlative default criminality, with respect to which a default model has become a supposition of violation *unless* consent is given. See Ruth A. Miller, *The Limits of Bodily Integrity: Abortion, Adultery, and Rape Legislation in Comparative Perspective* (Aldershot: Ashgate, 2007).
71. Stormer offers an account of this governmentality in "Prenatal Space," *Signs* 26, no. 1 (2000): 109–44, 135, discussed in Miller, *The Limits of Bodily Integrity*, 30.
72. Miller, *The Limits of Bodily Integrity*, 44. Miller offers several variants of this account of reproductive space as a preeminent modern political space and also an overlap of different regimes of reproduction. Women's bodies can have multiple statuses as private (understood as the property of their husbands and fathers), autonomous, and public (for example, in the sense that rape or pregnancy could be understood as collective, moral, national, moral, or public affronts or attacks on national integrity or collective future (ibid., 93–94). They can manifest overlaps of disciplinary, juridical-institutional, and biopolitical management (ibid., 88).

    One consequence of these overlaps is the problematic implications of the articulation of biopolitical sovereign spaces in women's bodies, deemed by her a sovereign (or biopolitical) right to regulate biology and sexuality (ibid., 88). With the emergence of the language of consent in the twentieth century, "'sexual liberty' was a right that could be possessed only by biopolitically defined citizens" (ibid., 94). Under those circumstances, she argues, consent has "little or nothing to do with 'choice' or 'freedom.'" Consent doesn't undo the biopolitical and public status of women's bodies in the sense that women's sexual and reproductive bodies occupy a biopolitical register— as seen when sexual crimes are understood as much as infringements on public as private interest, and womens' bodily integrity is understood to overlaps with national integrity, and so national borders as well as futures (ibid., 88–89).
73. Ibid., 44.
74. She sees the consequences of the *overlap* between regimes of consent and regimes of biopolitical interest in sexual and reproductive life, which mean that in a) the absence

4. IMMUNITY, BARE LIFE, AND THE THANATOPOLITICS OF REPRODUCTION 235

of expressed consent, sex in some contexts would be assumed to be rape and reproduction coerced. In a liberal regime of consent and contract, embodying the traditions of the private/public split, power would not be considered as primarily concerned with rights relating to bodily life. Reproductive and sexual life would be considered private matters. Matters of consent, autonomy of choice, and associated rights would be associated more with public transactions concerning property, contracts. In the absence of proof of consent, it might be assumed that a party is not using my car or my house *with* my consent. So when, by contrast, governmental and political interest extends to bodily life, and reproduction becomes a matter of *bio*political interest, Miller argues the consequence is as follows. In correlation (because of the concurrent tradition of liberal autonomy, freedom, and property rights) the language of consent extends to the sexual and reproductive body. In consequence, Miller argues we now live in a context of tacit assumption that sex and reproduction do not occur legitimately unless there is stated consent. Moreover, this has *also* become a *means and mode of biopolitical administration* of sex and reproduction.

One aspect of this governmentality relates to the (race hierarchizing) caesura in the biological continuum described by Foucault. Again Miller suggests the analysis can be extended to its "reproductive" variant. Since there will be a bifurcation between forms of reproduction considered to foster national interest or to weaken it, there will, Miller argues, also be a bifurcation in between the extent to which sex and reproduction are assumed to be coerced in the absence of explicit consent. She discusses "refugee sex" in camps and sexual contact between Bosnian women and Serbian men in the former Yugoslavia of the 1980s, arguing that in both cases the default assumption is that this is rape or coerced sex. Miller is not the only feminist to query the problematic results of a seemingly pro-feminist and positive focus on the importance of consent. But this is a specific and complex argument that the default models of violence, exposure, and likely criminality have concurrently become means of biopolitical administration of women's bodies, with a correlate bureaucratic and physical invasiveness of sexual and reproductive bodies. On this argument, it is seen when biopolitical interest in the life of the body and the level of population overlaps with new reproductive rights based on models of autonomy and establishment of "consent." Not all these analyses are developed, but they are governed by an attention to the phenomenon of overlapping models insofar as they may impact reproductive rights: sovereign individuality, legal personhood, discipline, biopower, and security.

75. My suggestion is that in lieu of the possibility of understanding embryonic life in such terms, instead women may be rendered "less than subjects," insofar as the possibility of making reproductive decisions may be available or be revoked or be denied, often by contrast to equivalent subjects who do access these contexts of decision making by virtue of civic or immigration status, race, religion, nation, or wealth. Again the argument is not that women have these rights and that they are denied, but rather that they are produced as subjects of denied (or absent) rights.

5. JUDITH BUTLER, PRECARIOUS LIFE, AND REPRODUCTION

Chapter epigraphs come from Judith Butler, *Frames of War: When Is Life Grievable?* (London: Verso, 2009), 7; Barbara Johnson, "Apostrophe, Animation, and Abortion," *Diacritics* 16, no. 1 (1986): 28–47, 33.

1. Judith Butler, *Frames of War: When Is Life Grievable?* (London: Verso, 2009), 15, hereafter *FW*.
2. With exceptions discussed in this chapter. In remarks about Agamben and Arendt in *Who Sings the Nation-State?* she proposes that biopolitics (and, in interconnection, sovereignty) would need to be understood more broadly than is indicated in their work. To see the function of sovereignty as separating life from the domain of the political or of citizenship presumes, she argues, "that politics and life join only and always on the question of citizenship and, so, restricts the entire domain of bio-power in which questions of life and death are determined by other means." Judith Butler and Gayatri Chakravorty Spivak, *Who Sings the Nation-State? Language, Politics, Belonging* (London: Seagull, 2007), 39–40.
3. For example, she mentions the focus by some recent biopolitical theorists on transformations in the paradigms of life (such as the shift to the molecular discussed, among others, by Nikolas Rose in *Politics of Life Itself*; see *FW* 17). Cary Wolfe groups her, along with Esposito and Agamben, with the "current avatars" of biopolitical thought. Cary Wolfe, *Before the Law: Humans and Other Animals in a Biopolitical Frame* (Chicago: University of Chicago Press, 2012), 3; but see her remark about biopolitical questions, "Maybe this is work for other scholars to do!," Judith Butler with Athena Athanasiou, *Dispossession: The Performative in the Political* (Cambridge: Polity, 2013), 169, and see 47. Butler refers often to biopolitical theory as contiguous with, or important, to her concerns, and yet not her primary point of focus, thus see also *Frames of War*: "it can be argued that processes of life themselves require destruction and degeneration, but this does not in any way tell us which sorts of destruction are ethically salient and which are not. To determine the ontological specificity of life in such instances would lead us more generally into a discussion of biopolitics, concerning ways of apprehending, controlling, and administering life, and how these modes of power enter into the very definition of life itself.... The bibliography on these important topics has grown enormously in recent years. My own contribution, however, is not to the genealogy of concepts of life or death" (*FW* 16–18).
4. Butler and Spivak, *Who Sings the Nation-State?* 37–38. In the context of a longer critical rejoinder to Arendt, this is also serving as a critical rejoinder to Agamben. In the previous chapter we explored the status of reproductivity in relation to bare life. But Butler's evocation here of the "means and legitimate uses of reproductive technology," as among the questions of life and power prompting her rejection of the view that life is ever "bare" (ibid., 37), does raise the question (not pursued by her) of how precariousness might, as an alternative category, apply here.

5. JUDITH BUTLER, PRECARIOUS LIFE, AND REPRODUCTION   237

5. Discussing the human acquisition of language, she describes the body as "alternately sustained and threatened through modes of address." Judith Butler, *Excitable Speech: A Politics of the Performative* (New York: Routledge, 1997), 5–6.
6. Ibid.
7. Judith Butler, *Psychic Life of Power: Theories in Subjection* (Stanford: Stanford University Press, 1997), 21, hereafter *PLP*.
8. Bonnie Honig offers a critical response to Butler's concept of precarious life in *Antigone, Interrupted* (Cambridge: Cambridge University Press, 2013), responding to Butler, "But there are other irrefutable generalizabilities that could be ontologized and on which we could build a politics as well: humans all eat, for example, and this too could ground an equality—a less minimal one—of social rights to food" (31). She attributes to Butler a "sentimental ontology of fragility" associated with a trend for which Honig has coined the term *mortalist humanism*.
9. According to the well-known Foucauldian formulation, "The man described for us, whom we are invited to free, is already in himself the effect of a subjection much more profound then himself" (*DP* 30).
10. This focus on a livable life has become stronger in Butler's work. While themes of survival and intelligibility were already present in *Gender Trouble*, in her revised introduction for the 1999 edition of *Gender Trouble*, it is noticeable that her references to gendering become references to a "gendered life," connecting to her ongoing interrogation of the conditions for livable lives. Judith Butler, *Gender Trouble: Feminism and the Subversion of Identity*, 2d ed. (New York: Routledge, 1999), viii.
11. Judith Butler, *Bodies That Matter: On the Discursive Limits of "Sex"* (New York: Routledge, 1993), 95, 133; and see also Judith Butler, "The Question of Social Transformation," in *Undoing Gender* (New York: Routledge, 2004), 204–31, 226. She was mindful, in the wake of *Gender Trouble*, to qualify what seemed to some an overly celebratory emphasis in that work's closing pages on the potential for gender play and parody. Butler sees gender normativity as effecting the conventional, the transgressive, and the illegible, with both positive and negative results. Possibilities for change are embedded in the slight and strong variability arising with the iterations of norms; but, insofar as these possibilities also include the transgressive or illegible, livability may, for some, be threatened. In *Gender Trouble's* revised introduction, she connects the making and living of gendered life to the question of how some lives do not count as fully valuable or, as she says, as "livable lives," "the violence of the foreclosed life, the one that does get named as 'living,' the one whose suspension implies an incarceration of life, or a sustained death sentence." One could unpack at length the many interconnecting resonances in Butler's work of life, "livable life," and their role in genealogies of life and death to which her work contributes (Butler, *Gender Trouble*, viii).
12. Butler describes an original and fundamental impingement by the other with reference to Laplanche's account of an infant flooded and overwhelmed by the other and its incomprehensible meanings. This inhabitation would precede anything resembling "mineness," or our taking any kind of shape as "subjects," "egos," or "selves." Judith Butler, *Giving an Account of Oneself* (New York: Fordham University Press, 2005), 77.

13. See both *Precarious Life* and also a remark in her exchange with Mills and Jenkins which links these problems: "the question of what I ought to do necessitates an inquiry into both the constitution of the 'I' and the manner of its 'doing.' The socially variable practice of subject production becomes an issue here, since populations are only differentially established as subjects, and power regimes operate in the production and de-production of subjects." Judith Butler, "Reply from Judith Butler to Mills and Jenkins," *differences* 18, no. 2 (2007): 180–95, 191–92; and Judith Butler, *Precarious Life: The Powers of Mourning and Violence* (London: Verso, 2006), hereafter *PL*.

14. In "The Question of Social Transformation" this question of gender is again connected to death: "to what extent does gender, coherent gender, secure a life as livable? What threat of death is delivered to those who do not live gender according to its accepted norms" (ibid., 205)? More generally this essay again reminds that embodying norms may well be a matter of life or death: "the question of how to embody the norm is thus very often linked to the question of survival, of whether life itself will be possible" (ibid., 217). She mentions a number of types of violence against the transgendered (ibid., 218). Moreover, and also important to her concept of the livable life, sometimes forms of violence might not even be recognized as such.

15. Butler takes Foucault to have neglected the phenomenon of desubjectivation. In *Precarious Life* she argues that this phenomenon should have been factored in the depiction of a disciplined subject compliant with the law, whose individuated relation to a standard for the human is a constitutive principle (*PL* 98). (Of course, one could add to this account—for, as described in Foucault's *Abnormal* lectures, Foucauldian discipline is also a normalization which makes, differentiates, grids, identifies, and includes abnormalities, the "monster," the figures who cannot be "disciplined" or appear indifferent to discipline.)

16. Butler and Spivak, *Who Sings the Nation-State?*, 4–8.

17. See in particular Judith Butler, "Is Kinship Always Heterosexual?" *differences* 13, no. 1 (2002): 14–44 and "The Question of Social Transformation."

18. Fiona Jenkins amplifies this possibility: "it becomes very tempting to try to apply a series of questions posed in many of (Butler's) essays to the case of foetal life." Like Butler, she acknowledges the difficulty: this could "be something that the Pro-Life, anti-abortion movement seeks to articulate." Fiona Jenkins, "Queering Foetal Life: Between Butler and Berlant," *Australian Feminist Law Journal* 30 (2009): 63–85, 65.

19. She reminds also that there are conceptual differences—and tensions—in the field of biopolitics between seeing life in anthropocentric or clinical or tissue-based or molecular terms, and these remain beyond the scope of her project.

20. The comment continues, "I don't know whether one can be a nominalist about life, since there are so many instances of living processes and beings. We have to enter into this complex array of problems, which means as well that social theory has to become more knowledgeable about debates in the life sciences." Jenkins notes that the applicability of Butler's arguments to fetal life also comes up in "The Question of Social Transformation." Again, Butler makes clear her view that, at least for the purposes of her own analysis, the "disenfranchised communities" to whom one might seek to extend

5. JUDITH BUTLER, PRECARIOUS LIFE, AND REPRODUCTION 239

the norms of sustaining viable life do not include the "unborn." Jenkins cites her on this point: "My argument against this conclusion has to do with the very use of 'life' as if we know what it means, what it requires, what it demands." The antiabortion activist seeks to assert dogmatically the value of (fetal) "human life," rather than joining Butler in exploring and affirming its ambiguity. Judith Butler with Nina Power, "Media Death - Frames of War." The Books Interview, New Statesman. (August 30, 2009) Original version at http://www.newstatesman.com/2009/08/media-death-frames-war-obama. (Accessed 12/18/2016)

21. See my chapter one, p20, for discussion of this formulation. Butler refers to Mbembe's term *necropolitics* (Butler with Athanasiou, *Dispossession*, 167) and, more generally, to the description by Mbembe, Patterson (*Slavery and Social Death*), and Gilmore (*Golden Gulag*) of humans whose proper place is constituted as that of "nonbeing," social death, higher rates of mortality, or death through negligence (Butler with Athanasiou, *Dispossession*, 19). My argument has been that these differentials are also seen in higher rates of mortality, harm, and death for women in contexts producing a differential (bio)political significance of their reproductive lives. The variability of visibility and grievability relating to this more specific phenomenon is a variant of precariousness. Spillers has indicated the need for it to be factored in Patterson's "social death." See Orlando Patterson, *Slavery and Social Death: A Comparative Study* (Cambridge: Harvard University Press, 1985), 206, 193; Hortense Spillers, "Mama's Baby, Papa's Maybe: An American Grammar Book," in *Black, White, and in Color: Essays on American Literature and Culture* (Chicago: University of Chicago Press, 2003), 203–29.

22. In chapter 4 I made mention of Cooper's interrogation of this possibility with respect to Agamben's "bare life," while arguing that this variant of pro-life politics can be understood as constructing the pseudo homo sacer for whom the woman's womb becomes a phantom variant of the "camp."

23. For two landmark essays on the question, see Rosalind Pollack Petchesky, "Fetal Images: The Power of Visual Culture in the Politics of Reproduction," *Feminist Studies* 13, no. 2 (1987): 263–92; and Donna Haraway, "Fetus: The Speculum in the New World Order," in *Modest_Witness@Second_Millennium.FemaleMan_Meets_OncoMouse: Feminism and Technoscience* (New York: Routledge, 1997), 173–212.

24. See Gail Kligman, "Political Demography: The Banning of Abortion in Ceausescu's Romania," in Rayna Rapp and Faye Ginsburg, *Conceiving the New World Order: The Global Politics of Reproduction* (California: University of California Press, 1995), 234–55, for its more complex account of the thanatopolitical differentials at work when race hierarchism will favor the reproduction of some over others.

25. On this see Jean L. Cohen, "Redescribing Privacy: Identity, Difference, and the Abortion Controversy," *Columbia Journal of Gender and Law* 3, no. 1 (1992): 43–117, 56–57; and Wendy Brown, "Reproductive Freedom and the Right to Privacy: A Paradox for Feminists," in *Families, Politics and Public Policy*, ed. Irene Diamond (New York: Routledge, 1983), 322–38, 332–34.

26. Ibid., 333.

27. Wolfe, *Before the Law*, 18–19.

28. This is to agree with Eva von Redecker who argues that Butler's precariousness would presuppose a status *as* human which must already be sufficiently in question to be tacitly *revocable*, see Eva von Redecker, *Zur Aktualität von Judith Butler: Einleitung in ihr Werk* (Wiesbaden: Verlag für Sozialwissenschaften, 2011).
29. See Butler's discussion of prisoners deemed less than human (*FW* 93), and of "Islamic populations destroyed in recent and current wars [who] are considered 'less than human,' or 'outside' the cultural conditions for the emergence of the human" (*FW* 125).
30. And see her comment in *Who Sings the Nation-State?*, concerning whether the public can "ever be constituted as such without some population relegated to the private and hence, the pre-political"? (ibid., 22). Butler continues here with a challenge addressed to Arendt's adherence to a distinction between the public, political sphere, and a pre-political private sphere. Discussing Arendt's critique in *Origins of Totalitarianism* of nation-states as working to disregard those who do not belong to them, Butler muses that Arendt might well have made a similar point about the "disregarding" effects of the "public," political sphere (Butler, *Who Sings the Nation-State?*, 22).
31. Jenkins, "Queering Foetal Life," 66.
32. Catherine Mills, "Technology, Embodiment, and Abortion," *Internal Medicine Journal* 35 (2005): 427–28, 427. It is true that, in dialogue with Mills, Jenkins places the emphasis on Mills's claim that, as technologically made, the fetus does newly and differently serve to make the woman a moral agent—one formulation proposed by Mills is that such technologies "transform the relations that we bear to each other, . . . and hence the ethical responsibilities that take hold in that relationality" (ibid.). It is still the fetus that both theorists consider (and speculatively, cautiously) as the possible candidate for terms such as vulnerability, grievability, precariousness (though it should be noted in this regard that Mills is concurrently arguing for a view of the fetus as nonseparable from the mother—and vice versa—in new forms of technologically rendered and stimulated intersubjective relationships and phenomenologies).
33. See Catherine Mills, *Futures of Reproduction: Bioethics and Biopolitics* (Dordrecht: Springer, 2011), 113–14. Mills also suggests this phenomenon is thinkable in terms of Esposito's concept of immunity.
34. Butler, "The Question of Social Transformation" 205, 225 (my emphasis).
35. Barbara Duden, Karen Barad, and Donna Haraway have been among the prominent voices in an immense literature here: with Haraway and Barad offering well-known alternatives for thinking about matter and agency in the context of ultrasound technological imaging. Barad also asks how materialization can be rethought so as to dislodge what she argues is a reinstallation of a "passive" matter by Butler in *Bodies That Matter*. These theorists also emphasize the differentials (geographical, class and wealth based, those relating to disability) of human value and women's value seen in the making of some pregnancies through such imaging. Barbara Duden offers a historical perspective, contributing to a genealogy of the fetus's mediation by medical, media, and technological makings and framings, in *Disembodying Women: Perspectives on Pregnancy and the Unborn* (Cambridge: Harvard University Press, 1993). Barad is among those (see also Haraway's "Fetus") who have called for a greater attention to uterine imaging

5. JUDITH BUTLER, PRECARIOUS LIFE, AND REPRODUCTION   241

as manifesting an interlocking of materiality, technology, and discourse, downplayed, she argues, by Butler, in a brief mention of the sonograms in *Bodies That Matter*, xvii. Here a degree of agency would be attributed not so much to the "fetus" (the latter not deemed to be a self-standing, unmediated entity) but perhaps to technologized matter interactively enfolding with the politics of gender and gendering in a differentiating politics (and economics) of visualization and formation. See Karen Barad, *Meeting the Universe Halfway: Quantum Physics and the Entanglement of Matter and Meaning* (Durham: Duke University Press, 2007), 191–94.

36. Rayna Rapp's *Testing Women, Testing the Fetus* remains a watershed work in describing this phenomenon. It engages specifically with the genetic counseling offered in clinical contexts in America in the course of amniocentric testing and related consultations surrounding possible or certain fetal genetic defects. These consultations have typically required decision making from mothers and parents—in conjunction with medical and genetic counselors, family, and other figures. Rapp is also attentive to differentiations based on class, culture, and race with respect to the expectations and approach by counselors, medical experts, and others to decision making, its possibility and conduct, and to interfacing with medical data and advice. Rapp's project is attentive to numerous ways in which decision making of this kind is framed. See Rayna Rapp, *Testing Women, Testing the Fetus: The Social Impact of Amniocentesis in America* (New York: Routledge, 1999).

37. Butler is relying on the redoubled senses of the term *normative*, which emerged early in her writing. See her comment about *Gender Trouble*:

> Some readers have asked whether *Gender Trouble* seeks to expand the realm of gender possibilities for a reason. . . . The question often involves a prior premise, namely, that the text does not address the normative or prescriptive dimension of feminist thought. "Normative" clearly has at least two meanings in this critical encounter, since the word is one I used often, mainly to describe the mundane violence performed by certain kinds of gender ideals. I usually use "normative" in a way that is synonymous with "pertaining to the norms that govern gender." But the term "normative" also pertains to ethical justification, how it is established, and what concrete consequences proceed therefrom. . . . It is not possible to oppose the "normative" forms of gender without at the same time subscribing to a certain normative view of how the gendered world ought to be.
> (Butler, *Gender Trouble*, xxi)

38. Butler, *Giving and Account of Oneself*, 9.
39. Amongst these, and in the context of recent and prominent debates in feminist theory, one would make particular mention of the controversial critique (with a Nietzschean inflection), of the making (and feminist deployment of) a concurrently punitive and self- lacerating moral subjectivity in Janet Halley's *Split Decisions: How and Why to Take a Break from Feminism* (Princeton: Princeton University Press, 2006).
40. Butler, *Giving and Account of Oneself*, 98–99. For example, in her account of the Nietzschean guilty conscience, Butler emphasizes the type of moral conscience

associated with a (disavowed) righteous vengefulness toward the other. This "injured and rageful subject . . . adopts a position of moral legitimacy for rageful and injurious conduct, and, through that moralization transmutes aggression into virtue" ("Reply from Judith Butler to Mills and Jenkins," 186). To Nietzsche's description of moral consciences of this kind, a description refuting the view that they seek triumph any less than other creatures, we can also add his concern for the stunted health and vitality of the creatures in whom bad conscience forms. He mentions the disoriented "sea animal," "imprisoned within the confines of society and peace," denying or reproving aggressive instincts, denied "external enemies and obstacles, and forced into the oppressive narrowness and conformity of custom," and whose old instincts of "pursuing, raiding, changing and destroying" have not thereby "suddenly ceased to make their demands!" So, since "all instincts which are not discharged outwardly *turn inwards*," they are directed instead back against the sea animal, forming a self-punishing form of conscience to its detriment. Here bad conscience is understood as a mode of "ripp[ing one]self apart," a raging against oneself. "That," he says, "is the origin of bad conscience" (*On the Genealogy of Morality*, 52, essay II, # 16). Friedrich Nietzsche, *On the Genealogy of Morality*, ed. Keith Ansell-Pearson, trans. Carol Diethe (Cambridge: Cambridge University Press, 2007), 56–57.

41. Dominique Memmi, *La seconde vie des bébés morts* (Paris: Editions de l'école des hautes études en sciences sociales, 2011), 159n9. (My translation.)

42. See Ewa Ziarek, "Bare Life on Strike: Notes on the Biopolitics of Race and Gender," *South Atlantic Quarterly* 107 (2008): 89–106, 96; Butler and Spivak, *Who Sings the Nation-State?*, 37; Ranjana Khanna, "Disposability," *differences* 20, no. 1 (2009): 181–98.

43. Foucault also discusses the decreased importance of the death penalty in France in the context of the increase in the importance and new techniques of biopower; see HS I 137–38).

44. From the perspective of those commentators for whom the thanatopolitical aspects of biopolitics amount to a blurring of the boundaries between biopolitical interest in life, the power to take life, and the power to make live, it might not appear mysterious that death penalties coincide perfectly well with the illegality of abortion, euthanasia, and suicide.

45. See also his comments on suicide HS I 138–39.

46. Memmi, *La seconde vie des bébés morts*, 166. (My translation.)

47. Estelle Ferrarese's analysis of the gendered politics of consent can be usefully added to this discussion. See her account of how a modern grammar of norms for consent and choice performable before another party concurrently differentiates between those entities whose consent (and its authenticity) is more or less likely to be in doubt, instituting inclusions and exclusions, centerings and decenterings of subjects in this regard. Estelle Ferrarese, "The Political Grammar of Consent: Investigating a New Gender Order," *Constellations* 22, no. 3 (2015): 462–72; and see the discussion of consent in Ruth A. Miller, *The Limits of Bodily Integrity: Abortion, Adultery, and Rape Legislation in Comparative Perspective* (Aldershot: Ashgate, 2007); in Elaine Scarry, "Consent and the Body: Injury, Departure, and Desire," *New Literary History* 21, no. 4 (1990): 867–96; and in Genevieve Fraisse, *Du Consentement* (Paris: Seuil, 2007).

48. See the discussion of Le Doeuff in chapter 4.
49. Memmi, *La seconde vie des bébés morts*, 165. (My translation.)
50. This is described by Brown in Wendy Brown with Christina Colegate, John Dalton, Timothy Rayner, and Cate Thill, "Learning to Love Again: An Interview with Wendy Brown," *Contretemps* 6 (2006): 25–42, 35–36. Brown responds to a question from Colegate concerning so-called Shared Responsibility Agreements used as a component of the Australian government's approach to welfare policy in indigenous affairs. An example of one such Shared Responsibility Agreement was the government's delivery of a petrol bowser to an indigenous community in exchange for undertakings to reduce trachoma through such measures as more assiduous cleaning of children's faces. The discussion leads to Brown's suggestion to think together her critique of the fictions of the sovereign subject *with* her critique of governmental disciplinary power. Of course, this isn't just a thinking together of modes of critique but also of modes of power. Subjects may be projected as possessing an always already failed sovereignty, understood in terms of irresponsibility. But such phenomena might also manifest some of the forms of docility and malleability associated with the disciplines. As Brown interprets this phenomenon, this is "the practice of making a subject whose sovereignty is granted on the condition that it is given up, not practiced . . . the site of a kind of sovereign subject that this practice of governmentality means to mow down, to erase." In particular, she suggests, it may be in the configurations of "race, gender, sexuality, class, subculture, . . nationality . . . religion . . . [that] the critiques comes together, in the recognition that the so-called production of the sovereign subject is actually the production of a very specified subject whose sovereignty is only recognized when it gratifies or responds to those specifications. Sovereignty is then internally deconstructed" (ibid., 36).
51. Carol Gilligan, *In a Different Voice: Psychological Theory and Women's Development* (Cambridge: Harvard University Press, 1993), hereafter *DV*.
52. Gilligan explains:

> In order to go beyond the question, "How much like men do women think, how capable are they of engaging in the abstract and hypothetical construction of reality?" it is necessary to identify and define developmental criteria that encompass the categories of women's thought. . . . But to derive developmental criteria from the language of women's moral discourse, it is necessary first to see whether women's construction of the moral domain relies on a language different from that of men and one that deserves equal credence in the definition of development. This in turn requires finding places where women have the power to choose and thus are willing to speak in their own voice.
>
> (*DV* 70)

She identified reproductive decision making in the wake of *Roe v. Wade* as one such place.

53. Barbara Johnson has written of her initial surprise, since abortion seemed precisely one of those issues about which "an even-handed comparison of the male and the female points of view is impossible." Yet, she continues, "this, clearly, turns out to be the point. There

is difference *because* it is not always possible to make symmetrical oppositions. As long as there is symmetry, one is not dealing with difference but with versions of the same." Barbara Johnson, "Apostrophe, Animation, and Abortion," *diacritics* 16, no. 1 (1986): 29–47, 33.

54. *DV* 69. Originally one of his research assistants, Gilligan was responding to Kohlberg's identification of four to six developmental stages of moral reasoning—amongst these, the highest level would be a capacity to formulate abstract, universally applicable principles. Kohlberg had not considered that sex difference might be relevant to the results of studies oriented toward the assessment of adult moral reasoning.

55. Among a number of overviews of subsequent feminist critique and sympathetic identification of widely recognized limits and problems in Gilligan's project, see the volume edited by Mary Jeanne Larrabee, *An Ethic of Care: Feminist and Interdisciplinary Perspectives* (New York: Routledge 1993); and see Joan Tronto's *Moral Boundaries: A Political Argument for an Ethic of Care* (New York: Routledge, 1993).

56. Ronald Dworkin, *Life's Dominion: An Argument About Abortion, Euthanasia, and Individual Freedom* (New York: Vintage 1994), 60.

57. Johnson, "Apostrophe, Animation, and Abortion," 33.

58. See, for example, the characterization of feminist reactions to the contours of pro-choice activism in the United States, "pro-choice activists have tended to ignore or trivialize the trauma of many women who undergo abortions. They have thus delivered into the hands of the pro-life contingent almost all concern with many women's tremendous emotional confusion, feelings of loss, and sense of complicity." Wendy Brown, "Reproductive Freedom and the Right to Privacy: A Paradox for Feminists," in Irene Diamond, ed., *Families, Politics and Public Policy* (New York: Routledge, 1983), 322–38, 322.

59. Johnson, "Apostrophe, Animation, and Abortion," 33.

60. To such tacit apprehensions of differential worth we could consider a number of aspects manifesting in the global commercial market in surrogacy, discussed later in this chapter, to which should be added the market in women's reproductive tissue, which can bear considerable health risks for the donor; see, for example, Catherine Waldby and Melinda Cooper, "The Biopolitics of Reproduction: Post-Fordist Biotechnology and Women's Clinical Labor," *Australian Feminist Studies* 23, no. 55 (2008): 57–73. Thus reproductive freedoms also become dividing practices of privilege: between those more likely to need the economic benefit of tissue sale or provision of surrogacy and those in a position to purchase these; between those whose abortions and pregnancies are, in a number of ways, or for a number of reasons, more likely to be supported and those for whom reproduction is less likely to signify rights and freedoms; and also those whose material support of the pregnancies of others may come to be equated with their own economic opportunity or, as in the discussion of *Google Baby* later in this chapter, their own means of "life-improvement."

61. Jenkins, "Queering Foetal Life," 65.

62. Ibid., 76.

63. I take this opportunity to thank an anonymous reader of the manuscript of this volume for Columbia University Press for recalling Butler's early interest in identifying a

more vitalist current in Foucault's understanding of life as well as for the point that this discussion of ontological tact might turn to David Caron's *The Nearness of Others: Searching for Tact and Contact in the Age of HIV* (Minneapolis: University of Minnesota Press, 2014). In discussions of living with AIDS, which articulate a wide range of careful, nuanced, subtly adjusting modes of living with others, Caron introduces the term *tact* as a means of thinking of a concurrent relationship of distance and proximity that is elaborated in a number of ways in *The Nearness of Others*: including the consensual flexibility and collective, attentive negotiability about the categories and meanings to which forms of life or death might be understood to belong and their malleability. The term also leads Caron to articulate a kind of negative ethics: "less about doing the right thing than not doing the wrong thing," a type of ethical gesture lacking a preestablished norm. Among the characteristics of the "ethics of tact" to which Caron speaks, he proposes they "can be determined only in specific situations that, like dysclosure, can never recur identically" (ibid., 308).

64. Memmi, *La seconde vie des bébés morts*, 183.
65. Memmi discusses just such regimes of flexibility in medical and expert comportment. Some might be expected to experience distress because their pregnancy is unwanted, others because a desired maternity was thwarted. Such flexibility allows Memmi and Jenkins to discuss the ambiguous threshold between fetal material as waste and as mourned. Where Memmi emphasizes the ambiguous status of fetus differently made depending on the context, Jenkins emphasizes the issues of waste, remainder, and grievability that may be overlooked, she argues, in pro-abortion politics. Often, where abortion is legal, "dealings with the aborted foetal body are effectively invisible," Memmi, *La seconde vie des bébés morts*. Of course these matters of invisibility and visibility are complex and relate to comportment as well as imaging. Think of how Memmi in fact discusses the ambiguous, constantly nuanced, responsive, discursive, and behavioral "making" negotiated by medical staff and others in terms of women's or parents' hopes and projects. A woman seeking an abortion might produce what all will consider biowaste she might never (in accordance with her own wishes) encounter. But when a miscarriage is made mournable or an abortion has different kinds of meanings, she may be offered more options. The comportment of those concerned will remake matter accordingly.
66. A phenomenon differently interpreted by Jenkins but these perspectives are not incompatible. (Jenkins, "Queering Foetal Life," 64).
67. Ibid.
68. There is a tradition in some philosophical and applied ethics treatments of abortion of positing the woman and the fetus as separate entities, with competing interests and moral claims which are then adjudicated. In "A Defense of Abortion" the philosopher Judith Jarvis Thompson famously suggested the thought experiment of a woman who finds she has been connected as the life support to a famous violinist and weighed their competing claims. She concludes that, *even if* the fetus were to be endowed with competing rights (such as a right to life), the woman cannot be seen as morally obligated to carry it to term, because a right to life does not extend to a right to use someone else's

body. Whatever the reasons a woman may choose to carry a fetus to term, there is not a moral claim on her to do so. See Judith Jarvis Thompson, "A Defense of Abortion," *Philosophy and Public Affairs* 1, no. 1 (1971): 47–66.
69. Jenkins, "Queering Foetal Life," 64.
70. Butler, *Giving an Account of Oneself*, 9.
71. Butler, "Reply from Judith Butler to Mills and Jenkins," 184.
72. Butler, *Giving an Account of Oneself*, 10.
73. Again: "Ethical deliberation is bound up with the operation of critique. And critique finds that it cannot go forward without a consideration of how the deliberating subject comes into being and how a deliberating subject might actually live or appropriate a set of norms," Butler, *Giving an Account of Oneself*, 8.
74. Reiterating a formulation of liberalism in these terms from Gayatri Spivak, Brown includes reproductive rights in her discussion of the conundrum of the rights we "cannot not want." See Wendy Brown, "Suffering Rights as Paradoxes," *Constellations* 7, no. 2 (2000): 230–41, 234; and see Gayatri Spivak, *Outside in the Teaching Machine* (New York: Routledge, 1993), 44–46.
75. See Brown, "Suffering Rights as Paradoxes"; and, among the diverse discussions of this issue, see Dorothy Roberts, *Killing the Black Body: Race, Reproduction, and the Meaning of Liberty* (New York: Vintage, 1998); Carole Pateman, "Race, Sex, and Indifference," in Carole Pateman and Charles Mills, *Contract and Domination* (Malden, MA: Polity, 2007), 134–64, 151; Haraway, "Fetus," 198; Gayatri Spivak, "A Literary Representation of the Subaltern: A Woman's Text From the Third World," in *In Other Worlds* (New York: Routledge, 2006), 330–69, 354–55.
76. Butler, "Is Kinship Always Already Heterosexual?," 22, 18. Butler has discussed a number of senses in which reproductive rights can delegitimate some subjects, or render others unthinkable, and institute hierarchies between those included and excluded. The reproductive rights claims of gay couples may come to seem immanent, possible, forthcoming, as distinct from "that [which] will never be eligible for a translation into legitimacy" (ibid., 18). Butler has both sexual illegitimacy and illegibilities of kinship in mind here.
77. Berlant's account of understandings of failures of the will is distinctive for having associated with these with a definition of biopower: "Biopower operates when a hegemonic bloc organizes the reproduction of life in ways that allow political crises to be cast as conditions of specific bodies and their competence at maintaining health or other conditions of social belonging; thus this bloc gets to judge the problematic body's subjects, whose agency is deemed to be fundamentally destructive. Apartheid-like structures from zoning to shaming are wielded against these populations, who come to represent embodied liabilities to social prosperity of one sort of another." See Lauren Berlant, *Cruel Optimism* (Durham: Duke University Press, 2011), 105–6.
78. See his ubiquitous discussions of power as productivity, for example, in Michel Foucault, "The Meshes of Power," trans. Gerald Moore, in *Space, Knowledge and Power: Foucault and Geography*, ed. Jeremy Crampton and Stuart Elden (Aldershot: Ashgate, 2007), 153–62.
79. Michel Foucault, "Body/Power," in *Power/Knowledge: Selected Interviews and Other Writings 1972–1977*, ed. Colin Gordon (New York: Pantheon, 1980), 55–62, 57.

5. JUDITH BUTLER, PRECARIOUS LIFE, AND REPRODUCTION   247

80. Michel Foucault, "The Eye of Power," in *Power/Knowledge*, 146–65, 162.
81. Michel Foucault, "The End of the Monarchy of Sex," in *Foucault Live, Collected Interviews, 1961–1984*, ed. Sylvère Lotringer (New York: Columbia University, 1989), 137–55, 143.
82. Referring to Lillian Faderman's *Surpassing the Love of Men*, he argues that the fact that women had been frustrated and isolated for centuries gave them the "real possibility of constituting a society, of creating a kind of social relation between themselves, outside the social world that was dominated by males." Michel Foucault, "Sex, Power, and the Politics of Identity," in *Ethics: Subjectivity, and Truth* (*Essential Works of Foucault, 1954–1984*, vol. 1), ed. Paul Rabinow (New York: New Press, 1998), 163–73, 168.
83. Foucault, "The End of the Monarchy of Sex," 144.
84. Foucault, "Body/Power," 56 (translation modified).
85. Most obviously, the Australian couple widely reported as having abandoned a twin born with Down syndrome to his Thai surrogate mother, Pattharamon Janbua, in Thailand in 2014, following the latter's refusal to abort the fetus on their request after it had been diagnosed with Down syndrome. A number of U.S. cases have been reported of clients requesting (or offering additional payment for) termination, selective or otherwise.
86. Butler, "Is Kinship Always Heterosexual?," 21.
87. Possibilities depicted phobically by Sylviane Agacinski; see Butler, "Is Kinship Always Heterosexual?," 36.
88. Surrogacy arrangements are not illegal in Australia, but cannot be commercial. However the Australian government will recognize the citizenship of a child born overseas through an international commercial surrogacy arrangement. For a full-length study of commercial international surrogacy clinics in India, see Amrita Pande, *Wombs in Labor: Transnational Commercial Surrogacy in India* (New York: Columbia University Press, 2014), which includes a comparative summary of national laws as of 2014 (14–15).
89. http://www.npr.org/templates/story/story.php?storyId=127860111 (accessed September 9, 2013), and see Pande, *Wombs in Labor*, 52. Chapter 3 and the epilogue to Pande's *Wombs in Labor* offers extensive analysis of the immediate and longer-term economic context of and impact on Indian surrogates.
90. See Pande, *Wombs in Labor*, chapter 4: "Manufacturing the Perfect Mother-Worker". Pande also offers an analysis of some of the unintended consequences and small resistances she located in surrogacy work, in an analysis consistent with the mood of the question "can we calculate?"
91. For early discussions on Foucault on death, see Judith Butler, "Sexual Inversions," in John Caputo and Mark Yount, eds., *Foucault and the Critique of Institutions* (University Park: Pennsylvania State University Press, 1993), 81–98; and for early discussions on Foucault on life, see Judith Butler, *Subjects of Desire: Hegelian Reflections in Twentieth-Century France* (New York: Columbia University Press, 2012 [1987]), 227, 231.
92. See Judith Butler, "What Is Critique: An Essay on Foucault's Virtue," in *The Judith Butler Reader*, ed. Sara Salih (Malden, MA: Blackwell, 2004), 302–21.
93. See Butler's commentary on this work: "the theory of responsibility that I sought to sketch in *Giving an Account of Oneself* . . . is not meant to be abstracted from social and political contexts and critical interrogation of norms." Moreover, she adds, "this

ethical call emerges insistently from scenes of political conflict" (Butler, "Reply from Judith Butler to Mills and Jenkins," 190).

94. Although *Giving an Account of Oneself* has, as Butler notes, been interpreted as her contribution to moral philosophy, her own understanding of its argument in this respect is that "questions of moral conduct and inquiry cannot be dissociated from social theory and that neither can be separated from the practice of critique" ("Reply from Judith Butler to Mills and Jenkins," 191). She has also emphasized that an interrogation of the framing or genealogical or indeed the political conditions of responsibility, of moral conduct, and of ethical struggles and calls need not be seen as invalidating ethical inquiry. Among her explorations of this point, see remarks in "Reply from Judith Butler to Mills and Jenkins" where she distances herself from one possible interpretation of her work: that norms operate through a normalizing violence, resulting in an ineluctable ontological violence attributable to normative constitution (ibid., 183). Even if this were so, she argues, the fact that a resulting ethics (particularly a nonviolent ethics) would then be "necessary but impossible" need not diminish its importance: "perhaps that paradox names the impasse from which any and all ethical struggle emerges" (ibid., 184).

95. Butler with Athanasiou, *Dispossession*, 169, and see 47.

96. Jasbir Puar, *Terrorist Assemblages: Homonationalism in Queer Times* (Durham: Duke University Press, 2007), 5, 22, 59.

97. Berlant, *Cruel Optimism*, 106.

98. For this reason, one would also need a circumspect response to the conclusions proposed in Cynthia Daniels's analysis of the twentieth-century U.S. legal history in which personhood and fetal rights have been progressively granted to embryos, in a series of legal cases whose precedents were partially set by parents claiming damages with respect to lost pregnancies resulting from accidents for which other parties (car drivers, state and local agencies who had failed to repair roads) were to blame. As the agent deemed to have suffered the loss in question shifted from the parent to the embryo "itself," the stage was set for impending legal configurations of women as entities against which the interests of fetuses could also be asserted with the language of criminal neglect, harm, or homicidal intent. The result has been a slew of "fetal homicide" cases against women, prosecution of women for exposing fetuses to substances they ingested, and new configurations of antiabortion measures, such as Arkansas's recent initiative to assign legal representation to fetuses. The question is whether the solution will be best found, as Daniels proposes, by a move away from seeing women and fetuses as having separate and competing individual interests to reconfiguration of reproduction in terms of collective responsibility. The argument of the present book is that these should not be seen as philosophical or political alternatives but as concurrent regimes. Thus the construction of the woman as a potential criminal actor with respect to an embryo is both a manufacture of private competing interest, but *also* a manufacture of the competing interest of state sovereignty, *and* it is a reconfiguration of the state's avowed, if highly conditional, interest in providing welfare services (as in the assignation of public legal representation to the fetus) and of governmental aspirations to administer heath and ensure optimal life (as seen in cases against women for exposure of fetuses to drugs

5. JUDITH BUTLER, PRECARIOUS LIFE, AND REPRODUCTION 249

in utero). Because of the capacity of these regimes to coexist, sometimes reinforcing each other, sometimes jostling against each other, one should be cautious of a solution aiming at a shift from one register to another (for example, a shift from individualized rights to the language and aspirations of collective interest). See Cynthia Daniels, *At Women's Expense: State Power and the Politics of Fetal Rights* (Cambridge: Harvard University Press, 1996).

99. Here we return to the formulation proposed about liberalism by Spivak in *Outside in the Teaching Machine*, 44–46; and amplified in Brown's discussion of the conundrum of rights for "articulating and redressing women's inequality and subordination in liberal constitutional regimes" (Brown, "Suffering Rights as Paradoxes," 230). One of the distinctive methodological insights of Brown's account of the rights we "cannot not want" is seen in its multiplication of the senses and dimensions in which there is a paradox of rights. The argument concerns a number of different ways of understanding the problem of paradox. That we would need to think together *all* such dimensions of paradox is a possibility that emerges as the senses of paradox accumulate. These dimensions (Brown includes reproductive rights) are parsed in the following terms: Rights mitigate but do not resolve subordinating powers. Or they may serve to regulate and distribute subordination. Rights can be "blind" (for example, race blind) and so enhance privilege. Or they can reinscribe a designation of subordination and so enhance subordination by means of that subordination. They differentially empower according to the privilege of those concerned. The rights of some may directly deprive others. They consolidate the fictions and norms of a lacking sovereign individuality. They disavow their own contingency or genealogical conditions. They attach subjects to injury. They deploy a discourse which was founded on the constitutive exclusion of those who later deploy it in their pursuit of inclusion. They may imply that a subordination is intelligible and reducible to its possible redress by rights.

And, among the many contributions of the argument, we see how an intensification of intersectionality is both required but will begin to breach its limits:

> As many feminist, postcolonial, queer, and critical race theorists have noted in recent years, it is impossible to pull the race out of gender, or the gender out of sexuality, or the colonialism out of caste out of masculinity out of sexuality. Moreover, to treat these various modalities of subject formation as simply additive or even intersectional is to elide . . . a production that does not occur in additive, intersectional, or overlapping parts, but through complex and often fragmented histories in which multiple social powers are regulated through and against one another. . . . the powers producing and situating socially subordinated subjects occur in radically different modalities, which themselves contain different histories and technologies, touch different surfaces and depths, form different bodies and psyches.
>
> (ibid., 236)

100. Derrida's rethinking of the event, the decision and the à-venir is a resource here suggesting a means of assuming their possibility, despite their constitutively resisting our

capacity to identify their specific taking place. See, for example, his account of the decision: "Who will ever be able to assure us that a decision as such has taken place?" This would be a decision which has 'truly' gone through the order of the incalculable. Jacques Derrida, "Force of Law: The 'Mystical Foundation of Authority,'" in Drucilla Cornell, Michael Rosenfeld, and David Gray Carlson, eds., *Deconstruction and the Possibility of Justice* (New York: Routledge, 1992), 25. See also his related discussion of justice: "justice again impl[ies] . . . non-gathering, dissociation, heterogeneity, non-identity with itself, endless inadequation, infinite transcendence. That is why the call for justice is never, never, fully answered. That is why no-one can say 'I am just.'" Jacques Derrida, *Deconstruction in a Nutshell: A Conversation with Jacques Derrida*, ed. John D. Caputo (New York: Fordham University Press, 1996), 17. And for his discussions of the event, as by definition exceeding my horizon of expectation, see Jacques Derrida with Bernard Stiegler, *Echographies of Television: Filmed Interviews*, trans. Jennifer Bajorek (London: Polity, 2002), 12–13.

101. See Michel Foucault, *The History of Sexuality*, vol. 2: *The Use of Pleasure*, trans. Robert Hurley (New York: Vintage, 1990); and see Michel Foucault, "On the Genealogy of Ethics: An Overview of Work in Progress," in *The Foucault Reader*, ed. Paul Rabinow (New York: Vintage, 2010), 340–72, 353–57; and Arnold Davidson, "Ethics as Ascetics: Foucault, the History of Ethics, and Ancient Thought," in Gary Gutting, ed., *The Cambridge Companion to Foucault* (Cambridge: Cambridge University Press, 1994), 115–40, 118.

INDEX

abjection, 41, 43–44, 59, 149
Abnormal (Foucault), 1, 30, 36, 83, 87, 114, 211*n*1, 212*n*7, 220*n*77, 238*n*15
abnormality. *See* normalization
abortion, 7, 40–41, 50–51; emotional life of woman, 168–69; exception, states of, 7, 36–37, 119–26, 133; Foucault, power and, 178–85; France, 125, 143, 159–64; as genocide, 4, 60, 209*n*61; "heartbeat bans," 123, 228*n*28, 228–29*n*29, 229*n*30, 229*nn*30, 31; illegal, dangers of, 154, 161; illegibility and, 164, 168, 176–78; as impediment to futures, 4, 65, 153; legal regimes, 120–26, 129; miscarriage, 171–72, 245*n*65; normalization of, 162–63; power and, 178–85; precarious right to, 120–26, 137; *Roe v. Wade*, 122–24, 127, 168; Romania, 154, 174–76; sex-selective, in China, 115; state criminal laws, 122–24; surrogacy and, 180–81, 244*n*60, 246*n*85, 247*n*88; third-term, 57; United States, 122–25; women as decision makers, 4–8, 36, 50–51, 104, 121, 126–27
absent concepts, 5–6, 10, 28, 61, 151; interpretive keys, 105, 110, 111, 115; oscillations in Foucault and Esposito, 105–16
administration of life, 2, 17, 24, 32, 35–36, 64, 73, 76–77, 96, 102–4, 106–12, 116–17, 136–42, 160; *Polizeiwissenschaft*, 35, 77, 95, 200–1*n*83; powers of death and, 105–9; precariousness and, 146–51, 154
adoption, 42–43
Adorno, Theodor, 10, 175–76
African American women, 60, 203*n*14, 209*nn*60, 61. *See also* racialization
After Tiller (Shane and Wilson), 57, 201*n*4, 205–6*n*32
Agamben, Giorgio, 7–11, 13–14, 32, 38, 72, 74, 103–4, 117–20, 126, 130, 185; biopolitics of modernity, 132–33; feminism and, 128–30; *homo sacer*, 127–28; overlaps with Foucault, 141–43; passive citizen, 133–35; sexual difference, neglect of, 128–32; *zoe* and *bios* distinction, 119, 130–32, 134, 159; Works: *Homo Sacer*, 103, 117–18, 127–32; *Remnants of Auschwitz*, 120. *See also* bare life
ages and epochs, 15, 20, 25–27, 31–32, 71, 195–96*n*23, 195*n*25

alliance, 31–32, 88–90, 220*n*74, 221–22*n*85. *See also* family spaces
ambivalence of madness, 25
analogy, 35–37, 38
anatomo-politics, 18, 23
anomie, 119–20, 124, 126–27, 132–33, 139
Antigone, 46, 47–48, 203*n*12, 204*nn*19, 20
antilife, 4, 42, 44–45, 70, 98, 100–1, 187, 208–9*n*58
antisociality, 4, 41, 101, 186; reproductive politics and, 57–59; *sinthom*osexual as figure of, 45–46
'Apostrophe, Animation, and Abortion' (Johnson), 144, 168, 243–44*n*53
archaeology, 17, 149, 194*n*13
Arendt, Hannah, 236*n*2, 240*n*30
Aristotle, 130

Barad, Karen, 163, 240–41*n*35
bare life, 7, 8–9, 39, 104, 118–20, 192*n*8; absent concepts, 10; Butler on, 147; citizenship and, 129–35; fetus and, 170–74; political value of, 159–61; women's reproductive life as, 127–28. *See also homo sacer*; life
The Beast and the Sovereign (Derrida), 31, 32–33
Beauvoir, Simone de, 55–56
Behrisch, Lars, 79
Bell, Vikki, 215*n*30
Berlant, Lauren, 7, 39, 163, 188, 205*n*28, 246*n*77
Bernasconi, Robert, 72, 98
Beyond the Pleasure Principle (Freud), 28
biopoliticization of women's reproductivity, 2, 7–8, 127–28
biopolitics/biopolitical, 2, 13–14, 221*n*81; bodies and populations, 66–70; dispersed, 35–37; excess, 108–9, 116–17; health concerns, 2, 4, 35–36, 51, 61, 62, 66, 74; life emerges with, 110–11, 117; modernity and, 132–33; paradoxes, 60, 107–9, 116; powers of death as underside of, 22, 31, 64–65, 95–97, 105–8; racism of, 68–69; reproduction, 112–13; reproductive futurism and, 61–63; reversal of politics of life into politics of death, 107–9, 111–13, 115; sexual difference and, 37–38; sexuality and, 32–33; sovereignty, relationship to, 19–20, 106–9, 116–18, 121, 141–43, 161; thanatopolitical, move to, 95–98, 242*n*44. *See also* biopower; thanatopolitics/thanatopolitical
biopower, 3, 20–22, 31–33, 86, 88–89, 93, 95, 105–9, 111; sexuality and, 61, 67, 73. *See also* biopolitics/biopolitical; power
bios, 119, 130–32, 159
Bios (Espositio), 105–7, 110, 111–15
Birds (Hitchcock), 46, 204*n*20
birthrate, 2, 3, 32, 35, 61, 64, 71, 77–78, 90, 93, 100, 114, 116, 136
The Birth of the Clinic (Foucault), 16–17, 145
Bloch, Ernst, 10
Bock, Gisela, 5, 116
Brown, Wendy, 13, 39, 59–60, 117, 154, 164, 226–27*n*18, 249*n*99
Butler, Judith, 3, 7, 9, 39, 102; Antigone, view of, 47; ethical life, 146, 155, 158–59, 170, 190; precariousness, view of, 146–51; Works: *Frames of War*, 9, 17, 144, 146, 149, 151–55, 186; *Gender Trouble*, 148, 237*nn*10, 11, 241*n*37; *Giving an Account of Oneself*, 148, 158, 170, 175–76, 185, 248*n*94; *Precarious Life*, 149–50, 156; *Subjects of Desire*, 145, 150

Cain, Herman, 60
calculability, 47–49, 55, 56, 59–61
camp, as anomic space, 119–20, 129, 132–33, 140, 142, 231*n*44, 231*n*45
Canguilhem, Georges, 74
Ceaușescu regime, 154, 174
Child, figure of, 40–45, 101, 211*n*72; Child of the Future, 49–51; as figure of continuity, 43–45; flexible possibilities for, 62–63; as

heteronormative fixation, 40; imaginary Child of gay parenting, 42–43; in James, 49–51; Tiny Tim figure, 43, 45, 48, 59
children, 1–2; European, as vulnerable, 98–99; feminist images of, 54–55; masturbating, 29–32, 64, 65–66, 73, 83–84, 96–97, 219n69; metabodies, 31–32, 34; moral duty toward, 80–81; mortality rates, 93
The Children of Men (James), 49–52
Chow, Rey, 67–68, 99
A Christmas Tale (Dickens), 46
citizenship, 129–32; living dead reproductive life, 136–37; passive, 133–35
classical age, 25–26. See also ages and epochs
clinic: France, changes in abortion law, 159–64; "outside," 173–76; precariousness and fetal life, 151–59
Clinton, Bill, 40
Cogito, 197–98n44, 198n45
colonialism, 33, 65–69, 98–100
Comstock Law, 122
Condorcet, Marquis de, 55–56, 207n43
conduct, 2, 3, 17, 23–24, 65, 99, 121; of conduct, 78, 79, 85; of consultation, 162–63; counterconduct, 189, 217–18n50, 223n94; reproductive futurism and, 35–36, 65; reproductive responsibilization and, 80–82, 143, 159, 161, 187
conservative defensiveness, 40, 42–45, 62
consultation, conducts of, 162–63
contemporary, 26–27. See also ages and epochs; present
contingent formations, 113, 173, 216n35, 220n73; ethical, 146, 155, 158–59, 163, 190; of life, 15–16, 35, 66, 69, 74, 146, 149, 187–88; of procreation, 71, 78, 80, 115, 146; of responsibilization, 66, 158–59, 176
Cooper, Melinda, 231n45
counterconduct, 189, 217–18n50, 223n94
critical history, 16

critical race theory, 128–29
critique, 150–1, 185, 246n73
Critique de la raison negre (Mbembe), 9

Daniels, Cynthia, 248–49n98
Das, Veena, 9
de Gouges, Olympe, 206n34, 207–8n45
Dean, Tim, 57–58
death, 4, 7–9; as collateral damage, 23; different forms, 17; of futures, 98–100; forms of political power and, 19–20, 22, 93, 118, 141, 160, 224n97; gay men as "culture" of, 42, 202n6; making of, 100–1; maternal failings as cause, 97, 177; murder, indirect forms, 22, 101, 115–16, 119, 137, 141–143, 154, 173–75, 207n44, 222–23n91; reversal of politics of life, 107–9, 111–13, 115; "slow death," 6–7; techniques of, 21–22; "vital," 22–23; women associated with delivery of, 5, 6, 36, 65. See also thanatopolitics
death, powers of, 22–23, 95–97, 102, 119, 185, 224n2; autodestruction, 107–10; as end point of biopower's process, 106–11; as underside of biopolitical, 22, 31, 64–65, 95–98, 105–8
death drive, 44–45, 52, 62, 198n51
death penalty, 6, 8, 20–23, 107, 159–60, 197n39, 228n25; differentiations of, 21–22; exception, states of, 7, 36–37; future impeded by, 34–36; justifications for, 22–23; women and, 6, 33–36
Death Penalty Seminar (Derrida), 6, 8, 32–33, 37, 197n40
decision making, 53, 121, 143, 153, 177, 184–89; decisional responsibility, 157–58, 163; Gilligan on, 164–68; Jenkins on, 170–74; Johnson on, 168–70; moral thought, 164–70
Declaration of Rights of Man and Citizen, 133–35
decompositions, 21–25. See also segmentations of power

deconstitution, 156, 159. *See also* desubjectivation; illegibility
"A Defense of Abortion" (Thompson), 245–46n68
Defense of Marriage Act (DOMA), 42
degeneracy, 16, 17, 31, 34, 65, 68, 216n39; debauched sexuality, 96–97; racialized, 98–100; "types," 66
dehumanization, 149–50, 155–56, 192n8
delegation, biopolitical, 161
delegitimation, 3, 59, 61, 184, 232n56, 246n76
Deleuze, Gilles, 86, 220n73
Démar, Claire, 53–54
demographics, 20, 72, 76, 78, 93–94, 110, 121
Derrida, Jacques, 6, 185, 198n51, 249n100; anesthetization, 8, 33; counter-readings of Foucault's figures, 25–26; deconstructions, 14–15; first essay on Foucault, 29–30; interrogation of Foucauldian present, 24–28; on relation of death penalty to biopolitics, 22; sexual difference addressed, 8, 37–38; survivance, 24, 38; Works: *The Beast and the Sovereign*, 31, 32; *Death Penalty Seminar*, 6, 33, 37; *Of Grammatology*, 30; *Politics of Friendship*, 33; "To Do Justice to Freud," 28, 31, 37
Des habitudes secrètes (Rozier), 83
Descartes, Rene, 25, 26, 29, 197–98n44, 198n45
desubjectivation, 3, 145, 156, 159, 185–86
Deuber-Mankowsky, Astrid, 128
différance, 30
disciplinary modes, 3, 18–20, 23, 36, 85, 88, 92, 94, 101, 195–96n25, 196–97n35; control of sexuality, 24, 72–73
Discipline and Punish (Foucault), 33, 103, 160
disposability, 7, 9, 124, 171, 172, 173, 182, 229n32
dissemination, 35–37, 94, 103, 224n97
domus, 131
Donzelot, Jacques, 83, 85, 95–96, 218n55, 221–22n85
Dorlin, Elsa, 5, 98, 99, 214n22

Duden, Barbara, 163, 240–41n35
Due Process Clause, 122
Dutot, Nicolas, 78
Dworkin, Richard, 52, 168, 208n49

economic concerns, 75–76; reproductive futurism, 41, 48–49, 59
Edelman, Lee, 4, 39, 40–63, 66, 70, 101, 191n2; queer negativity, 40, 50, 57–58, 210n64; *sinthom*osexual, 11, 45–48, 52–53, 63, 203n13, 204n17, 204n23. *See also* Child, figure of; *No Future* (Edelman); queer negativity
ego, conservative defensiveness, 40, 43–45
emergency, state of, 122, 126, 133
epistemological frame, 17, 149, 151, 152, 155
Eribon, Didier, 72
Esposito, Roberto, 5, 7, 13, 23, 39, 72, 74, 103–4, 109–13, 136, 154, 185; "forestalled life," 105–6, 114–16; Foucault, oscillations with, 105–16; interpretive keys, 105, 110, 111, 115; on state racism, 106–7, 225–26n13
Essai sur la police générale (Herbert), 79
Essay on the Principle of Population (Malthus), 80–81
ethical life, 146, 155, 158–59, 170, 175, 185–90, 247–48n93; hypergenealogy, 11, 185–87
eugenics, 17, 111, 113, 114, 124, 217–18n50
euthanasia, 137, 159–61
Evil Genius, 26, 198n45
exception, states of, 7, 36–37, 120–26, 133, 172; gender exceptionalism, 187, 214n25
exclusion, included, 132, 135, 140, 149
expert knowledges, 74, 76, 83, 85

failure, of author, 10. *See also* reserves, suspended.
failure, of sovereign subjects, 163–64, 177. *See also* responsibility
family spaces, 3, 39, 82–90, 218n55; control of sexuality, 75–76; divergence and incongruence in, 90–94; emergent forms, 82–83; as milieu, 90, 93; modes of

power and, 85–87, 219*n*61; mother as destructive figure, 99–100; subordination of mother, 84–85, 91–92
family values, 3, 40, 61, 70
Farge, Arlette, 86
Fassin, Didier, 13, 20, 74, 215–16*n*33
Fécondité (Zola), 66
feme covert, 135, 204*n*26
feminism, 41, 140; abortion, approaches to, 170–71; Agamben and, 128–32; critique of visual elimination of pregnant woman, 50–51; Foucault on, 178–79; rhetorical history, 53–55; *sinthom*osexual of, 55–57
Ferrarese, Estelle, 242*n*47
fetus: ambiguity of, 127, 152, 155, 159, 169–73; bare life and, 170–74; fetal motherhood, 205*nn*28, 30; grievability of, 171–73, 244*n*58; personhood rights, 123, 230*n*33, 248–49*n*98; precariousness and, 151–59; rights of, 123, 138, 139; ultrasound imaging, 157, 163, 177
finitude, human, 25
Forti, Simona, 7
Foucault, Michel: Derrida's engagement with, 8, 22–30; Esposito, oscillations with, 105–16; lack of attention to sexual difference, 37–38, 82–87; lexicon, 24–25; *No Future* and, 61–63; paradoxes in, 60, 105–9; power and abortion, 178–85; reserves, 14–16, 35; reserves, suspended, 28–32, 38–39, 65, 84–85, 101, 115–18; unstable oscillations in, 105–7, 110–11, 113, 115; Works: *Abnormal*, 1, 30, 36, 83, 87, 114, 211*n*1, 212*n*7, 220*n*77, 238*n*15; *The Birth of the Clinic*, 16–17, 145; Collège de France lectures, 1, 30, 69, 211*n*1; *Discipline and Punish*, 33, 103, 160; *History of Madness*, 25–30; *Le désordre des familles* (with Farge), 86; *The Order of Things*, 16–17, 74, 78–79; "The Political Technology of Individuals," 200–1*n*83; *Psychiatric Power*, 1, 30, 84–85, 87; *The Punitive Society*, 21, 145, 197*n*36; *Security, Territory, and Population*, 17–19, 24, 78–79, 87, 93–94; *Society Must Be Defended*, 18, 20, 72–73, 77, 88, 99, 102, 106–10, 114, 120, 224–25*n*6; See also *The History of Sexuality*, Volume 1 (Foucault)
4 Months, 3 Weeks, and 2 Days (Mungiu), 174–75
Fourteenth Amendment, 122
Frames of War (Butler), 9–10, 17, 144, 146, 149, 151–55, 156, 186
France: abortion law, 125, 159–64; colonialism, 98–100; Declaration of Rights of Man and Citizen, 133–35; globalist expansion, 33–34
Frank, Zippi Brand, 180–84, 189
French civil code, 84, 86
French Penal Code (1810), 125
French Revolution, 21, 33, 76, 86, 133–34
Freud, Sigmund, 25, 28, 198*n*45
futures, 1, 17, 202–3*n*12; abortion as impediment, 4, 65, 153; counterteleology, 47; death of, 98–100; death penalty as impediment, 34–36; masturbation as impediment, 29, 31; racial, 60, 98; risk of harm to, 116–17. See also reproductive futurism
Futures of Reproduction (Mills), 158

gathering, principle of, 15, 27–28, 32, 71, 198*n*51
gay marriage rights, 40, 42, 180, 202*n*7
gay reproductive rights, 180–84, 246*n*76. See also queerness
gay rights politics, 40–42
gender exceptionalism, 187, 214*n*25
Gender Trouble (Butler), 148, 237*nn*10, 11, 241*n*37
genealogy, 28, 68, 155; hypergenealogy, 11, 185–87
genetic perfectionism, 157
genocide: abortion as, 4, 60, 129, 209*n*61; ethnic rape, 132, 225*n*9

Germany, abortion access, 124–25, 230n33
Gilligan, Carol, 11, 52, 144, 164–68, 243n52, 244n54
Giving an Account of Oneself (Butler), 148, 158, 170, 175–76, 185, 248n94
Google Baby (Frank), 180–84, 189, 244n60
governmentality, 3–4, 39, 65, 72, 90; Butler's view, 150; children problematized, 93; excess, 108–9; intersection of race and sexuality, 69; new forms, 110; sex, management of, 74. *See also* power
Greek context, 130–31, 135
grievability, 145, 149–50, 152, 154–56, 168–69; of fetus, 171–73, 244n58

Habeas Viscus (Weheliye), 9, 214n22, 214–15n26, 227–28n24
Halberstam, Jack, 57–58, 61, 210n64
Halley, Janet, 72
Halperin, David, 72
Haraway, Donna, 163, 240–41n35
Harwood, Gwen, 168–69
health, biopolitical concerns, 2, 4, 36, 51, 61–62, 66, 74, 77, 87, 98, 107
"heartbeat bans," 123, 228n28, 228–29n29, 229nn30, 31
Herbert, Claude-Jacques, 79
heredity, 34, 74, 97–98
heteronormative reproductive values, 3, 40, 176
heterosexuality, 69; queerness said to impede, 42, 45–46, 57–58
history, 16, 32; consecutive modes, 18–20;
History of Madness (Foucault), 25–30
The History of Sexuality, Volume 1 (Foucault), 1–2, 5, 19–20, 27–28, 106, 114; alliance model, 32; Butler's view, 145; colonialism and race in, 68–69; *La Croisade des Enfants*, 39; parallel lives/readings, 72–75; procreative "hinge," 76–78; procreative hypothesis, 75–76; reproductive futurism and, 61–63; "terminal forms" of sexuality, 71

homo sacer, 117–18, 127–28, 231nn44, 47; citizenship, 130–32; living dead humanity, 135. *See also* bare life
Homo Sacer (Agamben), 103, 118–20, 127–32
homonationalism, 39, 69–70, 98, 187, 214n25
Honig, Bonnie, 204n20, 237n8
Huffer, Lynne, 29
Hugo, Victor, 6, 33–34, 35, 37
humanization, 157
Hyde amendment, 154
hypergenealogy, 11, 185–87
hysteric, 36, 65–66, 71, 75, 92, 217–18n50

illegibility, 148, 159, 164, 168–70; abortion and, 164, 168, 176–78; reproductive rights and, 52–53, 59, 143
immigrants, 50, 129, 205n27
immune paradigm, 14, 39, 103, 104, 105; reproductive immunities, 111–18
impediment, figures of, 4, 31, 65–66; death penalty and, 34–36, 38; queer, 43–46, 52, 56, 59
In a Different Voice (Gilligan), 11, 52, 164–68
incarceration, 21
included exclusion, 132–33, 135, 140, 149
individuation, 82, 84–85, 92, 150
infanticide, 113
interpretive keys, 17, 105, 110, 111, 115
intersectionality, 66–70, 213n11, 249n99
Italian philosophy, 2, 74. *See also* Agamben, Giorgio; Esposito, Roberto
ius soli and *ius sanguinis*, 134

James, P. D., 49–52
Jenkins, Fiona, 156–57, 170–76, 238–39n20, 240n32
Johnson, Barbara, 144, 168, 243–44n53
Jones, Donna V., 72

Khanna, Ranjana, 10, 160, 229n32
kinship relations, 47–48, 202–3n12, 204n19, 246n76
Klein, Ezra, 42

Kligman, Gail, 154
knowledge, objects of, 16–18
Kohlberg, Lawrence, 164, 244n54
Koopman, Colin, 27

La matrice de la race (Dorlin), 99, 214n22
La Volonté de Savoir, The Will to Knowledge (Foucault). See *The History of Sexuality, Volume I* (Foucault)
language, vulnerability and, 147–48
Lanjuinais, Jean-Denis, 134
law, 112, 118–26, 138
Le désordre des familles (Foucault and Farge), 86, 221–22n85
Le Doeuff, Michèle, 125, 162, 230n35
Left, discourse of life and, 146, 152
legibility of procreation, 45–46, 65. See also illegibility
Lemke, Thomas, 19, 195–96n25, 196n33
Lepore, Jill, 139
"lesbian movement," 178
lettres de cachet, 86
life, 3, 74–75, 200n78; contingent formations, 15–16, 35, 66, 69, 74, 146, 149, 163, 187–88; emerges with biopolitics, 110–11, 117; "forestalled," 105–6, 114–16; "not worth being lived," 104, 118–19, 141–42, 149; produced by biopolitics, 7, 110–11; of progress, 34. See also bare life; ethical life
Life Always group, 4
Life and Words (Das), 9
living dead humanity, 135–37
Logan, Katherine, 82, 84–85
Lorde, Audre, 43, 203n14
Love, Heather, 57–58, 61, 210n64

Ma loi d'avenir (Démar), 54
Mad for Foucault (Huffer), 29
madness, 25, 29, 198n45
Malabou, Catherine, 16
Malthus, Thomas Robert, 79–81, 100, 214n40, 217n46
Malthusian couple, 39, 64, 66, 80, 212–13n8

marriage, 79–81; gay marriage rights, 40, 42, 202n7
masturbation, 65–66; marsupial-like mother, 39, 63, 83; as mortal danger, 29–30; parents responsible for, 83–84; Rousseau's view, 30–31
maternity/motherhood: breast-feeding, 35, 37, 84, 91, 93, 96, 218n55; childlessness as tragic fate, 47–48; citizenship and, 129–30; expert knowledges and, 76, 83, 85, 93–94; as fetish, 49–51; health of, 158; idealized, 45; nationalism associated with, 65, 99; problematized, 36, 39, 82–95; redoubled role, 85, 96, 100; rejection of, 53–54. See also women
Mbembe, Achille, 7, 9, 39, 103, 224n97
McWhorter, Ladelle, 5, 98, 213n15, 214n22, 218–19n59
Medicaid, 154
Memmi, Dominique, 159–62, 171, 173, 183, 245n65
metabody, 31–32, 34
Miller, Ruth A., 105, 140, 142
Mills, Catherine, 10, 130, 131, 155–58, 163, 172, 176, 230n39, 240n32
miscarriage, 171–72, 245n65
modernity, 15, 19–20, 110; biopolitics of, 132–33; reproductive, 133–35
Moheau, Jean-Baptiste, 93
monarchy, 20, 86
moral agency, 51, 163, 186, 189–90, 240n32
moral duty, 80–81
moral thought, 57, 164–70, 244n54
mortality rates, 4, 16–17, 87, 93, 96
"The Mother" (Brooks), 168–69
Mottier, Véronique, 217–18n50
Mungiu, Cristian, 174–76
Muñoz, José, 10
murder, indirect forms, 21–23, 102–3, 118–19, 132–33; categories of vulnerable, 148–49; women exposed to, 100, 115–16, 137, 141–143, 154, 173–75, 207n44, 222–23n91

Murphy, Michelle, 100, 212*n*2, 217–18*n*50, 223*n*94

Nancy, Jean-Luc, 10
nationalism, 39, 50, 99–100, 205*nn*28, 30; feminist views, 54–55; homonationalism, 39, 69–70, 98, 187, 214*n*25
natural law, 81
Nazi camp, 119–20, 231*n*44, 231*n*45
Nazi state, 23, 88, 106–7, 112, 120, 195*n*24, 227–28*n*24
necropolitics/necropolitical, 7–8, 14, 65, 103, 212*n*2, 221*n*82
negativity, 40–41, 58, 203*n*16, 204*nn*17, 24, 210*n*64. *See also* queer negativity
Nietzsche, Friedrich, 241–42*n*40
No Future (Edelman), 11, 40–63; Child, figure of, 40–45, 49, 101, 211*n*72; Foucault, relationship with, 61–63; not antichild, but anti-Child, 44, 56; psychoanalytic orientation, 61–62
normalization, 19, 24, 69, 76, 87, 92, 94, 238*n*15
normativity, 169–70, 241*n*37
nuclear power, 106–9, 115

Of Grammatology (Derrida), 30
oikos, 130–31
Oksala, Johanna, 131
ontological tact, 11, 146, 163, 171–72, 183–84
optimization, 1, 2, 4, 23, 39; critical interrogation, 150; paradoxes, 107–8; thanatopolitical and, 95–96, 224*n*3. *See also* administration; biopolitics/biopolitical; governmentality
The Order of Things (Foucault), 16–17, 74, 78–79

panopticization, 19, 23, 61, 90
Panoptimism, 61, 210*n*65
paradoxes, 60, 105–9, 116, 117, 120, 127, 138, 140, 148
parent, 36–38, 42, 50; Foucault averts sexual difference, 37–38, 83–84
"parent's rights," 50
patriarchal power, 54, 131–32
penal order, 18
penetration metaphors, 20, 24, 31, 88–90, 110
personhood rights, 123, 230*n*33, 248–49*n*98
"petty" sovereigns, 150, 151
philanthropic movements, 96
Pinel, Philippe, 25, 198*n*45
Planned Parenthood, 60, 139, 209*n*60, 229*n*30
Plato, 113
The Policing of Families (Donzelot), 83, 85, 95–96, 221*n*81, 221–22*n*85
Politics of Friendship (Derrida), 33
Polizeiwissenschaft, 35, 77, 95, 200–1*n*83
Poovey, Mary, 123
population, 36, 200–1*n*83, 216*n*38; administration, 24; as biological collectivity, 17–18; bodies and, 66–70; confession and management of, 72–73; demographics, 20, 72, 76, 78, 93–94, 110, 121; duty to maximize health, 36; management, 149–50; masturbation saps vitality, 29, 31, 66; problematized, 100; procreation as necessary, 76–78; racialization and risk, 100–4; responsibility and, 78–85
post-Foucauldian theory, 2, 7, 9, 13–14, 103, 153
power, 7, 14, 147; body and, 179; decomposition of, 21–25; historically consecutive modes, 18–20; modes of, 1–2, 6–7, 22–23, 93, 118, 141, 160, 196–97*n*35, 224*n*97; patriarchal, 54, 131–32; resistance to, 178–80; segmentation of, 15, 21–25, 196–97*n*35; sovereign mode, 19–20, 85, 88–90, 97, 109, 110; techniques of, 15, 18–19, 24, 27, 85, 90, 93, 96. *See also* biopolitics/biopolitical; biopower
Power, Nina, 152
Precarious Life (Butler), 149–50, 156
precariousness, 7, 10, 17, 39, 104, 146, 187; abortion rights, 120–26, 137; Butler's

analysis, 146–51; fetus and, 151–59; maternal, 153–55, 157–58; "outside" clinic, 173–76; of women's reproductive life, 155–56

pregnancy. *See* maternity/motherhood

present, 14, 15, 18–20; ages and epochs destabilize, 25–26; contemporary, 26–27; Derrida's interrogation of Foucauldian, 24–28; fissured, 25–28; masturbatory, 31

privacy, right to, 122, 124

problematization, 3, 27; of children, 93; of mother, 36, 39, 82–95; of women, 100–1

procreative hypothesis, 1, 75–76

productive power, 89–90

progress, 33–34

pseudo homo sacer, 127–28

pseudosovereignty, 4–6, 36, 104, 120, 127–28, 153

Psychiatric Power (Foucault), 1, 30, 84–85, 87

The Psychic Life of Power (Butler), 147–48

psychoanalysis, 25, 26, 27

Puar, Jasbir, 7, 23, 39, 61, 187, 213*n*16, 214*nn*22, 25; Edelman, view of, 61, 62; *Terrorist Assemblages*, 66–70, 98

The Punitive Society (Foucault), 21, 145, 197*n*36

quality of life, 160, 186–87

queer negativity, 40–41, 50, 210*n*64; antilife, 4, 42, 44–45, 70, 98, 100–1, 187, 208–9*n*58; antisociality, 4, 41, 45–46, 57–59; "us," as fantasy beneficiary, 44–45, 51. *See also* negativity

queer theory, 2, 74, 214*n*22

queerness, 56; figural burden of, 43–44, 58; heterosexuality impeded by, 42, 45–46, 57–58; racialization and, 69–70. *See also* gay reproductive rights

racialization, 60, 62, 69–70, 98–100, 216*n*39, 225–26*n*13; bare life, 128–29; risk and reproduction, 100–4, 223*n*92

Rancière, Danielle, 221–22*n*85

rape, ethnic, 111, 132, 225*n*9

Rapp, Rayna, 241*n*36

Reform Act, 1974 (Germany), 124

Remnants of Auschwitz (Agamben), 120, 227*n*24

repressive hypothesis, 1–2, 7, 66, 89, 95

reproduction, 3; decision making, 53, 121, 143, 153, 158–64, 167, 170–74, 177, 184–89; immune paradigm, 111–15; living dead humanity, 135–37; of race and race hierarchy, 68–69; as threat, 4, 17, 36, 38–43, 50–51, 100–2, 116–17, 127–29, 185. *See also* administration of life

reproductive futurism, 4, 39, 40–63, 97; abjection of "others," 41, 43–44; biopolitics and, 61–63; burden shuffled to someone else, 58–59; calculability, 47–49, 55, 56, 59–61; denial of rights to queers and women, 42–43; different populations, 60; economic metaphors, 41, 48–49, 59; feminist views, 53–55; figural burden of queerness, 43–44, 58; imaginary Child of gay parenting, 42–43; imaginary continuity, 43–45; intelligibility, 46–49, 237*n*10; overpromising positive results, 54–57; Ponzi schemes, 40, 41, 49; reproductive rights discourse, 52–53; self-presence, 43–44; *sinthom*osexual, figure of, 11, 45–48; "us" as fantasy beneficiary, 44–45, 51. *See also* futures

reproductive rights, 139–41; illegibility and, 52–53, 59, 143. *See also* gay reproductive rights

reproductive rights politics, 36, 40–41, 50–51; as hypergenealogy, 185–87

Republican primary, 2011, 60

reserves: of proximity, 37–38; suspended, 11, 28–32, 37–38, 62, 65, 84, 115–18, 134, 186

resistance, 116, 128–29, 178–80; counterconduct, 189, 217–18*n*50, 223*n*94

responsibility: failed, 163–64, 177, 187–88; language of, 166–67

responsibilization, 3, 5, 39, 82, 115–16, 136; contingent formations, 66, 158–59, 176; fetus and, 157, 175–76; of pregnant women, 51, 186
right to have rights, 21
Roberts, Dorothy, 5
Roe v. Wade, 122–24, 127, 168
Roman legal system, 18, 20, 54, 131, 135
Romania, 154, 174–76
Romany women, 137, 154
Rose, Nikolas, 72
Rousseau, Jean-Jacques, 30–31
Rozier, P-M., 83

Santorum, Rick, 40
Savage, Dan, 40
Scalia, Antonin, 42
Schmitt, Carl, 119
Scott, Joan, 53, 206n34
security, 3, 19, 23–24, 90, 106
Security, Territory, and Population (Foucault), 17–19, 24, 78–80, 93–94
Sedgwick, Eve, 72
segmentations of power, 15, 21–25, 196–97n35
sexual difference: Agamben neglects, 128–30, 131–32; biopolitical and, 37–38; death penalty as problem of, 8; Foucault averts, 37–38, 82–87, 217–18n50
sexuality: alliance and, 31–32, 88–90, 220n74; biopolitics and, 32–33; disciplinary control of, 24, 73; as formation of death in life, 28–29; as intersection, 66–70; penetration metaphors, 20, 24, 31, 88–90; "terminal forms," 71; of text, 31, 32
sexuality studies, 2
Shalala, Donna, 41
Shane, Martha, 57, 205–6n32
Shared Responsibility Agreement, 243n50
Sieyès, Emmanuel-Joseph, 134
Simons, Jon, 217–18n50
*sintho*mosexual, 11, 45–48, 63, 203nn13, 204nn17, 23; Antigone, 46, 47–48; of feminism, 55–57

slow death, 6–7, 39
Smith, Adam, 79
social ontology, 146
socially dead, 148
Society Must Be Defended (Foucault), 18, 20, 23, 31, 68, 72–73, 77, 88, 96–97, 99, 102, 106–10, 117, 119–20, 224–25n6
sovereign mode, 19–20, 85, 88–90, 97, 109, 110
sovereign power of death, 8, 21–23, 195n24, 224n2; as privative, 102–3, 107
sovereignty, 3; biopolitical, relationship to, 19–20, 106–9, 116–18, 121, 141–43, 161; family space and, 85–87; Foucault and Agamben on, 118–20; phantasmatic, 33, 104, 117, 161–62, 164, 225n10, 226–27n18; weakened, 117–18; women's power over reproductive life, 4–6, 121
spatial organizations, 18–19
state, control over bare life, 159–61
Stewart, Potter, 154
Stoler, Ann, 68, 98–99, 129, 205n27, 213n16
subjectivation, 145, 147–48, 155–59, 185; abjection and, 41, 43–44, 59, 149; desubjectivation, 3, 145, 156, 159, 185–86; of fetus, 155–56; unmaking, 120, 149, 155–56, 171, 173, 227n20
Subjects of Desire (Butler), 145, 150
subordination, 9, 147–48, 249n99; of mother, 84–86, 91–92
Supreme Court, 123
surrogacy, 179–84, 244n60, 246n85, 247n88
surveillance, 73, 90–91, 178
survival, 88; imaginary continuity, 43–45
survivance, 24, 38
suspended reserves, 11, 28–32, 37–38, 62, 65, 84, 115–18, 134, 150, 186
suspension, 15, 28, 38, 70

The Taming of the Shrew (Shakespeare), 46
temporality, 14, 15. *See also* ages and epochs
terrorist assemblage, 9, 98
Terrorist Assemblages (Puar), 66–70

text/textuality, 30, 32
thanatopolitical drift, 103–4
thanatopoliticization, 225*n*12; of "life," 115; of reproduction and maternity, 36, 112–16
thanatopolitics, as term, 153
thanatopolitics/thanatopolitical, 7–8, 11, 65, 95–98, 105–43, 153, 185; as biopolitical, 102; dividing practices, 102; eightfold definition, 65, 102–4; fetus, figure of, 153; framing vignettes, 111–13; hypothesis, 5, 7; life "not worth being lived," 104, 118–19, 141–42, 149; living dead humanity, 135; sovereign power and, 102–3; thresholds, 103, 114; woman, 140–41; women and collective futures, 36–37. *See also* biopolitics/biopolitical theory, limits of, 6. *See also* suspended reserves
Thompson, Judith Jarvis, 245–46*n*68
threshold, 15, 17, 26, 31; mother as, 97, 223*n*92; reproduction as, 36, 114; thanatopolitical and, 103, 114
Tiny Tim figure, 43, 45, 48, 59
"To Do Justice to Freud" (Derrida), 28, 31, 37
transactional unities, 15, 16–18, 194*nn*11, 13
transformation, 19–20, 25–26
Tronto, Joan, 166
Trumbull, Robert, 28, 198*n*51
Tuke, Samuel, 25, 198*n*45

ultrasound imaging, 123, 157, 163, 177
universal rights, 55, 135
urban planning, 23–24
"us," as fantasy beneficiary, 44–45, 51

Veil law (France), 125
violence. *See* murder, indirect forms
viruses, unmanageable, 108, 109
vitality, 22–23, 29, 31, 66
von Justi, Johann, 77, 200–1*n*83
von Redecker, Eva, 240*n*28
vulnerability, 147–49, 157

Walled States (Brown), 117
war, 22, 152, 156
Weheliye, Alex, 9, 72, 128, 214*n*22, 214–15*n*26, 227–28*n*24
wet nurses, 35, 90, 93, 96–97
Wheeler, Anna, 207*n*44
The Will to Knowledge (Foucault). *See The History of Sexuality*, Volume I (Foucault)
Wilson, Lana, 57, 205–6*n*32
Wollstonecraft, Mary, 54–55, 56, 208*n*47
women: animal devotions, 56; citizenship and, 129–35; death associated with, 5, 6, 36, 50–51, 65, 97–98; death penalty, 6, 33–36; pretensions of interest in, 4–5; problematization of, 100–1; as pseudo homo sacer, 127–28; pseudosovereignty, 4–6, 36, 104, 120, 127–28, 153; queer figures, 45–46; redoubled roles, 85, 96, 100, 120, 121, 127; thanatopoliticized, 140–41; women-as-life-principle, 5, 6, 34, 36, 38, 153–54. *See also* mother; *sinthom*osexual

Ziarek, Ewa, 128–29, 137, 231*n*47, 232*n*56
zoe, 119, 130–32, 134, 159. *See also* bare life